MAKE PYTHON TALK

Build Apps with Voice Control and Speech Recognition

by Mark Liu

**no starch
press**

San Francisco

Printed in the United States of America

First printing

25 24 23 22 21   1 2 3 4 5 6 7 8 9

ISBN-13: 978-1-7185-0156-0 (print)
ISBN-13: 978-1-7185-0157-7 (ebook)

Publisher: William Pollock
Production Manager: Rachel Monaghan
Production Editor: Paula Williamson
Developmental Editor: Liz Chadwick
Cover Illustrator: Gina Redman
Interior Design: Octopod Studios
Technical Reviewer: Noah Spahn
Copyeditor: Sharon Wilkey
Compositor: Jeff Lytle, Happenstance Type-O-Rama
Proofreader: Paula Fleming
Indexer: JoAnne Burek

For information on book distributors or translations, please contact No Starch Press, Inc. directly:
No Starch Press, Inc.
245 8th Street, San Francisco, CA 94103
phone: 1.415.863.9900; info@nostarch.com
www.nostarch.com

Library of Congress Control Number: 2021938060

[S]

Dedicated to Ivey, Andrew, and all
MS Finance students (past, present, and
future) at the University of Kentucky.

About the Author

Dr. Mark H. Liu is the founding director of the Master of Science in Finance program at the University of Kentucky, where he holds the title of Associate Professor of Finance with tenure. He has a Ph.D. in finance from Boston College, and has been published in top finance journals, including *Journal of Financial Economics*, *Journal of Financial and Quantitative Analysis*, and *Journal of Corporate Finance*. Dr. Liu has more than 20 years of coding experience in C++, SAS, Stata, and Python and runs Python workshops for Finance master students at the University of Kentucky. He has also incorporated Python in finance courses he is teaching.

About the Technical Reviewer

Noah Spahn is presently enjoying the role of Software Engineer for the Computer Security Group at UCSB (known as SecLab) and their world-famous hacking team: Shellphish. Prior to his current academic role, he ran his own consulting business, allowing him to work on a wide variety of projects, with a broad spectrum and languages, and collaborate with varying teams. Fluency in Python has opened many doors for Spahn, providing the opportunity to contribute to the areas of natural sciences (oceanography, ecohydrology, seismology), computer science (network traffic analysis, machine learning, binary analysis), open-source projects (NASA, Kubernetes, and others), as well as many practical applications. Spahn holds a Master of Software Engineering degree from California State University, Fullerton. He has taught courses in Python at the University of California and Santa Barbara's interdisciplinary Collaboratory, and has taught an upper-division course on the concepts of programming languages at Westmont College. Spahn is glad to teach anyone who is interested in learning.

BRIEF CONTENTS

CONTENTS IN DETAIL

PART II: LEARNING TO TALK   53

3
SPEECH RECOGNITION   55

PART III: INTERACTIVE GAMES 167

9
GRAPHICS AND ANIMATION WITH THE *TURTLE* MODULE 169

10
TIC-TAC-TOE 189

11
CONNECT FOUR 207

12
GUESS-THE-WORD GAME 227

13
SMART GAMES: ADDING INTELLIGENCE 241

PART IV: GOING FURTHER 269

14
FINANCIAL APPLICATIONS 271

15
STOCK MARKET WATCH 295

ACKNOWLEDGMENTS

Many people have helped to make this book a reality. A portion of this book was developed while I was preparing Python workshops for MS Finance students at the University of Kentucky in the past few years. Several Finance master and Ph.D. students helped tremendously in the process: Joe Farizo, James Keyser, Blake Best, and especially my teaching assistants at the time Mike Farrell and Patrick Mullins. I'd like to thank all MS Finance students for keeping me motivated to learn new Python skills in order to show them how useful and interesting coding is.

I'd also like to thank Bill Pollock and Barbara Yien at No Starch Press for guiding me through the editorial process. Special thanks to my developmental editor Liz Chadwick, whose pursuit for perfection has greatly improved the book. She helped me find the delicate balance between over-explaining and not enough detail.

Many thanks to the technical reviewer of the book Noah Spahn. He doesn't simply check if the code works correctly, he also makes sure the scripts are as efficient as they can be. A case in point is that he pushed me to find a way to make the self-made modules in different chapters consistent. This prompted me to use the self-made Python package in the book. He went way beyond just checking the scripts, and frequently edited the writing to help explain technical details in the book.

Last but not least, I'd like to thank my wife Ivey Zhang and my son Andrew Liu for being so supportive in this journey. In the past couple of years, I probably have spent more time with the book than with them over the weekends and holidays. I am indebted to them the most.

INTRODUCTION

Banks are essentially technology firms.
—Hugo Banziger, former chief risk officer at Deutsche Bank

 Python is currently the world's most popular coding language, having overtaken more long established languages like Java and C. Once you start to code in Python, it's easy to see why. The two main advantages of Python are its simplicity and openness. Python code is relatively close to plain English, so with only a little experience, you can often guess what a script is trying to accomplish.

Python is open source, meaning not only that the software is free to use for everyone but also that other users can create and alter libraries. In fact, Python has a vast ecosystem from which you can get resources and help from members in the community. Python programmers can share their code with one another, so instead of building everything from scratch, you can import modules designed by others, as well as share your modules with others in the Python community.

When people heard that I was writing a Python book on speech recognition and text to speech, their reaction was generally the same: "I thought you were a *finance* professor." My typical answer is the Hugo Banziger quote that opens this chapter, made shortly after the 2008 financial crisis. Nowadays, you can replace *banks* with corporations in any other industry—car manufacturers, retailers, anything really—and the quote still rings true. Technology is in every aspect of our lives these days. The future is here and now.

Python has been the world's most popular coding language since 2018. Long before that, Python was the leading programming language in the finance world, with applications in financial services, portfolio management, algorithmic trading, cryptocurrency, and so on.

NOTE *The article "Python Is Becoming the World's Most Popular Coding Language" in* The Economist *(https://www.economist.com/graphic-detail/2018/07/26/python-is-becoming-the-worlds-most-popular-coding-language/) has details on the increasing popularity of Python.*

When talking to potential employers of my Master of Science in Finance (MSF) students, I was told that they have people who know finance, but not coding—and people who know coding, but nothing about finance. They wanted to hire people who understood both. As a result, we started to incorporate Python into the MSF curriculum.

The reactions from the finance students were mixed. Many students found Python user-friendly and versatile, while others wondered why they needed to bother learning Python when they could do everything in Microsoft Excel. So I started to show them cool skills in Python that are impossible in Excel, such as obtaining real-time stock prices via voice commands, creating a talking graphical US stock market watch, and so on. I wanted to show that Python can accomplish more than Excel, that the barrier to entry is not very high, and most important, that it's fun!

In this book, I focus on speech recognition and text-to-speech functionality in fun and genuinely useful applications, such as a voice translator, a voice-controlled online radio, a virtual personal assistant, voice-controlled graphical games, and so on. My aim is to teach Python skills that are applicable and adaptable in real life, while keeping the skeptical students of Python interested in what they're doing.

About This Book

This book both *is* and *isn't* an introductory book on Python. While it's not intended as a full tutorial in Python basics, it is written simply enough that a total beginner can follow along. You'll learn how to install Python on your computer and write your very first script. You'll also learn the basic rules of Python, how functions and modules work, and various data types every Python user needs to know. With this, you'll be able to accomplish most simple tasks in Python.

At the same time, this book *isn't* an introductory book in Python. I'll provide a Python refresher that will prepare you for later chapters, but it isn't a comprehensive introduction. Several wonderful books cover all the basics of Python. One example is *Python Crash Course* by Eric Matthes (No Starch Press, 2019).

Beyond the refresher, the purpose of this book is to improve your skills and build real working applications you can use in your daily life. This book also eases you into more advanced topics, such as making your own Python modules and packages. In Chapter 3, you'll learn how to use a function in a self-made module to contain all speech recognition functionality and related code so that you don't have to repeat the code every time you convert speech to text. In Chapter 5, you'll create a package from which you can import the function in the module to convert speech to text in all chapters that need this feature (which is pretty much all the remaining chapters in the book). Along the way, you'll learn how Python modules and packages work.

The end-of-chapter exercises are a great tool for practicing concepts and checking that you really understand them. You'll find the answers at the end of the book.

The code in this book is all cross-platform, so it should work in Windows, Mac, or Linux. I'll address the differences in the three operating systems whenever there are any.

What's in This Book?

This book is divided into four parts. Part I discusses how to install Python, as well as the basic Python rules and skills you'll need in later chapters. Part II introduces you to speech recognition and text-to-speech functionality, including how to install and fine-tune the required modules. You'll also use the speech recognition and text-to-speech functionalities to create a virtual personal assistant.

Part III covers interactive games. You'll learn to create graphical games and add text-to-speech and speech recognition features to make them talk and take voice commands. In Part IV, we build some applications to follow the financial markets, and we'll see how to make Python talk and listen in major world languages. The last chapter of the book builds our ultimate virtual assistant by adding the interactive games and the voice translator to it. Here's an overview of the book:

Part I: Getting Started

Chapter 1: Setting Up Python, Anaconda, and Spyder

You'll install the Python software required for the book and start running Python scripts, even if you know nothing about coding. We'll also talk about basic operations in Python.

Chapter 2: Python Refresher

You'll learn how to use the built-in Python functions and how to import modules in the Python Standard Library. You'll then learn how functions and modules work and how to create your own. I'll discuss ways of installing these modules on your computer. Finally, you'll learn about virtual environments, their uses, and how to create and activate them.

Python uses strings, lists, dictionaries, and tuples as collections of elements to accomplish certain tasks. In this chapter, you'll learn about these four types of collections and see examples of their uses.

Part II: Learning to Talk

Chapter 3: Speech Recognition

You'll install modules related to speech recognition in Python, then create a script to have Python recognize your speech and print it out. You'll use voice control to complete several tasks, such as taking voice dictation, opening web browsers, opening files, and playing music on your computer. To save space in your scripts, you'll learn how to put all code related to speech recognition into a custom local module so that the final script is concise, short, and clean.

Chapter 4: Make Python Talk

Here, you'll learn how to make Python talk back to you in a human voice. You'll install the text-to-speech module and teach Python to speak aloud whatever you enter into Spyder. We'll also add the speech recognition feature and get Python to repeat whatever you say. We'll store all code related to text-to-speech functionality in another custom module.

Chapter 5: Speaking Applications

You'll put the speech recognition and text-to-speech functionality from Chapters 3 and 4 to use in a couple of applications. First, you'll parse text to extract news summaries from National Public Radio (NPR) and have Python read them out to you. You'll also build a script to extract information from Wikipedia based on your voice inquiries and speak the answers. Finally, you'll learn how to traverse files in a folder with your voice, with the aim of building your very own Alexa. You'll be able to say, "Python, play Selena Gomez," and a song by Selena Gomez that's saved on your computer will play.

Chapter 6: Web Scraping Podcasts, Radios, and Videos

You'll learn the basics of web scraping. I'll cover how HyperText Markup Language (HTML) works to construct web pages. You'll parse HTML files and extract information. Then you'll use these skills to voice-activate podcasts, live radio stations, and videos on various websites.

Chapter 7: Building a Virtual Personal Assistant

You'll create your own virtual personal assistant (VPA), similar to Amazon's Alexa. Whenever you need assistance, you can say "Hello, Python" to wake up your VPA; you'll also use voice commands to put it in standby mode. The VPA can act as a timer and an alarm clock, tell jokes, and send email 100 percent hands-free.

Chapter 8: Know-It-All VPA

Here you'll add know-it-all functionality to your VPA. Specifically, you'll tap into the vast knowledge base in the computational engine WolframAlpha and use Wikipedia as a backup if WolframAlpha can't answer your question. Your know-it-all VPA is capable of answering almost any question for you.

Part III: Interactive Games

Chapter 9: Graphics and Animation with the Turtle Module

Our goal in Part III is to build voice-controlled graphical games such as tic-tac-toe, Connect Four, and guess-the-word. You'll do all these in the *turtle* module. In this chapter, you'll learn the basic *turtle* commands that will let you set up a turtle screen, draw shapes, and create animations.

Chapter 10: Tic-Tac-Toe

You'll build a voice-controlled tic-tac-toe game to put all the new skills you've learned so far into practice. You'll draw a game board, check for valid moves, and detect if a player has won. You'll then add the speech recognition and text-to-speech features and set up the game so you play against your own computer.

Chapter 11: Connect Four

You'll next build a voice-controlled Connect Four game. You'll draw the board, animate the effect of a disc falling from the top of a column to the lowest available cell, and use Python logic to enforce a new set of game rules. Then you'll add speech functionality to the game.

Chapter 12: Guess-the-Word Game

You'll build a voice-controlled, graphical guess-the-word game that is an adaptation of the popular hangman game. This is an interesting challenge because when playing guess-the-word, players often exchange information verbally at a fast pace, so you'll need to fine-tune the script's listening abilities.

Chapter 13: Smart Games: Adding Intelligence

In the one-player version of tic-tac-toe or Connect Four, the computer always randomly selects a move. In this chapter, we'll build smart games by using two techniques that will get you to think about how to break down and solve problems in programming. The first is the think-three-steps-ahead approach, which has the computer following the path that most likely leads to a victory after three moves. The second method uses machine learning. You'll simulate a million games in which both players select random moves. With this data, the computer will learn at each move and select the one most likely to lead to a winning outcome.

Part IV: Going Further

Chapter 14: Financial Applications

These programming skills and speech recognition and text-to-speech techniques can be applied to any aspect of your life. Here, I'll show you how to adapt your skills to monitoring the financial markets. You'll then be able to generalize these techniques and apply them to your own area of interest, whatever that may be. You'll build three projects: an app that tells you the up-to-date stock price of any publicly traded company; a script that builds visualizations of stock prices; and an app that uses recent daily stock prices to calculate returns, run regressions, and perform detailed analyses.

Chapter 15: Stock Market Watch

You'll create a graphical, speaking app that watches the US stock market live and updates you aloud whenever a chosen stock exceeds certain preset thresholds. To build the necessary skills, you'll first create a graphical Bitcoin watch by using *tkinter* to display live price information.

Chapter 16: Use World Languages

So far, we've taught Python how to speak and listen in English. But Python can understand many other world languages. In this chapter, you'll first teach Python to talk in several other languages with the modules you've been using. I'll then introduce a useful module called *translate*, which can translate one language to another. You'll use it to build a translator that changes whatever you speak into another language of your choice.

Chapter 17: Ultimate Virtual Personal Assistant

You'll load up your virtual personal assistant with the interesting projects in this book, like voice-controlled games, translators, music players, and so on. You'll first add a chatting functionality to the VPA so you can carry out a daily conversation with the script. The whole idea of a VPA is its convenience, so we'll adjust these projects so that all added functionalities are 100 percent hands-free.

Appendix A: Install Modules to Play Audio Files

Since the focus of the book is on making Python talk and listen, playing audio files is important. This appendix presents a few modules you can use to play audio files, along with their advantages and disadvantages.

Appendix B: Answers to End-of-Chapter Exercises

This appendix provides suggested answers to all the exercises at the end of the chapters. You can use these answers to check your own and for help if you get stuck on any of the questions.

PART I

GETTING STARTED

1

SETTING UP PYTHON, ANACONDA, AND SPYDER

 Even if you've never coded before, this chapter will guide you through installing the Python software you need to start running Python scripts for this book. We'll be using Anaconda and Spyder, so we'll discuss the advantages of choosing this Python distribution and development environment, respectively. I'll guide you through the installation process based on your operating system, whether that's Windows, Mac, or Linux. Then you'll learn how to start coding in the Spyder editor. We'll discuss basic Python rules and operations at the end.

Before you begin, set up the folder */mpt/ch01/* for this chapter on your computer. All scripts in this chapter (and later chapters) are available at the book's resources page, *https://www.nostarch.com/make-python-talk/*.

Introducing Anaconda and Spyder

There are many ways to install Python and run scripts. In this book, we'll use Anaconda and Spyder.

Anaconda is an open source Python distribution, package, and environment manager. It is user friendly and provides for the easy installation of many useful Python modules that otherwise can be quite a pain to compile and install yourself. We'll start by downloading the Anaconda distribution of Python that comes bundled with Spyder.

Spyder is a full-featured integrated development environment (IDE) for writing scripts. It comes with many useful features such as automatic code completion, automatic debugging, code suggestions, and warnings.

Installing Anaconda and Spyder

Python is a cross-platform programming language, meaning you can run Python scripts whether you use Windows, Mac, or Linux. However, the installation of software and modules can be slightly different depending on your operating system. I'll show you how to install various modules in your operating system. Once these are properly installed, Python code works the same in different operating systems.

Install Anaconda and Spyder in Windows

To install Anaconda in Windows, go to *https://www.anaconda.com/products/individual/* and download the latest version of Python 3 for Windows.

I recommend using the graphical installer instead of the command line installer, especially for beginners, to avoid mistakes. Make sure you download the appropriate 32- or 64-bit package for your machine. Run the installer and follow the instructions all the way through.

Find and open the Anaconda navigator, and you should see a screen like Figure 1-1 (if you need to, search for *Anaconda navigator* in the search bar).

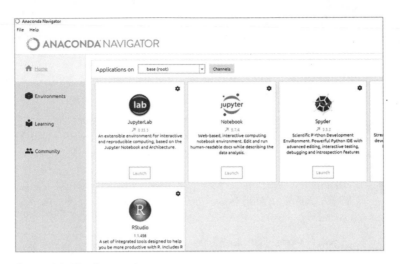

Figure 1-1: The Anaconda navigator

Click the **Launch** button under the Spyder icon. If Spyder is not already installed, click **Install** to install the Spyder development environment. After it finishes, click **Launch**.

Install Anaconda and Spyder in macOS

To install Python via Anaconda for macOS, go to *https://www.anaconda.com/products/individual/*, scroll down, and download the latest version of Python 3 for Mac. Choose the graphical installer and follow the instructions through.

Open the Anaconda navigator by searching for *Anaconda navigator* in Spotlight search. The screen for the Anaconda navigator in macOS should look similar to Figure 1-1, perhaps with slight differences.

To launch Spyder, click **Launch** under the Spyder icon (if you see an **Install** button instead, click it to install Spyder first).

Install Anaconda and Spyder in Linux

The installation of Anaconda and Spyder in Linux involves more steps than for other operating systems. First, go to *https://www.anaconda.com/products/individual/*, scroll down, and find the latest Linux version. Choose the appropriate x86 or Power8 and Power9 package. Click and download the latest installer bash script. For example, the installer bash script during my installation was *https://repo.anaconda.com/archive/Anaconda3-2020.11-Linux-x86_64.sh*. This link will change over time, but we'll use this version as our example.

By default, the installer bash script is downloaded and saved to the *Downloads* folder on your computer. You should then install Anaconda as follows using the path for your bash script if it is different.

```
bash ~/Downloads/Anaconda3-2020.11-Linux-x86_64.sh
```

After pressing ENTER, you'll be prompted to review and approve the license agreement. The last question in the installation process is this:

```
installation finished.
Do you wish the installer to prepend the Anaconda3 install location to PATH
in your /home/mark/.bashrc ? [yes|no]
[no] >>>
```

You should type **yes** and press ENTER in order to use the `conda` command to open Anaconda in a terminal.

WARNING   *Since the default choice is no in this step, it's easy to make a mistake by pressing ENTER without typing in* **yes**. *If that occurs, enter the following command in the terminal:*

    `gedit /home/your user name here/.bashrc`

You'll need to enter your actual username in the path. My username is mark, *so my full path is* /home/mark/.bashrc. *Once you execute this command, the* .bashrc *file should open. Enter this as a new line at the end of the file:*

    `export PATH=/home/your user name here/anaconda3/bin:$PATH`

Then save and close the file.

Now you need to activate the installation by executing this command:

```
source ~/.bashrc
```

To open Anaconda navigator, enter the following command in a terminal:

```
anaconda-navigator
```

You should see the Anaconda navigator on your machine, similar to Figure 1-1. To launch Spyder, click the **Launch** button under the Spyder icon (if you see an **Install** button instead, click it to install Spyder first).

Using Spyder

To get you up and running, we'll build a really simple script in Spyder. Then I'll run through a few basic concepts that'll be useful to know before you start coding for real.

Write Python in Spyder

As mentioned earlier, Spyder is a full-featured IDE. Let's start with a simple script. After you launch the Spyder development environment, you should see a layout like Figure 1-2.

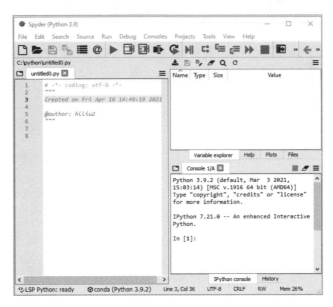

Figure 1-2: Spyder development environment

Spyder comes with several predefined layouts, and you can customize layouts according to your preferences. The default layout has three panels. Let's examine that default.

At the left is the *Spyder editor*, in which you can write Python code. At the top right is the *variable explorer*, which shows the details of the data generated by your script. As scripts become quite complicated, the variable explorer becomes a valuable asset in double-checking the values stored in your variables.

At the bottom right is the *interactive Python (IPython) console*, which shows the output of the script or executes snippets of Python code. The IPython console is also where you enter input for scripts that require user information. It also displays error messages if you make a mistake in your script.

Now let's start coding. Go to the Spyder editor window (again, the default location is on the left) and enter this:

```python
print("This is my very first Python script!")
```

Click **File ▶ Save As** and save the file as *my_first_script.py* in your chapter folder.

There are three ways to run scripts, and all lead to the same outcome:

1. Go to the **Run** menu and select **Run**.
2. Press F5 on your keyboard.
3. Press the green triangle icon ▶ in the icons bar.

Run the script and you should see something like Figure 1-3. The output, shown in the IPython console, is a simple printed message: This is my very first Python script! Congratulations—you have written and successfully run your first Python script!

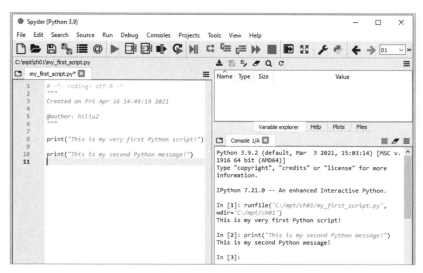

Figure 1-3: Running a script in the Spyder development environment

Inspect Code in Spyder

Besides running an entire script, Spyder has the ability to run code line by line or block by block. Running a piece of a script at a time is useful for carefully following the execution of a script, to verify that it does exactly what you intended it to do. Go back to the *my_first_script.py* example and add another line:

```
print("This is my second Python message!")
```

Place your cursor over this second line and press F9, and you should see the output shown in Figure 1-4.

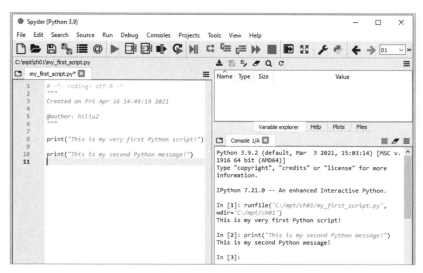

Figure 1-4: Running just one line of code in the Spyder editor

As you can see, only the highlighted line is executed. Here's the output:

```
This is my second Python message!
```

Now press F5, and you'll see that every line in the script is executed:

```
This is my very first Python script!
This is my second Python message!
```

To run a particular block of code, highlight those lines of code and press F9.

Understanding Coding in Python

Before we get into the coding concepts of Python, you need to understand a few general things. This section introduces Python syntax and basic mathematical operations.

Python Syntax

First, Python is case-sensitive. You should take great care when it comes to uppercase and lowercase letters. The variables X and Y are different from the variables x and y. The strings "Hello" and "hello" are also different from each other.

Second, indentations are significant in Python. Nonprinting characters like tabs must be consistently applied throughout a script. If you have experience with another programming language, like C or Java, you may notice the lack of brackets and semicolons in Python; this is by design. Blocks of code are defined by indentation. An unintended space in the code will likely betray your intentions, as we'll see in Chapter 2 when we discuss indentations in conditional executions, loops, and functions.

Third, Python uses single quotation marks and double quotation marks (mostly) interchangeably. For example, placing a sequence of characters inside single quotes has the same effect as if we put them in double quotes (unless one of the characters is an escape character or a single quote).

Fourth, Python lets you make notes, known as *comments*. One popular way to write a comment uses the hash mark (#). Everything in the same line after # will not be executed. It's good practice to make notes in your scripts so others can more easily understand what the code is doing—and to remind yourself of the decisions you've made when you revisit the code after a few weeks or a few months. For example, in the very first line in *my_first_script.py*, we have this:

```
# -*- coding: utf-8 -*-
```

Since this line starts with #, Python ignores it, understanding that it's a comment and not code to execute.

When you have a comment that can't fit on one line, you can place the comment in triple quotation marks ("""), and everything between the first set of quotes and the last set will not be executed by the Python script. For example, in lines 2 to 6 in *my_first_script.py*, we have this:

```
"""
Created on Fri Apr 16 14:49:19 2021

@author: hlliu2
"""
```

All those lines are ignored by Python.

Basic Operations in Python

Python is capable of basic math operations. For example, to calculate 7 multiplied by 123, you enter the following in the Spyder editor:

```
print(7*123)
```

Place your cursor in this line, press F9, and you will get an output of 861. Table 1-1 provides the other basic math operations in Python.

Table 1-1: Basic Math Operators

Operators	Action
+	Addition: print(5+6) will give you a result of 11.
-	Subtraction: print(9-4) will give you a result of 5.
/	Division: print(9/3) will give you a result of 3.
**	Exponent: print(5**3) will give you a result of 125.
%	Remainder: print(13%5) will give you a result of 3 because 13 = 5 × 2 + 3.
//	Integer quotient: print(13//5) will give you a result of 2 because 13 = 5 × 2 + 3.

These operations have *precedence*, meaning they will execute in a particular order. That order of operations is as follows: operations within parentheses have highest priority, followed by exponents, then multiplication and division, which have the same priority and are executed from left to right. Addition and subtraction have the least priority and are treated equally, so whichever comes first is executed first.

For more complicated mathematical operations, such as cosine in trigonometry or the natural logarithm, we need to import modules, which I'll cover in Chapter 2.

Summary

In this chapter, you learned how to install Python and Spyder via Anaconda. You also learned to run Python scripts by using Spyder.

In Chapter 2, we'll discuss the Python skills that you need for the rest of the book. You'll learn the four main value types and how to convert one type to another. We'll look at conditional execution and loops as well as how functions and modules work in Python, allowing you to accomplish more-complicated tasks.

End-of-Chapter Exercises

1. Add a line of code to *my_first_script.py* so that it prints out a third message that says `Here is a third message!`

2. What is the output from each of the following Python statements? First write down the answers and then run the commands in Spyder to verify.

```
print(2)
print(3**2)
print(7//3)
print(7/3)
print(7%3)
print(2+2)
print(10*2)
```

3. What is the command line in the Spyder editor if you want to find the result of 55 multiplied by 234?

2

PYTHON REFRESHER

This chapter is a refresher on basic Python. The purpose of this chapter is not to comprehensively review all the basic commands in Python. Instead, I'll provide you with the Python skills that are most important to the rest of the book.

Specifically, you'll learn the four Python variable types (strings, integers, floats, and Booleans) and how to convert one type to another. Functions are useful tools in programming languages, and you'll learn to use built-in functions in Python and to import modules in the Python Standard Library.

You'll also learn how functions work and how to define your own functions. Many modules we use in this book are not in the Python Standard Library, and you'll learn different ways of installing these modules on your computer.

We'll discuss how modules work and how to create your own self-made modules. You'll then learn about a virtual environment, why it's useful, and how to create and activate one.

Python uses strings, lists, dictionaries, and tuples as collections of elements to accomplish complicated tasks. In this chapter, you'll learn these four types of collections, one by one. You'll also see examples of their uses.

Before you begin, set up the folder */mpt/ch02/* for this chapter. As in Chapter 1, all scripts in this chapter are available at the book's resources page, *https://www.nostarch.com/make-python-talk/*.

NEW SKILLS

- Understanding different types of variables and converting one type to another
- Using Python built-in functions and importing modules to a script
- Learning various ways of installing third-party modules
- Creating your own functions and modules
- Creating and activating a virtual environment
- Using strings, lists, dictionaries, and tuples to accomplish complicated tasks

---

Variables and Values

A *variable* is a reserved memory location to store values in Python (and in other programming languages). We can assign values to variables and use the variable name to recall the associated value. Python has four types of values: strings, floats, integers, and Booleans.

Strings

A *string* is a sequence of characters inside quotation marks, often used to represent text. Here are some examples of strings:

```
Name1 = 'University of Kentucky '
Name2 = "Gatton College 2021"
```

You can find out the type that a variable contains by using the type() function. Enter the following in the Spyder editor:

```
print(type(Name1))
print(type(Name2))
```

After execution, you'll see the following output:

```
<class 'str'>
<class 'str'>
```

This means both variables have string values. You can add or multiply strings, but not in the traditional mathematical sense; instead, you can join strings or repeat them. For example, say you run the following two lines of code in the Spyder editor:

```
print(Name1+Name2)
print(Name1*3)
```

You will see the following output:

```
University of Kentucky Gatton College 2021
University of Kentucky University of Kentucky University of Kentucky
```

The plus sign joins two strings together, while multiplying a string by 3 means to repeat the characters in the string three times. Note that I've deliberately left an empty space at the end of the string University of Kentucky, so that when they join together, there is a space between the strings.

Floats

Floating-point numbers, also known as just *floats*, are a number type that's equivalent to decimal numbers in mathematics. Here are two examples of floats:

```
x = -17.8912
y = 0.987
```

You can use the round() function to restrict a float to a certain number of digits after the decimal point. Floats can be positive, negative, or zero. Run the following code:

```
print(type(x))
print(type(y))
print(round(x,3))
print(round(y,1))
```

You will have the following output:

```
<class 'float'>
<class 'float'>
-17.891
1.0
```

Floats are used to perform calculations.

Integers

Integers are another number type; they can't have decimal places and so must be whole numbers. Integers are used mainly for indexing purposes in Python. Integers can be positive, negative, or zero. Here are some examples of integers:

```
a = 7
b = -23
c = 0
```

It is important to know that floats always have decimals, while integers do not. You never need to tell Python what type you want to use; instead, it can tell by the information you give it. Python knows you're using an integer if you enter a number without any quote marks and without decimal places. Even if you round a float number to zero digits after a decimal, you would still get a decimal point and a 0 trailing the number. Run the following code:

```
print(type(a))
print(type(b))
print(type(c))
print(round(7.346,1))
print(round(7.346,0))
```

You will have the following output:

```
<class 'int'>
<class 'int'>
<class 'int'>
7.3
7.0
```

The output shows that all three variables, a, b, and c, are integers. You will not get an output of 7 from print(round(7.346,0)), because using the decimal is Python's way of telling an integer apart from a float.

Bools

Booleans, or *bools*, are binary variables that can take only the value of True or False. Note that the first letter in True or False must always be uppercase. We use bools to find out truths about our code and make logical statements. As an example, run these two lines of code that compare two numbers:

```
print(4 > 5)
print(10 >= 6)
```

You will get the following output:

```
False
True
```

The results show that the logic statement 4 > 5 is False, while the logic statement 10 >= 6 is True. The values True or False (without quotes) are not strings but are special values reserved by Python. Try the following commands:

```
print('4 > 5')
print(type(4 > 5))
print(type('4 > 5'))
```

Here's the output:

```
4 > 5
<class 'bool'>
<class 'str'>
```

As you can see, once you put 4 > 5 inside quotation marks, it becomes a string variable instead of a bool.

Bools can also be represented with 1 (or, in reality, anything that's nonzero) for True and 0 for False. Run this code:

```
print(int(True))
print(int(False))
print(float(True))
print(str(False))
```

It outputs the following:

```
1
0
1.0
'False'
```

The bool() function converts any nonzero value to True and 0 to False. Run the following:

```
print(bool(1))
print(bool(-2))
print(bool(0))
print(bool('hello'))
```

And you will get this:

```
True
True
False
True
```

Convert Variable Types

You can convert the type of a variable by using the functions str(), int(), bool(), and float(), but only if the type you're trying to convert is compatible with the resulting type. For example, you can convert the string variable "17" to an integer or a float by using int("17") or float("17"), because 17 is a number that can be recognized as an integer or float. However, you cannot convert the string "Kentucky" to either an integer or a float.

Consider the following lines of code:

```
print(int(17.0))
print(int("88"))
print(int("3.45"))
print(str(17.0))
print(float(-4))
```

The output is the following:

```
17
88
ValueError: invalid literal for int() with base 10: '3.45'
'17.0'
-4.0
```

Bool values True and False can be converted to integers 1 and 0, respectively, because 1 and 0 are often used to represent True and False. While the float number 17.0 and string variable "88" can be converted to integers, the string variable "3.45" can't be converted to an integer because it has values after the decimal point.

You can convert almost anything into a string variable; for example, the float number 17.0 can be converted to the string variable "17.0". You can also convert any integer to a float: for example, the integer -4 can be converted to the float -4.0.

Rules for Variable Names

Certain rules exist for naming variables, and not everything can be used as a variable name. A variable name must start with a letter (either uppercase or lowercase) or an underscore (_). For example, you can't use 8python as a variable name because it starts with a number.

The only special character a variable name can have is the underscore, so special characters such as @ or & are not allowed. See the Python naming conventions at *https://www.python.org/dev/peps/pep-0008/#id34/*.

Variable names can't be Python keywords or Python built-in functions. To get the list of all keywords, run these two lines of code in the Spyder editor:

```
from keyword import kwlist
print(kwlist)
```

The output is a full list of Python keywords:

```
['False', 'None', 'True', 'and', 'as', 'assert', 'async', 'await', 'break',
'class', 'continue', 'def', 'del', 'elif', 'else', 'except', 'finally',
'for', 'from', 'global', 'if', 'import', 'in', 'is', 'lambda', 'nonlocal',
'not', 'or', 'pass', 'raise', 'return', 'try', 'while', 'with', 'yield']
```

Variable names can, however, *contain* keywords. For example, first_break and class1 are valid variable names, even though break and class are not.

Variable names should not be Python built-in functions. Figure 2-1 lists those functions, which are found in the Python documentation at *https://docs.python.org/3/library/functions.html*. You would do well to familiarize yourself with the list and avoid using these terms as variable names.

NOTE   *More information about Python built-in functions and their definitions can be found in the Python documentation.*

Built-in Functions				
abs()	delattr()	hash()	memoryview()	set()
all()	dict()	help()	min()	setattr()
any()	dir()	hex()	next()	slice()
ascii()	divmod()	id()	object()	sorted()
bin()	enumerate()	input()	oct()	staticmethod()
bool()	eval()	int()	open()	str()
breakpoint()	exec()	isinstance()	ord()	sum()
bytearray()	filter()	issubclass()	pow()	super()
bytes()	float()	iter()	print()	tuple()
callable()	format()	len()	property()	type()
chr()	frozenset()	list()	range()	vars()
classmethod()	getattr()	locals()	repr()	zip()
compile()	globals()	map()	reversed()	__import__()
complex()	hasattr()	max()	round()	

Figure 2-1: List of Python built-in functions

Loops and Conditional Execution

Loops and conditional statements let you make decisions in your code, so that certain code will run if a particular thing happens.

Conditional Execution

The if statement allows your code to take particular actions based on whether a condition is met. Consider the following lines of code:

```
x = 5
if x > 0:
    print('x is positive')
else:
    print('x is nonpositive')
```

Here, x > 0 is the condition. If the value of x is larger than 0, the condition is met, and the script prints the message x is positive. Conditionals in Python always need a colon (:) after the conditional statement. If the condition is not met, the script moves to the else branch and prints x is nonpositive.

We can also have more than two conditions by using the elif keyword. Consider the following code:

```
x = 5
if x > 0:
    print('x is positive')
elif x == 0:
    print('x is zero')
else:
    print('x is negative')
```

Python uses the double equal sign (==) as a comparison operator, to distinguish it from value assignments when we use a single equal sign (=). This script has three possible outcomes, depending on which condition is met: x is positive, x is zero, or x is negative.

If we require more than three conditions, the first condition must follow the if statement, the last condition must come after the else statement, and all conditions between should have the elif keyword:

```python
score = 88
if score >= 90:
    print('grade is A')
elif score >= 80:
    print('grade is B')
elif score >= 70:
    print('grade is C')
elif score >= 60:
    print('grade is D')
else:
    print('grade is F')
```

The script prints out the letter grade based on the value of the score: A if the score is greater or equal to 90; if not, B if the score is above 80, and so on.

Loops

One great advantage of computers is their ability to repeat the same tasks many times at a fast rate. This is known as *looping*, or *iterating*, in programming. Python has two types of loop: the while and the for loop.

The while Loop

A while loop is used to execute a block of code as long as a certain condition is met. Here we use the while statement to create a loop that adds 1 to the variable n every time it loops until n reaches 3. Then the loop exits, and the script prints finished. Save this as *whileloop.py*:

```python
n = 0
while n < 3:
    n = n+1
    print(n)
print('finished')
```

We first assign n a value of 0. Then, the script starts the while loop with the condition n < 3. As long as the condition is met, the loop keeps running. Notice the colon, which tells Python to expect the indented lines that follow as part of the loop. Those lines will execute every time the loop runs. The last line, which is not indented, runs only after the loop exits.

In the first iteration, the value of n increases from 0 to 1, and the updated value of n is printed out. In the second iteration, the value of n increases to 2, and the updated value of n is printed out. In the third iteration, the value of n increases to 3, and 3 is printed out. When the script goes to the fourth iteration, the condition n < 3 is no longer met, and the loop stops. After that, the last line is executed. As a result, we see the following output from *whileloop.py*:

```
1
2
3
finished
```

The while loop is most useful when we don't know the number of iterations we need beforehand, even though it can also be used to perform the same tasks as a for loop. Later in this book, we often use the statement while True to create an infinite loop that puts the script in standby mode.

The for Loop

The for loop is generally used when you want to execute a block of code a fixed number of times. The following script, *forloop.py*, is an example of a for loop that does the same as the while loop we just made, adding 1 to the variable n until n reaches 3:

```
for n in range(3):
    n = n + 1
    print(n)
print('finished')
```

We start by using range(), a built-in function in Python, to produce a range of values from 0 to 2 (Python always begins counting from 0). The line tells the script to loop through the three values, one value per loop, and execute the next two lines of code for each value, adding 1 to n per loop. When the range has been used up, the loop exits, and we print finished.

The code in *forloop.py* produces the same output as *whileloop.py*.

Loops in Loops

You can place a loop inside another loop. This is known as *nesting*. Nested loops are useful when, for each iteration in the outer loop, you need to repeat certain jobs for each iteration in the inner loop. The example script *loop_in_loop.py* loops through a list and a tuple, printing each member of the list with each member of the tuple, one pair per iteration:

```
for letter in ["A", "B", "C"]:
    for num in (1, 2):
        print(f"this is {letter}{num}")
```

First, we start the outer loop with for, and then the first indented line starts the inner loop. The script takes the first value in the outer loop, goes through all iterations in the inner loop, and prints a message at each iteration. It repeats the process again with the second value of the outer loop.

We need to indent the content of the inner loop twice so the script knows which lines belong to which loops. The final output from *loop_in_loop.py* is shown here:

```
this is A1
this is A2
this is B1
this is B2
this is C1
this is C2
```

Notice that we use the f"{}" string-formatting approach. The string f"this is {*letter*}{*num*}" tells Python to replace whatever is in the curly brackets with the actual value of the variable mentioned.

NOTE *Using f-strings to format strings works only in Python versions 3.6 or newer. If you're using an older version of Python, use the syntax "this is {0}{1}".format(letter, num) instead.*

You can nest loops pretty much indefinitely, and the script will iterate through all values in the innermost loop for each combination of values in the medium and outer loops. However, nesting too many loops can make your code difficult to read and isn't generally recommended practice.

Loop Commands

Loops have a few commands that are useful for controlling the way your loops behave—namely, continue, break, and pass. These commands allow you to make decisions within a loop by using the if statement.

continue

The continue command tells Python to stop executing the rest of the command for the current iteration and to go to the next iteration. You use continue when you want to skip certain actions when certain conditions are met in a loop. For example, the script *forloop1.py* uses the continue command to skip printing the number 2 and go to the next iteration:

```
for n in (1, 2, 3):
    if n == 2:
        continue
 ❶ print(n)
print('finished')
```

When the value of n is 2, line ❶ will not be executed because the continue command tells the script to skip it and go to the next iteration. The output from this script is as follows:

```
1
3
finished
```

break

The break command tells Python to break the loop and skip all remaining iterations. You use break when you want to exit the loop. The example script *forloop2.py* uses the break command to exit the for loop when the number reaches value 2:

```
for n in (1, 2, 3):
    if n == 2:
        break
    print(n)
❶ print('finished')
```

When the value of n is 2, the whole loop stops and the script goes to line ❶ directly. The output is therefore as follows:

```
1
finished
```

Later in this book, we'll frequently use the break command to tell the script to stop the infinite loop generated by the statement while True.

pass

The pass command tells Python to do nothing, and it is used when a command line is needed but no action needs to be taken. We often use it along with try and except, and we'll revisit this command later in this book. The script *forloop3.py* uses a pass command to tell the script to take no action when the value of the number is 2:

```
for n in (1, 2, 3):
    if n == 2:
        pass
    print(n)
print('finished')
```

When the value of n is 2, no action needs to be taken. Therefore, here's the output from the preceding script:

```
1
2
3
finished
```

This is the same as the output from *forloop.py*.

Strings

A *string* is a sequence of characters inside single or double quotation marks. The characters in the string can be letters, numbers, whitespace, or special characters. We'll discuss how elements in a string are indexed, how to slice them, and how to join multiple strings together.

String Indexing

The characters in strings are indexed from left to right, starting at 0. This is because Python uses *zero-based indexing*, so the first element is always indexed as 0 instead of 1.

You can access characters in a string by using the square bracket operator and the index of the character you want:

```
msg = "hello"
print(msg[1])
```

Since e is the second character in the string "hello", the output is this:

```
e
```

Python also uses *negative indexing*, which starts from the end of the string. The last character in the string can be indexed as [-1], the second-to-last one as [-2], and so on. This is useful when you have a long string and want to locate characters at the end of it.

To find the third-to-last character of the string msg, you'd use this:

```
print(msg[-3])
```

Here's the output:

```
l
```

String Slicing

Slicing a string means taking out a subset of characters. We again use the square bracket operator:

```
msg = "hello"
print(msg[0:3])
```

This will output the following:

```
hel
```

The code msg[*a*:*b*] gives you the substring from position *a* to position *b* in the string msg, where the character in position *a* is included in the substring but the character in position *b* is not. Therefore, msg[0:3] produces a substring of the first three characters in the string msg.

NOTE *If you omit the starting position when slicing a string, the default starting position is the first character. If you omit the ending position, the default is the last character. Therefore, msg[:3] gives you the same result as msg[0:3], and msg[0:] is equivalent to msg[:] (both produce the original string).*

String Methods

I'll cover a few common string methods we'll use throughout this book.

replace()

The replace() method replaces certain characters or substrings in the string with other characters. It takes two arguments: the character you want to replace and the character to replace it with. For example:

```
inp = "University of Kentucky"
inp1 = inp.replace(' ','+')
print(inp1)
```

We use replace() to replace all whitespaces with the plus sign. The output from the preceding script is shown here:

```
University+of+Kentucky
```

This method will be useful later in the book, when we deal with the speech recognition feature. We'll use replace() to change the voice text from the speech engine to a suitable format for the script.

lower()

The lower() method converts all uppercase letters in a string to lowercase. Since Python strings are case-sensitive, converting all letters to lowercase when matching strings means we won't miss uppercase substrings that should match.

Say we want to capture the spoken phrase "department of education" via a speech recognition module. We can't be sure whether the phrase will be captured as Department of Education or not. You can use lower() to convert the phrase to an all lowercase string to avoid mismatches, like so:

```
inp = "Department of Education"
inp1 = "department of education"
print(inp.lower() == inp1.lower())
```

The script tests whether the two strings inp and inp1 are the same when we ignore case-sensitivity. Here's the output:

```
True
```

find()

You can use find() to locate the position of a character in a string. The method returns the index of the character in the string.

Enter the following lines of code into the Spyder editor and save it as *extract_last_name.py*; then run it:

```
email = "John.Smith@uky.edu"
pos1 = email.find(".")
print(pos1)
```

```
pos2 = email.find("@")
print(pos2)
last_name = email[(1+pos1):pos2]
print(last_name)
```

The string variable `email` has a pattern: it consists of the first name, the dot, and the last name, followed by @uky.edu. We use this pattern to locate the positions of the dot and the at sign, then retrieve the last name based on those two positions.

First, we get the position of . and define it as a variable pos1. Then, we find the position of @ and define it as pos2. Finally, we slice the string and take the characters between the two positions, returning the substring as the variable last_name.

Running the script should produce this:

```
4
10
Smith
```

The indexes of . and @ in the email are 4 and 10, respectively, and the last name is Smith.

You can also use the string method find() to locate a substring. The method returns the starting position of the substring in the original string. For example, if you run the following lines of code

```
email = "John.Smith@uky.edu"
pos = email.find("uky.edu")
print(pos)
```

you'll get the following output:

```
11
```

The output says that the substring uky.edu starts with the 12th character in the email.

NOTE *If a character or a substring is not in a string, the output is -1 instead of an error message. For example, email.find("$") will give you an output of -1. We will use this feature later in this book to identify cases where something is not in a string.*

split()

The split() method splits a string into multiple strings, using the specified separator. Enter the following code in Spyder and run it:

```
msg = "Please think of an integer"
words = msg.split()
print(words)
```

The output is as follows:

```
['Please', 'think', 'of', 'an', 'integer']
```

The default *delimiter* (a fancy name for *separator*) is a whitespace (' '). You can also specify the delimiter when you use split(). Let's revisit the example of extracting the last name from an email address, naming the new script *split_string.py*, as in Listing 2-1.

```
email = "John.Smith@uky.edu"
(name, domain) = email.split('@')
(first, last) = name.split('.')
print(f"last name is {last}")
```

Listing 2-1: Using a delimiter to split up an email address

We first split the email into two parts by using @ as the delimiter and assign the name and domain to a tuple. (We'll discuss the definition of a *tuple* later in this chapter.) As a result, the first element in the tuple, the variable name, is a substring: John.Smith. The script then splits John.Smith into the first name and the last name, using . as the delimiter, and saves them in the tuple (*first, last*). Finally, we print out the second element in the tuple as the last name.

The output is shown here:

```
last name is Smith
```

join()

The join() method joins several strings into one, as in this script, *join_string.py*:

```
mylink = ('&')
strlist = ['University', 'of', 'Kentucky']
joined_string = mylink.join(strlist)
print(joined_string)
```

We define & as the variable mylink, to be used as our separator. The strlist is a list of the three words that we want to join together. We use join() to combine the three words into one single string. Note that you need to put join() after the separator. Finally, we print out the joined string:

```
University&of&Kentucky
```

Lists

A *list* is a collection of values separated by commas. The values in a list are called *elements*, or *items*, and they can be values, variables, or other lists.

Create a List

To create a new list, you simply put the elements in square brackets:

```
lst = [1, "a", "hello"]
```

We define the list lst with three elements: an integer number 1 and two strings. Note that list() is a built-in function in Python, so you cannot use list as a variable name or list name. I suggest that you use a descriptive name to help future readers understand the code.

You create an empty list by using a pair of square brackets with nothing in it:

```
lst1 = []
```

Or you can use the list() function:

```
lst2 = list()
```

Access Elements in a List

You can access the elements of a list by using the bracket operator:

```
lst = [1, "a", "hello"]
print(lst[2])
```

This will produce the following:

```
hello
```

Here, lst[2] refers to the third element in the list, because Python is like most computer programming languages, which start counting at zero.

You can traverse the elements of a list by using a loop:

```
for x in range(len(lst)):
    print(lst[x])
```

This give us the following:

```
1
a
hello
```

We use the built-in function len() to return the length of the list, which is 3 in this case. The built-in function range() returns values 0, 1, and 2 here.

Use a List of Lists

A list can use lists as its elements. This is useful for mapping element positions to coordinates in a two-dimensional space. Here is one example:

```
llst = [[1,2,3,5],
        [2,2,6,8],
        [2,3,5,9],
        [3,5,4,7],
        [1,3,5,0]]
print('the value of llst[1][2] is ', llst[1][2])
```

```
print('the value of llst[3][2] is ', llst[3][2])
print('the value of llst[1][3] is ', llst[1][3])
```

Here's the output:

```
the value of llst[1][2] is  6
the value of llst[3][2] is  4
the value of llst[1][3] is  8
```

The list llst itself contains five lists. To find the value of llst[1][2], the code first looks at the second item in the outer list llst, which is the list [2, 2, 6, 8]. The third element of that list is 6; hence llst[1][2] = 6.

Now let's draw a corresponding picture in a two-dimensional space, as in Figure 2-2.

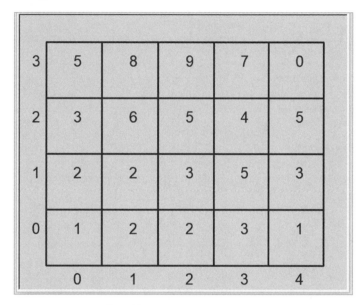

Figure 2-2: Map a list of lists to a two-dimensional space

We'll use this in Part III to create boards for our interactive games.

Add or Multiply Lists

You can use the plus (+) and multiplication (*) operators on lists, but not in the mathematical sense. For example, run the following lines of code:

```
lst = [1, "a", "hello"]
print(lst + lst)
print(lst * 3)
```

You should see the following output:

```
[1, "a", "hello", 1, "a", "hello"]
[1, "a", "hello", 1, "a", "hello", 1, "a", "hello"]
```

The plus operator joins two lists into a larger list. The multiplication operator repeats the elements in the list. If you multiply a list by 3, the elements will appear three times.

List Methods

I'll introduce several useful list methods here that we'll use in later chapters of this book.

enumerate()

The enumerate() method prints out all elements in a list with their corresponding indexes. Assume we have the following list names:

```
names = ['Adam','Kate','Peter']
```

The following lines of code

```
for x, name in enumerate(names):
    print(x, name)
```

will generate this output:

```
0 Adam
1 Kate
2 Peter
```

The first element at index 0 is Adam, the second at index 1 is Kate, and so on.

You can choose the start value to be 1 instead of 0 with start=1, like so:

```
names = ['Adam','Kate','Peter']
for x, name in enumerate(names, start=1):
    print(x, name)
```

The output is as follows:

```
1 Adam
2 Kate
3 Peter
```

append()

You can append an element to the end of a list by using the append() method. Consider this script, *list_append.py*:

```
lst = [1, "a", "hello"]
❶ lst.append(2)
print(lst)
```

This code is appending the element 2 to the existing list lst, producing this:

```
[1, "a", "hello", 2]
```

The new lst now has four elements.

You can append only one element at a time, and it is added to the end of the list by default. Appending two elements will lead to an error message. Change line ❶ in the script *list_append.py* to the following:

```
lst.append(2, 3)
```

You'll get the following error message:

```
TypeError: append() takes exactly one argument (2 given)
```

However, you can append multiple elements as a list. Add square brackets around the two numbers as follows:

```
lst.append([2, 3])
```

You'll get the following output:

```
[1, "a", "hello", [2, 3]]
```

The new list has four elements.

To add two or more elements to the existing list, you should use the plus operator. For example, to add 2 and 3 as two separate elements to the list, you can use the following line of code:

```
lst + [2, 3]
```

The output will be as follows:

```
[1, a, "hello", 2, 3]
```

remove()

You can remove an element from a list by using remove():

```
lst = [1, "a", "hello", 2]
lst.remove("a")
print(lst)
```

We remove the element that was at index 1, resulting in this:

```
[1, "hello", 2]
```

The new list no longer has element a. You can remove only one element at a time.

index()

You can find the position of an element in a list by using the index() method:

```
lst = [1, "a", "hello", 2]
print(lst.index("a"))
```

From this we get the following:

```
1
```

The result tells you that the element a has an index of 1 in the list.

count()

You can count how many times an element appears in a list by using count():

```
lst = [1, "a", "hello", 2, 1]
print(lst.count(1))
print(lst.count("a"))
```

This produces the following:

```
2
1
```

This tells us that the element 1 has appeared in the list twice, while the element a has appeared once.

sort()

You can sort the elements in a list by using sort(). The elements must be the same type (or at least convertible to the same type). For example, if you have both integers and strings in a list, trying to sort the list will lead to the following error message:

```
TypeError: '<' not supported between instances of 'str' and 'int'
```

Numbers are sorted from the smallest to the largest. Adding reverse=True inside the method as an option will reverse the ordering. Here's an example:

```
lst = [5, 47, 12, 9, 4, -1]
lst.sort()
print(lst)
lst.sort(reverse=True)
print(lst)
```

This will output the following:

```
[-1, 4, 5, 9, 12, 47]
[47, 12, 9, 5, 4, -1]
```

Letters are sorted in alphabetic order, and they come after numbers. Consider this example:

```
Lst = ['a', 'hello', 'ba', 'ahello', '2', '-1']
lst.sort()
print(lst)
```

The output is shown here:

```
['-1', '2', 'a', 'ahello', 'ba', 'hello']
```

Use Built-in Functions with Lists

We can use several Python built-in functions on lists directly, including min(), max(), sum(), and len(). These produce the minimum value, the maximum value, the total sum, and the length of the list, respectively, like so:

```
lst = [5, 47, 12, 9, 4, -1]
print("the range of the numbers is", max(lst)-min(lst))
print("the mean of the numbers is", sum(lst)/len(lst))
```

Here's the output:

```
the range of the numbers is 48
the mean of the numbers is 12.666666666666666
```

list()

You can use the list() function to convert a string to a list of characters:

```
msg = "hello"
letters = list(msg)
print(letters)
```

The output is as follows:

```
['h', 'e', 'l', 'l', 'o']
```

Interestingly enough, Python strings can be treated just like lists of characters.

Dictionaries

A *dictionary* is a collection of key-value pairs. We create a dictionary by placing the elements inside curly brackets, as shown in Listing 2-2.

```
scores = {'blue':10, 'white':12}
```

Listing 2-2: Creating a dictionary with two key-value pairs

The dictionary scores has two key-value elements, separated by a comma: the first element is the key blue and the value 10, denoted by their position and separated by a colon. The second element is 'white':12.

To create an empty dictionary, you use dict() or a pair of curly brackets with nothing within them:

```
Dict1 = dict()
Dict2 = {}
```

You can add a new element to the existing dictionary as follows:

```
Dict3 = {}
Dict3['yellow'] = 6
print(Dict3)
```

The line `Dict3['yellow'] = 6` assigns a value of 6 to the key yellow. The new Dict3 contains the element 6, which is accessible by the key yellow.

Access Values in a Dictionary

You access values in a dictionary by using the bracket operator. The key value in each pair acts as the index. For example, we can access the values in scores, built in Listing 2-2, as follows:

```
print(scores['blue'])
print(scores['white'])
```

This will give you the following results:

```
10
12
```

We can also use the get() method. The advantage of using get() is that it uses None as a default value when a user requests a key that isn't in the dictionary, rather than returning an error. Consider the following script, *get_score.py*:

```
scores = {'blue':10, 'white':12}
print(scores['blue'])
print(scores['white'])
print(scores.get('yellow'))
print(scores.get('yellow',0))
```

This produces the following:

```
10
12
None
0
```

Since the key yellow is not in scores, the method get('yellow') returns a value of None. Further, when you put the option 0 in the method, get('yellow', 0) returns a value of 0.

Use Dictionary Methods

You can use the keys() method to produce a list of all keys in a dictionary:

```
scores = {'blue':10, 'white':12}
teams = list(scores.keys())
print(teams)
```

This gives us the following:

```
['blue', 'white']
```

We can use `values()` to produce a list of all values in a dictionary:

```
points = list(scores.values())
print(points)
```

The output is shown here:

```
[10, 12]
```

We can use `items()` to get the list of each key-value pair as a tuple (see "Tuples" on page 37).

```
print(list(scores.items()))
```

This produces the following result:

```
[('blue', 10), ('white', 12)]
```

How to Use Dictionaries

The values in a dictionary can be any type of variable, a list, or even another dictionary. Here we have a dictionary that uses lists as values:

```
scores2 = {'blue':[5, 5, 10], 'white':[5, 7, 12]}
```

The value for each key is a three-element list. The three values represent the scores each player got in the first half and second half of the game and the total score, respectively. To find out how many points the white team got in the second half, you can call this:

```
print(scores2['white'][1])
```

The advantage of a dictionary is that its key can be any value, not necessarily an integer. This makes dictionaries useful in many situations. For example, *most_freq_word.py* uses a dictionary to count words:

```
news = (
'''Python is an interpreted, high-level, and general-purpose programming
 language. Python's design philosophy emphasizes code readability with
 its notable use of significant whitespace.
 Its language constructs and object-oriented approach aim to help
 programmers write clear, logical code for small- and large-scale
 projects.
''')
wdcnt = dict()
wd = news.split()
for w in wd:
    wdcnt[w] = wdcnt.get(w, 0) + 1
print(wdcnt)
```

```
for w in list(wdcnt.keys()):
    if wdcnt[w] == max(list(wdcnt.values())):
        print(w)
```

We define news as a string variable with a short paragraph. We then create an empty dictionary wdcnt. Next, we split the string into a list of separate words. We then count the frequency of each word and store the information in the dictionary, with the word as the key and the word count as the value. Because we use get(), if a word is not already in the dictionary as a key, the second argument in get() assigns a value of 0 to the word.

Finally, we print out the words that have the highest frequency. The result is as follows:

```
{'Python': 1, 'is': 1, 'an': 1, 'interpreted,': 1, 'high-level': 1, 'and': 3,
 'general-purpose': 1, 'programming': 1, 'language.': 1, "Python's": 1,
 'design': 1, 'philosophy': 1, 'emphasizes': 1, 'code': 2, 'readability': 1,
 'with': 1, 'its': 1, 'notable': 1, 'use': 1, 'of': 1, 'significant': 1,
 'whitespace.': 1, 'Its': 1, 'language': 1, 'constructs': 1,
 'object-oriented': 1, 'approach': 1, 'aim': 1, 'to': 1, 'help': 1,
 'programmers': 1, 'write': 1, 'clear,': 1, 'logical': 1, 'for': 1,
 'small-': 1, 'large-scale': 1, 'projects.': 1}
and
```

It turns out that the most frequent word in the news article is and, which is used three times.

Switch Keys and Values

Sometimes you'll want to switch the positions of keys and values. Now let's take the term *dictionary* literally and suppose you have the following English-to-Spanish dictionary that uses the English word as the key and the Spanish translation as the value:

```
spanish = {'one': 'uno', 'two': 'dos', 'three': 'tres'}
```

You want to create a Spanish-to-English dictionary instead. You can accomplish this by using the following line of code:

```
english = {y:x for x,y in spanish.items()}
```

The command x,y in spanish.items() retrieves all the key-value pairs in spanish. The command y:x for x,y switches the positions of the keys and values. You must put curly brackets around everything to the right of the equal sign so that the script treats it as a dictionary. To verify, enter this:

```
print(english)
```

You will have the following output:

```
{'uno': 'one', 'dos': 'two', 'tres': 'three'}
```

Combine Two Dictionaries

To combine two dictionaries x and y into one large dictionary z, you assign z = {**x, **y}:

```
spanishenglish = {**spanish, **English}
```

The result is a new dictionary called `spanishenglish` with six elements: three pairs from `spanish` and three pairs from `english`.

Tuples

A *tuple* is a collection of values separated by commas, similar to a list—with the big difference that a tuple cannot be changed after it's defined (that is, tuples are immutable). Elements of a tuple exist inside parentheses instead of square brackets to distinguish the tuple from a list. Here we make a tuple and attempt to modify it:

```
tpl = (1, 2, 3, 9, 0)
tpl.append(4)
print(tpl)
```

We get the following error message:

```
AttributeError: 'tuple' object has no attribute 'append'
```

Because tuples are immutable, we cannot use methods like `append()` or `remove()` on them. We cannot sort the elements in a tuple either.

The elements of a tuple are indexed by integers, and we can access them by using the bracket operator:

```
tpl = (1, 2, 3, 9, 0)
print(tpl[3])
print(tpl[1:4])
```

Our output is shown here:

```
9
(2, 3, 9)
```

We saw examples of assigning values to a tuple in *split_string.py* (Listing 2-1).

You can compare two tuples. This process begins with comparing their first elements. If the first elements are the same, we check whether the second elements match. If the second elements are also the same, we go to the third elements, and so on, until we find a difference.

Run the following lines of code in your Spyder editor:

```
lt = [(1, 2), (3, 9), (0, 7), (1, 0)]
lt.sort()
print(lt)
```

And you'll see this output:

```
[(0, 7), (1, 0), (1, 2), (3, 9)]
```

Functions

A *function* is (ideally) a block of code designed to do a task. There are many functions that do many things, but it is commonly considered best practice to have a function that performs only one task (and does not make changes to other variables). Some functions have defined parameters (inputs). We can assign the function code to a variable name so we don't have to repeat the same code every time we need that task done. Instead, we just call the function and enter the inputs.

Functions also improve readability, making the code more organized, less cluttered, and less error-prone.

Use Built-in Python Functions

Python comes with many built-in functions that you can readily use, including print() from Chapter 1. Here I'll discuss a couple of built-in functions we'll use frequently in this book.

The range() Function

The range() function is used to produce a list of integers. We introduced range() when we discussed loops on page 21. We know that, for example, range(5) produces the values [0, 1, 2, 3, 4]. The default starting value generated by the function range() is 0, because Python uses zero indexing, but you can also specify the starting value. For example, range(3, 6) produces the list of the following three values: [3, 4, 5].

The default increment value is 1, but you can also specify the increment as the optional third argument. For example, the code

```
for x in range(-5, 6, 2):
    print(x)
```

will give this output:

```
-5
-3
-1
1
3
5
```

The third argument in range(-5, 6, 2) tells the script to increase the value by 2 for each element.

If the increment value is a negative integer, the values in the list decrease. For example, range(9, 0, -3) produces the list [9, 6, 3].

The input() Function

Text-to-speech is the process of converting written text into human voice, so it's important to know how Python takes written text inputs, using a built-in function called input().

Run the following script in Spyder:

```
color = input('What is your favorite color?')
print('I see, so your favorite color is {}'.format(color))
```

You should see a screen similar to Figure 2-3.

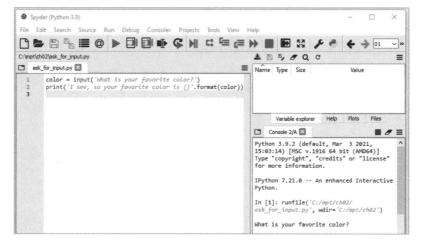

Figure 2-3: A screenshot of what happens when Python is asking for input

As you can see in Figure 2-3, the script asks for your input in the lower-right IPython console. It waits for you to type some text and press ENTER before it continues to run. If you enter **blue**, the script will output the following:

```
What is your favorite color? blue
I see, so your favorite color is blue.
```

You can ask for multiple inputs, like so:

```
FirstName = input('What is your first name?\n')
LastName = input('What is your last name?\n')
print(f'Nice to meet you, {FirstName } {LastName }.')
```

The script asks for two inputs. The sequence \n is an escape character, inserting a new line below the question "What is your first name?"

Define Your Own Functions

In addition to using built-in functions, we can build our own. I'll show you how to create a function, and this process will also show you how functions work. Functions can take one or more inputs, known as *arguments*, or no input at all.

A Function with No Argument

We'll start by building a function that prints the message Finished printing. This function takes no input:

```
def TheEnd():
    print('Finished printing')
for i in (1, 2, 3):
    print(i)
TheEnd()
```

We use def to signify a function definition, give a function name, and follow it with empty parentheses and a colon. The colon tells Python to expect the body of the function. All indented lines that follow are considered part of the function.

The script prints three numbers, after which we call the function. The output is as follows:

```
1
2
3
Finished printing
```

As you can see, the command line in the function is executed only when the function is called, not when it is defined.

A Function with One Argument

Now we'll write a function that takes one input. We need to write a thank-you note to 50 people. The message is the same except for the recipient's name. We'll define a function to print the message, and we need to supply only the name for each message when we call it. We first define a function called msgs() as follows:

```
def msgs(name):
    print(f"Thank you, {name}, I appreciate your help!")
```

The name of the function is msgs, with the variable name as its only input. If we call the function twice as follows:

```
msgs("Mary")
msgs("Bob")
```

the output will be this:

```
Thank you, Mary, I appreciate your help!
Thank you, Bob, I appreciate your help!
```

To write the 50 thank-you notes, you can call the function 50 times: once with each name.

A Function with Multiple Arguments

Functions can have two or more arguments as inputs. Consider the script *team_sales.py* in Listing 2-3, which defines a function that needs three inputs.

```
def team_sales(sales1, sales2, sales3):
    sales = sales1 + sales2 + sales3
    return sales
print(team_sales(100, 150, 120))
```

Listing 2-3: Defining a function with three arguments

We define a function to calculate the total sales from a team with three members. The function uses the sales from individual members, sales1, sales2, and sales3, as the three arguments. We calculate the total team sales, sales, by summing the three individual sales numbers. We then tell the script the output of the function by using the return command. As a result, when the function team_sales() is called, you get the sum of the three sales.

If the individual sales are 100, 150, and 120, when we call the function team_sales(), we'll get an output of 370.

A Function That Takes an Unknown Number of Arguments

Sometimes the number of inputs is unknown. For example, you want to define a function to calculate the total sales made by a group of salespeople, but different groups have different numbers of salespeople. You can define a single function for this purpose that works regardless of the size of the group by using the argument *args, which allows you to pass multiple values of variable length to a function. Listing 2-4, *total_sales.py*, accomplishes the job.

```
def total_sales(*args):
    total = 0
    for arg in args:
        total = total + arg
    return total
--snip--
```

Listing 2-4: First part of total_sales.py

We start total_sales(), which takes *args as the argument. We set the value of the variable total to 0 and then loop through each element in the argument args. For each element in the argument, we add it to the variable total. We output the total sales of the group. Test it out with Listing 2-5.

```
--snip--
print(total_sales(200,100,100,100))
print(total_sales(800,500,400))
```

Listing 2-5: Second part of the script total_sales.py

From this, we get the following:

```
500
1700
```

As you can see, the function takes the one argument, *args, but you can put as many elements in the function as you want.

Modules

You are not limited to just the Python built-in functions. The Python Standard Library has many modules that provide other functions you can call from your own code.

Import Modules

We'll discuss three ways of using a function from a module and the pros and cons of each approach.

Import the Module

The first way is to import the entire module. For example, to find the value of the cosine of a 30-degree angle, you can first import the *math* module. Then you can use the cos() function from the module by calling both the module name and the function name: math.cos().

Enter the following code in Spyder:

```
import math
print(math.cos(30))
```

You'll have an output of 0.15425144988758405.

You have to import the module before you call `math.cos()`. If you don't import *math* and just run this command:

```
print(math.cos(30))
```

Python will give you an error message:

```
NameError: name 'math' is not defined
```

Also, you must always put the module name in front of the function name when you call the function. Enter the following two lines of code in Python:

```
import math
print(cos(30))
```

You'll get this error message:

```
NameError: name 'cos' is not defined
```

This is because Python doesn't know where to find the cos() function, even though you have imported the *math* module.

Import the Functions

If you want only one or two functions from a certain module, you can save time by importing just those one or two functions. This approach allows you to use the function name without having to append the module name. Enter the following two lines of code:

```
from math import cos, log
print(cos(30)+log(100))
```

You'll get the correct output, 4.759421635875676. We don't need to use `math` because we told the script where to look for the two functions. This is particularly useful if you need to use the function dozens or hundreds of times in your script.

Use Asterisk Import

If your script relies heavily on many functions in a module, you can potentially save time by importing all functions from the module by using asterisk import: `from module import *`. However, many in the Python community have cautioned against this approach because the import * statement can pollute your namespace, potentially interfering with functions you define (or functions from other modules). We won't use this method in the book.

Create Your Own Modules

In Listing 2-3, we defined team_sales() in *team_sales.py* and then called the function. You might need to calculate the total sales in many scripts. You can do so without rewriting the code in each script by building the function into a module.

Let's first create a script called *create_local_module.py*, as shown in Listing 2-6.

```
def team_sales(sales1, sales2, sales3):
    sales = sales1 + sales2 + sales3
    return sales
```

Listing 2-6: Code for the local module

This script defines team_sales() but does not call it. Next, create the new script *import_local_module.py* in Listing 2-7 and save it in the same folder as *create_local_module.py*.

```
from create_local_module import team_sales
print(team_sales(100, 160, 200))
print(team_sales(200, 250, 270))
print(team_sales(150, 120, 200))
```

Listing 2-7: Code to import the local module

When you import a module, Python first looks in the directory the importing script is stored in, so the module must be in the same folder. This kind of module is known as a *local module*.

If you run the script, you'll get the following results:

```
460
720
470
```

The team_sales() function correctly calculates the total sales for three teams.

Local modules work the same as modules in the Python Standard Library, but they need to be stored in the folder Python expects them to be in.

For modules that you download, Python stores the file path of the downloaded module behind the scenes and follows that path when you import it. For example, the *tkinter* package is in the Python Standard Library we'll use later in this book. When you install it, the files are placed under a specific path, which is something like the following on Windows:

```
C:\Users\ME\Anaconda3\envs\MYEV\Lib\tkinter
```

It's buried like this so you don't accidentally alter or misplace it, which would mean you could no longer use it.

Use Third-Party Modules

One of the main advantages of Python is that programmers can share modules with one another for free. Many of these modules are not in the Python Standard Library, including the module we'll rely on for the text-to-speech and the speech recognition functionality. These external modules, known as *third-party modules*, can be installed separately. Before you do that, you need to check that the module isn't already installed.

Check Installed Modules

All modules in the Python Standard Library are automatically installed on your machine when you install Python. Other modules may also be installed when you download various software or modules. For example, when you install *pandas* in Chapter 14, about 23 other supporting modules will be installed because *pandas* depends on them.

You can check whether a module is installed on your computer already with the following in your Spyder editor:

```
help("modules")
```

This will provide you with the list of all modules installed on your computer. However, it can take a long time for Python to list all the modules and for you to check them.

NOTE *For a list of all modules in the Python Standard Library, go to* https://docs.python .org/3/library/. *The list is constantly changing because more and more modules are added to the library over time.*

Alternatively, you can check whether a module is installed by trying to import it:

```
import ModuleName
```

To check whether *pandas* is installed on your computer, run `import pandas`, and if you receive no error message, the module is already installed. If the output shows `ModuleNotFoundError`, you need to install it. Let's see how.

Pip Install Modules

The *gTTS* module we'll use in Chapter 4 is not included in Python Standard Library, so we'll pip install it. Open the Anaconda prompt (in Windows) or a terminal (in Mac or Linux), and enter this:

```
pip install gTTS
```

Follow the onscreen instructions all the way through, and the *gTTS* module will be installed.

Conda Install Modules

If you can't find the module you want through pip install, try conda install.

We'll install the *yt* module by using the following in the Anaconda prompt (in Windows) or a terminal (in Mac or Linux):

```
conda install yt
```

Many people think pip install and conda install are the same, but they're not. Pip is the Python packaging authority's recommended tool for installing packages from the Python packaging index. You can install Python software only by using pip install. In contrast, Conda is a cross-platform package and environment manager that installs not only Python software but also packages in C or C++ libraries, R packages, or other software.

As you build more and more projects in Python, you'll install many modules. Some modules may interfere with other modules, and different projects may use different versions of the same module. To avoid problems of clashing modules, I recommend you build a virtual environment for each project. A *virtual environment* is a way to isolate projects from each other.

Create a Virtual Environment

To create a virtual environment, open an Anaconda prompt (in Windows) or a terminal (in Mac or Linux). We'll name the virtual environment for the projects in this book *chatting*. Enter the following command:

```
conda create -n chatting
```

After pressing ENTER, follow the instructions onscreen and press **y** when the prompt asks you y/n. Once you have created the virtual environment on your machine, you need to activate it.

Activate the Virtual Environment in Windows

In the Anaconda prompt (in Windows) or a terminal (in Mac or Linux), type this:

```
conda activate chatting
```

In Windows, you'll see the following on your Anaconda prompt:

```
(chatting) C:\>
```

You can see the (chatting) prompt, which indicates that the command line is now in the virtual environment *chatting* that you've just created.

On a Mac, you should see something similar to the following in the terminal (the username will be different):

```
(chatting) Macs-MacBook-Pro:~ macuser$
```

In Linux, you should see something similar to this on your terminal (the username will be different):

```
(chatting) mark@mark-OptiPlex-9020:~$
```

NOTE   *If you're using some versions of Linux, use* activate chatting *instead of* conda activate chatting *to activate the virtual environment. You might not see the* (chatting) *part on your terminal even if the virtual environment is activated.*

Set Up Spyder in the Virtual Environment in Windows

Now we need to install Spyder in the new virtual environment. First make sure you've activated the virtual environment. Then run this command:

```
conda install spyder
```

To then launch Spyder, execute the following command in the same terminal with the virtual environment activated:

```
spyder
```

Summary

In this chapter, you learned the four variable types and how to convert one type to another. You also learned how functions work in Python. You learned three ways to import a module into a script and the pros and cons of each approach.

You also created your own functions. You created a local module and imported it to a script to make clean and concise code. Finally, you created and activated a virtual environment in order to separate packages in different projects.

In Chapter 3, you'll learn how to install speech recognition–related modules to make Python understand the human voice.

End-of-Chapter Exercises

1. Assume:

```
name1 = 'Kentucky '
name2 = "Wildcats"
```

What is the output from each of the following Python statements? First write down the answer and then run the command in Spyder to verify.

```
print(type(name1))
print(type(name2))
print(name1 + name2)
print(name2 + name1)
print(name2 + ' @ ' + name1)
print(3 * name2)
```

2. Assume:

```
x = 3.458
y = -2.35
```

What is the result from each of the following Python statements?

```
print(type(x))
print(type(y))
print(round(x, 2))
print(round(y, 1))
print(round(x, 0))
```

3. Here are some examples of integers:

```
a = 57
b = -3
c = 0
```

What is the result from each of the following Python statements?

```
print(type(b))
print(str(a))
print(float(c))
```

4. What is the output from each of the following Python statements?

```
print(type(5==9))
print('8<7')
print(5==9)
print(type('8<7'))
print(type('True'))
```

5. What is the output from each of the following Python statements?

```
print(int(-23.0))
print(int("56"))
print(str(-23.0))
print(float(8))
```

6. What is the output from each of the following Python statements?

```
print(int(True))
print(float(False))
print(str(False))
```

7. What is the output from each of the following Python statements?

```
print(bool(0))
print(bool(-23))
print(bool(17.6))
print(bool('Python'))
```

8. Are the following variable names valid, and why?

```
global
2pirnt
print2
_squ
list
```

9. The loop command break is used in the following script. What should the output be? First write down the answer and then run the command in Spyder and verify.

```
for letter in ("A", "B", "C"):
    if letter == "B":
        break
    for num in (1, 2):
        print(f"this is {letter}{num}")
```

10. The loop command continue is used in the following script. What should the output be? First write down the answer and then run the command in Spyder and verify.

```
for letter in ("A", "B", "C"):
    if letter == "B":
        continue
    for num in (1, 2):
        print(f"this is {letter}{num}")
```

11. The loop command pass is used in the following script. What should the output be? First write down the answer and then run the command in Spyder and verify.

```
for letter in ("A", "B", "C"):
    if letter == "B":
        pass
    for num in (1, 2):
        print(f"this is {letter}{num}")
```

12. What is the output from each of the following commands? First write down the answer and then run the command in Spyder to verify it.

a.

```
for i in range(5):
    print(i)
```

b.

```
for i in range(10, 15):
    print(i)
```

c.

```
for i in range(10, 15, 2):
    print(i)
```

13. What is the value of team_sales(50, 100, 120) according to the defined function in this chapter?

14. Change the module import method in the script *import_local_module.py* from the from *module* import *function* method to the import *module* method. Name the new script *import_local_module1.py* and make sure it produces the same output.

15. Grades for the midterm project of eight groups in a class are in a list midterm = [95, 78, 77, 86, 90, 88, 81, 66]. Use Python built-in functions on the list to calculate the range and the average of the grades.

16. Assume inp = "University of Kentucky", and determine inp[5:10], inp[-1], inp[:10], and inp[5:].

17. If email = John.Smith@uky.edu, what is email.find("y")?

18. Assume llst = [[1,2,3,5],[2,2,6,8],[2,3,5,9],[3,5,4,7],[1,3,5,0]]. What are the values of llst[2], llst[2][2], and llst[3][0]?

19. What is the output from each of the following Python statements?

```
[1, "a", "hello", 2].remove(1)
[1, "a", "hello", 2].append("hi")
```

20. Assume scores2 = {'blue':[5, 5, 10], 'white':[5, 7, 12]}. What is scores2['blue'][2]?

21. Here is an example of a tuple: tpl = (1, 2, 3, 9, 0). What is tpl[3:4]?

22. You have a list lst = [1, "a", "hello", 2]. Create a dictionary with four key-value pairs: the key is the position of each element in lst, and the value is the element at that position.

PART II

LEARNING TO TALK

3

SPEECH RECOGNITION

In this chapter, we'll begin interacting with Python through speech. We'll first install the *SpeechRecognition* module; the installation process can be a source of frustration and will therefore require some careful attention. You'll then create a script to let Python recognize your speech and print it out to ensure that the voice recognition function works smoothly on your computer.

You'll use voice control to complete several tasks, including voice dictation, opening web browsers, opening files, and playing music on your computer. You'll put all code related to speech recognition into a custom local module so the final script is concise and easy to read.

Before you begin, set up the folder */mpt/ch03/* for this chapter. All scripts in this chapter are available at the book's resources page, *https://www.nostarch.com/make-python-talk/*.

Install the SpeechRecognition Module

Installing the *SpeechRecognition* module can be tricky, even to the point of frustration. Don't panic; we'll discuss how to install it in Windows, Mac, and Linux. Installing the *SpeechRecognition* module takes an extra step compared to most modules because it relies on the *pyaudio* module, which we'll have to install manually. The *pyaudio* module provides bindings for the cross-platform audio input/output library *portaudio*.

You cannot `pip install` the *pyaudio* module in the Anaconda prompt either. Instead, you need to `conda install` it.

NOTE   *Even though we have gone to great lengths to test the steps required to install these modules on a variety of hardware and software platforms, there is a chance that something might not work on your system. If this happens, be sure to check the errata page for updates, search the forums for the Python packages, or contact the author.*

In Windows

First, you need to activate the virtual environment *chatting* from Chapter 2. Go to your Anaconda prompt and enter the following:

```
conda activate chatting
```

You should see a modified prompt:

```
(chatting) c:\>
```

Note that the (chatting) in the prompt indicates that you are now in the virtual environment *chatting*. If the command hasn't worked, return to Chapter 2 for full instructions on how to create and activate a virtual environment.

Next, enter the following in the Anaconda prompt:

```
(chatting) c:\> pip install SpeechRecognition
```

If you then try to import it and run a script, Spyder will tell you that you need the *pyaudio* module for the *SpeechRecognition* module to run correctly.

With the virtual environment *chatting* activated, run the following in your Anaconda prompt:

```
(chatting) c:\> conda install pyaudio
```

Follow the instructions all the way through.

In Mac or Linux

First, activate the virtual environment *chatting*. Open a terminal and enter and execute the following:

```
conda activate chatting
```

Next, execute the following in the terminal:

```
pip install SpeechRecognition
```

If you now try to import *SpeechRecognition* and run a script, Spyder will tell you that you need *pyaudio* for *SpeechRecognition* to run correctly. With the virtual environment *chatting* activated, run the following command in your terminal:

```
conda install pyaudio
```

Follow the instructions all the way through.

Test and Fine-Tune SpeechRecognition

We'll next test and fine-tune the *SpeechRecognition* module so Python can take your voice commands.

Import SpeechRecognition

To import *SpeechRecognition* in your Python scripts, use the following command:

```
import speech_recognition
```

Note that there is a small difference in the module name when you install it and when you import it: one is *SpeechRecognition* and the other is *speech_recognition*. Make sure you don't miss the underscore in the module name when you import it.

You also need to have a microphone plugged into the computer if you're using a desktop. Most laptops come with a built-in microphone, but sometimes having an external one is convenient so you can speak close to the microphone and avoid ambient noise.

If you have multiple microphone devices on your computer, make sure your Python script is using the right one as the input device. Better yet, make sure that your microphone is indeed working by testing it first with other applications on your computer (for example, Voice Recorder in Windows, Voice Memos or QuickTime Player in Mac, or Audacity in Linux).

Test SpeechRecognition

Next, let's test the hardware and software. Enter Listing 3-1 into your Spyder editor and save it as *sr.py*, or you can download the file from the book's resources.

```python
import speech_recognition as sr
speech = sr.Recognizer()
print('Python is listening...')
with sr.Microphone() as source:
    speech.adjust_for_ambient_noise(source)
    audio = speech.listen(source)
    inp = speech.recognize_google(audio)
print(f'You just said {inp}.')
```

Listing 3-1: Testing SpeechRecognition

We import the *SpeechRecognition* module. Next, we call `Recognizer()` to initiate a *Recognizer* instance from the module so that your script is ready to convert voice to text. We save it as the variable `speech`. We also print a message that lets you know the microphone is ready to receive speech input.

If a module has a long name, writing out the full module name in the script is time-consuming (and can reduce the code's readability). You can use a shorter alias instead. For example, `import speech_recognition as sr` *allows you to use* `sr` *instead of* `speech_recognition` *whenever you refer to the module.*

We tell the script that the source of the audio comes from the microphone using `Microphone()`. We use the `adjust_for_ambient_noise()` method to reduce the impact of the ambient noise on your voice input. The script captures the voice input from the defined microphone, converts it into text, and saves in `inp`. We print out the value of `inp`.

Note in this script, the *Recognizer* instance uses `recognize_google()`for recognizing speech from the audio source. This method uses the Google Web Speech application programming interface (API) and requires a good internet connection. Other methods available to the *Recognizer* instance in the *SpeechRecognition* module include `recognize_bing()`, which uses Microsoft Bing Speech; `recognize_ibm()`, which uses IBM Speech to Text; and so on. The only method that works offline is `recognize_sphinx()`, which uses the services of CMU Sphinx. However, the accuracy with `recognize_sphinx()` is not nearly as good as with `recognize_google()`, so we'll use `recognize_google()` throughout this book.

Run *sr.py* and say something simple, like "Hello" or "How are you?", to test if Python correctly prints out your voice input. You should see the following if you say, "How are you?":

```
Python is listening...
You just said how are you.
```

If the script is working, you've successfully installed the speech recognition feature. If not, double-check the previous steps and make sure your microphone is connected properly. Also make sure that you are in a relatively quiet area with a good internet connection.

Notice that Python converts almost all voice input as lowercase text, which can be a good feature since string variables are case-sensitive. This way, Python won't miss a command because of capitalization.

TRY IT OUT

Run *sr.py* and try speaking a few simple phrases to the microphone to make sure the script understands you.

Fine-Tune the Speech Recognition Feature

Now you'll fine-tune the speech recognition code to make it more user-friendly for the rest of the book. We'll use try and except on a few common errors to allow the execution of the code to continue after encountering errors, instead of causing the script to crash.

The common error `UnknownValueError` happens when the Google speech recognition server cannot understand the audio, either because the speech isn't clear or because of ambient noise. The error `RequestError` happens when the Google speech recognition request fails, either because of a bad internet connection or because the server is too busy. The error `WaitTimeoutError` happens when the script doesn't detect any audio from the microphone for a long period.

Without using try and except, the script crashes, and you have to start the script all over again. By using the exception-handling constructs, the script will continue without crashing. The errors I mentioned aren't harmful enough to be worth handling, so our scripts will just allow those errors to pass.

Listing 3-2, *stand_by.py*, uses an infinite loop to first stand by and then repeatedly take voice inputs and print them out. This way, we don't have to rerun the script every time we want the script to take our voice inputs.

```
import speech_recognition as sr

speech = sr.Recognizer()
while True:
    print('Python is listening...')
    inp = ""
```

```
    with sr.Microphone() as source:
        speech.adjust_for_ambient_noise(source)
 ❶ try:
            audio = speech.listen(source)
            inp = speech.recognize_google(audio)
        except sr.UnknownValueError:
            pass
        except sr.RequestError:
            pass
        except sr.WaitTimeoutError:
            pass
 ❷ print(f'You just said {inp}.')
    if inp == "stop listening":
        print('Goodbye!')
        break
```

Listing 3-2: Code for stand_by.py

We start a while loop to put the script in standby. This way, after taking your voice input, the script prints out what you said and starts listening again. At each iteration, the script prints Python is listening so you know it's ready. We define the variable inp as an empty string at the beginning of each iteration. Otherwise, if the user doesn't say anything for a while, the script will retrieve the inp value from the previous iteration. By clearing the string, we avoid any potential mix-ups.

We use exception handling when connecting to the Google speech-recognition server ❶. If there is an UnknownValueError, a RequestError, or a WaitTimeoutError, we let the script continue without crashing.

At each iteration, the script prints what you said so that you can check if the speech recognition software has correctly captured your voice ❷.

Finally, we don't want the script to run forever, so we add a condition to stop it. When you say, "Stop listening," the if branch is activated, the script prints Goodbye!, and the while loop stops.

Here's a sample output, with my voice input in bold:

```
Python is listening...
You just said hello.
Python is listening...
You just said how are you.
Python is listening...
You just said today is a Saturday.
Python is listening...
You just said stop listening.
Goodbye!
```

Next, you'll put the speech recognition feature to use in several projects. Some are practical and useful, and others are for building up skills for later chapters.

NOTE   *Sometimes the speech recognition takes a long time to process, especially if there is ambient noise and the internet connection is slow. Try to test the script in a quiet place with a good internet connection.*

Perform a Voice-Controlled Web Search

Our first project is a script to navigate the web by using voice. You'll learn to use the *webbrowser* module to open a browser on your computer. Then you'll add voice-control functionality to open the browser and perform various searches online.

Use the webbrowser Module

The *webbrowser* module gives you tools to open a website by using the default browser on your computer. The module is in the Python Standard Library, so no installation is needed.

To test the *webbrowser* module on your computer, enter the following lines of code in your Spyder editor and run them:

```
import webbrowser
webbrowser.open("http://"+"wsj.com")
```

We use "http://"+ inside the open() function so that you need to input only the main body of the web address instead of the full URL. This is to prepare you for voice activation in the next section. The web browser will automatically correct the URL if it uses *https://* instead of *http://* or if *www* is in the full URL.

A new web browser window should open on the *Wall Street Journal* website. Microsoft Edge is the default browser on my computer, and the result is shown in Figure 3-1.

Figure 3-1: Result of using the webbrowser.open("http://"+"wsj.com") *command*

Add Voice Control

Now we'll add the speech recognition feature. Save Listing 3-3 as *voice_browse.py*.

```
import webbrowser
import speech_recognition as sr

speech = sr.Recognizer()
❶ def voice_to_text():
    voice_input = ""
    with sr.Microphone() as source:
        speech.adjust_for_ambient_noise(source)
        try:
            audio = speech.listen(source)
            voice_input = speech.recognize_google(audio)
        except sr.UnknownValueError:
            pass
        except sr.RequestError:
            pass
        except sr.WaitTimeoutError:
            pass
    return voice_input
❷ while True:
    print('Python is listening...')
    inp = voice_to_text()
    print(f'You just said {inp}.')
    if inp == "stop listening":
        print('Goodbye!')
        break
    elif "browser" in inp:
        inp = inp.replace('browser ','')
        webbrowser.open("http://"+inp)
        continue
```

Listing 3-3: Code for voice_browse.py

We import the two modules needed for this script: *webbrowser* and *SpeechRecognition*. At ❶, we define the voice_to_text() function, which contains most of the steps in *stand_by.py*: it starts with the empty string voice_input, converts the audio from the microphone to text, and puts it in voice_input. It also makes exceptions for the UnknownValueError, the RequestError, and the WaitTimeoutError. Once called, the function will return the value stored in voice_input.

The script starts an infinite loop to continuously take voice input ❷. At each iteration, it prints Python is listening... so you know it's ready.

WARNING *Don't start speaking into the microphone before you see the message* Python is listening...*, or part (or even all) of your speech may not be captured by the speech recognition software.*

We call `voice_to_text()` to capture your voice input and save the converted text in `inp`. Note that I intentionally use a different variable name for the local variable `voice_input` and the global variable `inp` to avoid confusion.

If you say, "Stop listening" to the microphone, the `if` branch is activated. The script prints `Goodbye!` and stops running. If the word *browser* is in your voice command, the `elif` branch is activated. The script then puts `http://` and whatever you say next in the address bar and opens the web browser. For example, if you say "browser abc.com," the `replace()` method will change "browser" and the space after it to an empty string, which effectively changes `inp` to `abc.com`.

Here's one sample output, with my voice input in bold:

```
Python is listening...
You just said browser cnn.com.
Python is listening...
You just said browser pbs.org.
Python is listening...
You just said stop listening.
Goodbye!
```

The associated web browser pop-ups are as shown in Figure 3-2.

Figure 3-2: One of the sample outputs from voice_browse.py

You use the word *browser* instead of *browse* to ensure that the script understands you: if you say "Browse" to your microphone, Python might convert it to `brows` instead. You may encounter several instances where slight adjustments will need to be made. Since everyone has a different voice, microphone, and diction (accent, inflection, and intonation), your adjustments will likely be different from mine.

> **TRY IT OUT**
>
> Run *voice_browse.py* and use it to visit *http://nbc.com/*.

Perform a Google Search

We'll now modify *voice_browse.py* so you can voice-activate a Google search. All you need to change is this one line of code from *voice_browse.py*:

```
webbrowser.open("http://"+inp)
```

Change it to this:

```
webbrowser.open("http://google.com/search?q="+inp)
```

Then save the modified script as *voice_search.py*. (You can also download it from the book's resources page.)

Here we are using the fact that whenever Google performs a search, it puts the search term after *http://google.com/search?q=* and uses it as the URL in the address bar. For example, when you search `how many liters are in a gallon` in Google, you get the same result as if you entered the URL *http://google.com/search?q=how many liters are in a gallon*.

Run *voice_search.py* in your Spyder editor. Ask a question, like "Browser yards in a mile," into the microphone. The script should open your default browser, perform a Google search for `yards in a mile`, and show a result similar to Figure 3-3.

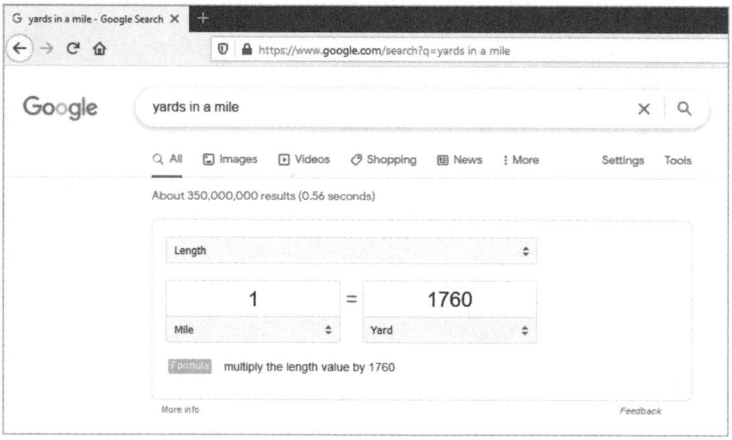

Figure 3-3: The result when you say "browser yards in a mile"

You can also use the script in any way you use Google, for example, as a voice-controlled dictionary. If you want to know the exact definition of the word *diligence*, you can say, "Browser define diligence."

Open Files

With the capability of speech recognition in a Python script, you can do many things with voice control. We'll build a script to open various types of files, including text files, PDF files, and music files.

Use the os and pathlib Modules to Access and Open Files

You can use the *os* and *pathlib* modules to access files and folders on your computer. The *os* module accesses operating system functionalities such as *go to a folder, open a file*, and so on. However, the commands differ across operating system. For example, to open a file, the command is explorer in Windows, open in Mac, and xdg-open in Linux.

To make your scripts portable cross-platform, we'll use the *platform* module, which lets the script automatically identify your operating system and then choose the appropriate command for you. The *pathlib* module allows you to find out the file paths and specify a file or folder path. Luckily, *pathlib* is cross-platform, so you don't have to worry about a forward slash or backslash. All three modules—*os, pathlib*, and *platform*—are in the Python Standard Library, so no installation is needed.

In your chapter folder, create a subfolder called *files* and save a file *example.txt* in it. Then enter Listing 3-4 in your Spyder editor and save it as *os_platform.py*.

```python
import os
import pathlib
import platform

myfolder = pathlib.Path.cwd()
print(myfolder)
myfile = myfolder/'files'/'example.txt'
print(myfile)
if platform.system() == "Windows":
    os.system(f"explorer {myfile}")
elif platform.system() == "Darwin":
    os.system(f"open {myfile}")
else:
    os.system(f"xdg-open {myfile}")
```

Listing 3-4: Code for os_platform.py

We import the modules, then use `Path.cwd()` from *pathlib* to find the current working directory of the script. We'll use this as the starting path to navigate from.

We then specify the path and name of the file we want to open. In the *pathlib* module, we use a forward slash to denote subfolders no matter what operating system you are using. The command `/'files'` tells the script to go to the subfolder *files*, and `/'example.txt'` indicates which file to define as *myfile*.

The `system()` method from the *os* module executes the command in a subshell. The `explorer` command opens a folder or a file on your computer in Windows. However, if you're using Mac, the `system()` method in the *os* module uses the `open` command, and in Linux, the command is `xdg-open`. Therefore, the script opens the file *example.txt* in the subfolder *files*.

For example, say you're using Windows and have saved the script in your chapter folder *C:\chat\mpt\ch03*. After running the script, you'll have the following output in the IPython console:

```
C:\chat\mpt\ch03
C:\chat\mpt\ch03\files\example.txt
```

At the same time, the file *example.txt* should open.

Open Files via Voice Control

We'll now demonstrate how to open various file types, like MP3; Microsoft Word, PowerPoint, and Excel; and PDF files. Before running the following script, save an MP3 file, a Word file, a PowerPoint file, an Excel file, and a PDF file in the subfolder *files* you just created in your chapter folder. Name the five files *presentation.mp3, lessons.docx, graduation.pptx, book.xlsx,* and *desk. pdf,* respectively. It's best if the files are not too large.

NOTE *You need to have proper software installed on your computer to open the five files. To make sure, you can double-click each one to see if it opens on your computer. If you don't have software to open all file types, try only the ones that you can open.*

Listing 3-5 shows *voice_open_file.py*, which can also be downloaded from the book's resources page.

```
import os
import pathlib
import platform

import speech_recognition as sr

speech = sr.Recognizer()
directory = pathlib.Path.cwd()

❶ def voice_to_text():
    voice_input = ""
    with sr.Microphone() as source:
        speech.adjust_for_ambient_noise(source)
        try:
```

```
                    audio = speech.listen(source)
                    voice_input = speech.recognize_google(audio)
                except sr.UnknownValueError:
                    pass
                except sr.RequestError:
                    pass
                except sr.WaitTimeoutError:
                    pass
        return voice_input
    def open_file(filename):
        if platform.system() == "Windows":
            os.system(f"explorer {directory}\\files\\{filename}")
        elif platform.system() == "Darwin":
            os.system(f"open {directory}/files/{filename}")
        else:
            os.system(f"xdg-open {directory}/files/{filename}")
❷ while True:
        print('Python is listening...')
        inp = voice_to_text().lower()
        print(f'You just said {inp}.')
        if inp == "stop listening":
            print('Goodbye!')
            break
        elif "open pdf" in inp:
            inp = inp.replace('open pdf ','')
            myfile = f'{inp}.pdf'
            open_file(myfile)
            continue
        elif "open word" in inp:
            inp = inp.replace('open word ','')
            myfile = f'{inp}.docx'
            open_file(myfile)
            continue
        elif "open excel" in inp:
            inp = inp.replace('open excel ','')
            myfile = f'{inp}.xlsx'
            open_file(myfile)
            continue
        elif "open powerpoint" in inp:
            inp = inp.replace('open powerpoint ','')
            myfile = f'{inp}.pptx'
            open_file(myfile)
            continue
        elif "open audio" in inp:
            inp = inp.replace('open audio ','')
            myfile = f'{inp}.mp3'
            open_file(myfile)
            continue
```

Listing 3-5: Code for voice_open_file.py

As with *voice_browse.py*, we define voice_to_text() to convert your voice command to text ❶. We also define open_file() to identify your operating system and use the proper command, explorer, open, or xdg-open, to open the file on your computer. Note that while the Windows operating system uses a backward slash (\) to go to a subfolder, Mac and Linux use a forward slash (/) for that purpose.

The script is then put in standby mode by using a `while` loop ❷. Within the loop, the microphone first detects your voice and converts it into text. Since we put the `lower()` method after `voice_to_text()`, all letters in the variable `inp` will be lowercase to avoid mismatch due to capitalization.

NOTE *The* `lower()` *method will not affect the opening of files later in the script because the command in the* `os.system()` *method is not case-sensitive. For example, the file* presentation.mp3 *will still open even if you use the filename* Presentation.MP3.

If you say, "Stop listening," the script prints `Goodbye!` and stops running. If the words *open pdf* are in your voice command, the first `elif` branch is activated. The script then replaces `open pdf` with an empty string so only the filename is left in `inp`. The script goes to the subfolder and opens the proper PDF file. For example, when you say, "Open PDF desk," the file *desk.pdf* will open on your computer.

When you say, "Open Word lessons," the second `elif` branch is activated. The same principle works for Excel files and PowerPoint files. And when you say, "Open audio presentation," the audio file *presentation.mp3* will start playing on your computer, using the default MP3 player.

Here is the output from my interaction:

```
Python is listening...
You just said open pdf desk.
Python is listening...
You just said open word lessons.
Python is listening...
You just said
Python is listening...
You just said open excel book.
Python is listening...
You just said open powerpoint graduation.
Python is listening...
You just said open audio presentation.
Python is listening...
You just said stop listening.
Goodbye!
```

TRY IT OUT

Save a comma-separated values (CSV) file as *payments.csv* and an MP4 file as *recording.mp4* in the subfolder *files* in your chapter folder. Then add two additional `elif` branches in *voice_open_file.py* so that your computer will open the CSV file when you say, "Open data payments," and will open the MP4 file when you say, "Open video recording."

Create and Import a Local Module

As you have probably noticed, the three scripts *voice_browse.py*, *voice_search.py*, and *voice_open_file.py* share a large chunk of the same code: the code to import the speech recognition module and define the voice_to_text() function.

To make our scripts more efficient, we'll put all command lines related to speech recognition in a local module. We can then import the module in any script that uses the speech recognition feature.

Create the Local Module mysr

Enter Listing 3-6 in your Spyder editor and save it as *mysr.py*. Alternatively, you can download it from the book's resources page.

```
# Get rid of ALSA lib error messages in Linux
❶ import platform
import speech_recognition as sr

if  platform.system() == "Linux":
    from ctypes import CFUNCTYPE, c_char_p, c_int, cdll

    # Define error handler
    error_handler = CFUNCTYPE\
    (None, c_char_p, c_int, c_char_p, c_int, c_char_p)
    # Don't do anything if there is an error message
  ❷ def py_error_handler(filename, line, function, err, fmt):
      pass
    # Pass to C
    c_error_handler = error_handler(py_error_handler)
    asound = cdll.LoadLibrary('libasound.so')
    asound.snd_lib_error_set_handler(c_error_handler)


# Now define the voice_to_text() function for all platforms
❸ import speech_recognition as sr


def voice_to_text():
    voice_input = ""
    with sr.Microphone() as source:
        speech.adjust_for_ambient_noise(source)
        try:
            audio = speech.listen(source)
            voice_input = speech.recognize_google(audio)
        except sr.UnknownValueError:
            pass
        except sr.RequestError:
            pass
        except sr.WaitTimeoutError:
            pass
    return voice_input
```

Listing 3-6: Code for the self-made module mysr

You can ignore the first part of the code ❶ if you aren't using Linux. The Advanced Linux Sound Architecture (ALSA) configuration, which is coded in the C programming language, spits out warning messages like these every time the *pyaudio* module is imported:

```
ALSA lib pcm.c:2212:(snd_pcm_open_noupdate) Unknown PCM cards.pcm.rear
ALSA lib pcm.c:2212:(snd_pcm_open_noupdate) Unknown PCM cards.pcm.center_lfe
ALSA lib pcm.c:2212:(snd_pcm_open_noupdate) Unknown PCM cards.pcm.side
ALSA lib audio/pcm_bluetooth.c:1613:(audioservice_expect)
BT_GET_CAPABILITIES failed : Input/output error(5)
ALSA lib audio/pcm_bluetooth.c:1613:(audioservice_expect)
BT_GET_CAPABILITIES failed : Input/output error(5)
ALSA lib audio/pcm_bluetooth.c:1613:(audioservice_expect)
BT_GET_CAPABILITIES failed : Input/output error(5)
ALSA lib audio/pcm_bluetooth.c:1613:(audioservice_expect)
BT_GET_CAPABILITIES failed : Input/output error(5)
ALSA lib pcm_dmix.c:957:(snd_pcm_dmix_open)
The dmix plugin supports only playback stream
ALSA lib pcm_dmix.c:1018:(snd_pcm_dmix_open) unable to open slave
```

We create an error handler in Python ❷ and pass it to C so that you won't see any error messages when you import *pyaudio*. The details are beyond the scope of this book, so it's okay if you don't understand this part. Just leave the error handler in the module *mysr*, and it won't affect your understanding for the rest of the book.

Starting at ❸, we import the *SpeechRecognition* module, initiate the Recognizer() class, and define the voice_to_text() function.

Note that if you run *mysr.py*, nothing will happen. This is because we just define voice_to_text() in this script and don't call it.

Import mysr

Let's revisit *stand_by.py* and modify it to use *mysr*. Save Listing 3-7 as *stand_by1.py*.

```
# Make sure you put mysr.py in the same folder as this script
from mysr import voice_to_text

while True:
    print('Python is listening...')
  ❶ inp = voice_to_text()
    print(f'You just said {inp}.')
    if inp == "stop listening":
        print('Goodbye!')
        break
```

Listing 3-7: Code for stand_by1.py

We've replaced all speech recognition–related code with just one line: from mysr import voice_to_text. This line tells the script to go to the local module *mysr* and import voice_to_text() to be used in the current script.

Whenever you need to convert speech to text, you simply call voice_to_text() ❶.

TRY IT OUT

Run *stand_by1.py* and say two simple phrases as you did in the "Try It Out" exercise on page 61 and see if you get the same results. After that, say, "Stop listening" to end the script.

Summary

In this chapter, we installed the *SpeechRecognition* module and used try and except to handle potential errors. In this way, we prevent the script from closing when we would rather it continue. We tested the voice control functionality with a few projects: voice-controlled web surfing and voice-controlled web search.

You learned how to use the *os* module to open files and the *pathlib* module to navigate through the file path, as well as the *platform* module to make your Python code cross-platform.

Finally, you put all code related to speech recognition into a self-made local module so that your scripts look concise, short, and clean. We'll use this module throughout the rest of the book.

End-of-Chapter Exercises

1. Modify *stand_by.py* so that you end the while loop by saying, "Quit the script" instead of "Stop listening," and when the while loop ends, the script prints Have a great day!

2. Modify *voice_open_file.py* so that when you say, "Open text filename," *filename.txt* will open on your computer.

3. Modify *voice_open_file.py* so that it imports voice_to_text() from the local *mysr* module.

4

MAKE PYTHON TALK

In this chapter, you'll learn how to make Python talk back to you in a human voice. You'll first install the text-to-speech module based on your operating system and then teach Python to speak aloud whatever you enter on your computer. You'll also add the speech recognition feature you learned in Chapter 3 and get Python to repeat your own speech. Finally, you'll build a real-world application to use voice inputs to ask Python to calculate the area of a rectangle and tell you the answer in a human voice.

To save space, you'll put all text-to-speech-related code in a self-made module. Once you do that, you can import the module into any script that needs the text-to-speech feature.

You'll also learn how to ask Python to read a long text file, such as a news article, aloud. Before you begin, set up the folder */mpt/ch04/* for this chapter. As in previous chapters, you can download the code for all the scripts from *https://www.nostarch.com/make-python-talk/*.

NEW SKILLS

- Installing speech-related modules depending on your operating system
- Adjusting properties of your text-to-speech module
- Creating a module that is portable cross-platform
- Combining the text-to-speech module with speech recognition so a computer can repeat what you said
- Making the computer solve a problem and answer you in a human voice

---

Install the Text-to-Speech Module

Python has two commonly used text-to-speech modules: *pyttsx3* and *gTTS*. If you use Windows, you'll install *pyttsx3* and use it throughout the book. In the Windows operating system, the *pyttsx3* module works offline, has a human-like voice, and lets you adjust the speech properties—namely, the speed, volume, and gender of the voice output.

However, the *pyttsx3* module works differently in Mac and Linux. The voice sounds robotic, and the speech properties are not easily adjustable. Therefore, you'll install *gTTS* if you use Mac or Linux. The *gTTS* module requires an internet connection since it uses the Google Translate text-to-speech API. Further, *gTTS* does not play the sound directly. It saves the voice as an audio file or file-like object. You'll have to use your own audio player to hear the voice. The voice generated by *gTTS* is very human-like.

In Chapter 2, you built a virtual environment called *chatting*, which you then used for speech recognition in Chapter 3. You'll install the *pyttsx3* or *gTTS* module in the same virtual environment so your script will have both the speech recognition and text-to-speech features.

Setup

If you are using Windows, go to the "Install *pyttsx3* in Windows" section and skip the "Install *gTTS* in Mac or Linux" section. Otherwise, skip the "Install *pyttsx3* in Windows" section and go to the "Install *gTTS* in Mac or Linux" section.

Install pyttsx3 in Windows

The *pyttsx3* module is not in the Python standard library, so you'll need to install it via pip.

If you haven't already set up your *chatting* virtual environment, go back to Chapter 2 now and follow the instructions to do so. Then activate the virtual environment *chatting* in the Anaconda prompt by executing the following:

```
conda activate chatting
```

With your *chatting* virtual environment activated, enter this:

```
pip install pyttsx3
```

Follow the instructions onscreen to finish the installation.

Install gTTS in Mac or Linux

The *gTTS* module is not in the Python standard library, so you'll need to install it via pip.

If you haven't already set up your *chatting* virtual environment, go back to Chapter 2 now and follow the instructions to do so. Then activate the virtual environment *chatting* in a terminal by executing the following:

```
conda activate chatting
```

With your *chatting* virtual environment activated in your terminal, enter this command:

```
pip install gTTs
```

Follow the instructions onscreen to finish the installation.

Test Your Text-to-Speech Module

Before beginning, you'll check that your text-to-speech module is properly installed and working. Based on your operating system, skip the sections that don't apply to you.

Run a Sample Script in Windows

With your virtual environment activated and Spyder open, copy the script *test_pyttsx3.py* into your editor and save it in your chapter folder. If you prefer, you can download the file from the book's resources through *https:// www.nostarch.com/make-python-talk/*.

```
import pyttsx3
engine = pyttsx3.init()
engine.say("hello, how are you?")
engine.runAndWait()
```

First, import the *pyttsx3* module to the script. Then use init() to initiate a text-to-speech engine in the *pyttsx3* module and call it engine. The say() function in the *pyttsx3* module converts the text to a speech signal and prepares to send it to the speaker. The `runAndWait()` function then sends the actual speech signal to the speaker so you can hear the sound. The `runAndWait()` function also keeps the engine running so that when you want to convert text to speech later in the script, you don't need to initiate the engine again.

To understand how each line of code functions, run *test_pyttsx3.py* line by line by using the F9 key.

NOTE   *The* `say()` *function in the* pyttsx3 *module only converts the text to a speech signal and prepares to send it to the speaker. It does not do the actual speaking. To hear the sound, use* `runAndWait()`, *which sends the speech signal to the speaker.*

If the module is correctly installed, when you finish running the whole script, you should hear a voice saying, "Hello, how are you?" If not, recheck the instructions and make sure that the speaker on your computer is working properly at the right volume. I'll discuss later in this chapter how to customize the speed, volume, and voice gender associated with the *pyttsx3* module.

Run a Sample Script in Mac or Linux

You'll use the gtts-cli tool (*cli* stands for *command line*) to convert text to speech, instead of converting text to an audio file, and then play it. The gtts-cli tool is faster than the alternative method. Once you install the *gTTS* module, the gtts-cli tool is available in the command line in your virtual environment. The gtts-cli tool converts the text to a file-like object, and you have to choose which audio player to play it. I find that the mpg123 player works well.

First, you need to install the mpg123 player on your computer. If you are using Mac, run the following command in a terminal:

```
brew install mpg123
```

If you are using Linux, run the following two commands on a terminal:

```
sudo apt-get update
sudo apt-get install mpg123
```

Once you're finished, with your virtual environment activated, run the following command in a terminal:

```
gtts-cli --nocheck "hello, how are you?" | mpg123 -q -
```

If you have correctly installed everything, you should hear a voice saying, "Hello, how are you?" If not, recheck the instructions and make sure that the speaker on your computer is working properly at the right volume. Further, since you have installed the *gTTS* module in your virtual environment, you have to run the preceding command with your virtual environment activated. Otherwise, it won't work.

The nocheck option in this command is to speed up execution. The q flag instructs the module not to display copyright and version messages, even in an interactive mode. Make sure you don't miss the hyphen at the end of the command.

Next, you'll use the *os* module in Python to execute commands in a subshell.

Copy the *test_gtts.py* script into your Spyder editor and save it in your chapter folder. The script is also available at the book's resources through *https://www.nostarch.com/make-python-talk/*.

```
import os

os.system('gtts-cli --nocheck "hello, how are you?" | mpg123 -q -')
```

First import the *os* module to the script. Then use system() to execute a command in a subshell to achieve the same effect as running the command in a terminal. As a result, the gtts-cli tool is used to convert text to a file-like object. After that, the mpg123 player plays the sound object so you can hear a human voice.

NOTE   *You don't need to explicitly import the gTTS module in* test_gtts.py *because you use the gtts-cli tool in the command line, even though the gTTS module is used.*

If you've done everything correctly, you should hear a voice saying, "Hello, how are you?"

Convert Text to Voice in Windows

Now let's practice converting written text input into a human voice in Windows. With your virtual environment activated and Spyder open, copy the script *tts_windows.py*, as shown in Listing 4-1, into your editor and save and run it.

```
import pyttsx3

engine = pyttsx3.init()
❶ while True:
    inp = input("What do you want to covert to speech?\n")
    if inp == "done":
        print(f"You just typed in {inp}; goodbye!")
        engine.say(f"You just typed in {inp}; goodbye!")
        engine.runAndWait()
        break
  ❷ else:
        print(f"You just typed in {inp}")
        engine.say(f"You just typed in {inp}")
        engine.runAndWait()
        continue
```

Listing 4-1: Converting text to voice in Windows

After importing the *pyttsx3* module and initiating a text-to-speech engine, start an infinite loop to take user text input ❶. In each iteration, the script asks for text input at the IPython console. If you want to stop the script, enter done, and the script will print and say in a human voice, "You just typed in done; goodbye!" After that, the loop stops, and the script quits running.

If the text input is not done, the else branch runs ❷, and the script speaks your text input out loud in a human voice. After that, the script goes to the next iteration and takes your text input again.

The following is sample output from the script (user input is in bold):

```
What do you want to covert to speech?
Python is great!
You just typed in Python is great!

What do you want to covert to speech?
Hello, world!
You just typed in Hello, world!

What do you want to covert to speech?
done
You just typed in done; goodbye!
```

Convert Text to Voice in Mac or Linux

Now we'll practice converting written text input into a human voice in Mac or Linux. With your virtual environment activated and Spyder open, copy the script *tts_mac_linux.py* (Listing 4-2) into your editor, and save and run it.

```
import os

while True: ❶
    inp = input("What do you want to covert to speech?\n")
    if inp == "done":
        print(f"You just typed in {inp}; goodbye!")
        os.system(f'gtts-cli --nocheck "You just typed in {inp}; goodbye!" | mpg123 -q -')
        break
    else: ❷
        print(f"You just typed in {inp}")
        os.system(f'gtts-cli --nocheck "You just typed in {inp}" | mpg123 -q -')
        continue
```

Listing 4-2: Converting text to voice in Mac and Linux

After importing the *os* module so you can run commands in a subshell, start an infinite loop to take user text input ❶. In each iteration, the script asks for text input at the IPython console. If you want to stop the script, enter done, and the script will print and say in a human voice, "You just typed in done; goodbye!" After that, the loop stops, and the script quits running.

If the text input is not done, the else branch runs ❷, and the script speaks your text input out loud in a human voice. After that, the script goes to the next iteration and takes your text input again.

The following is sample output from the script (user input is in bold):

```
What do you want to covert to speech?
Python is great!
You just typed in Python is great!

What do you want to covert to speech?
Hello, world!
You just typed in Hello, world!

What do you want to covert to speech?
done
You just typed in done; goodbye!
```

Repeat After Me

We'll start with a simple script that hears what you say aloud and repeats it in a human voice. This script serves two purposes. First, you'll learn how the script takes your voice inputs and which words are easiest for the script to understand—some uncommon words won't be understood. Second, you'll learn how to put both the speech recognition and text-to-speech features in the same script so you can communicate with the computer through human voices only.

We'll also make the script portable cross-platform. The script will automatically choose the *pyttsx3* module if you are using Windows and the *gTTS* module otherwise.

Start a new script, name it *repeat_me.py*, and enter the code in Listing 4-3. Make sure to save it in your chapter folder. You'll also need to copy your *mysr.py* file from Chapter 3 and paste it into the same folder, as you'll need voice_to_text() from that script.

```
# Make sure you put mysr.py in the same folder as this script
from mysr import voice_to_text

import platform ❶
if platform.system() == "Windows":
    import pyttsx3
    engine = pyttsx3.init()
else:
    import os

while True:
    print('Python is listening...')
    inp = voice_to_text() ❷
    if inp == "stop listening":
        print(f'You just said {inp}; goodbye!')
        if platform.system() == "Windows":
```

```
            engine.say(f'You just said {inp}; goodbye!')
            engine.runAndWait()
        else:
            os.system(f'gtts-cli --nocheck "You just said {inp}; goodbye!" | mpg123 -q -')
        break

    else:
        print(f'You just said {inp}')
        if platform.system() == "Windows": ❸
            engine.say(f'You just said {inp}')
            engine.runAndWait()
        else:
            os.system(f'gtts-cli --nocheck "You just said {inp}" | mpg123 -q -')
        continue
```

Listing 4-3: Repeating aloud

WARNING　*Remember to put* mysr.py *in the same folder as Listing 4-3. Otherwise, the speech recognition feature won't work! Yes, I've said this before, but it's important enough to bear repeating.*

First, import the voice_to_text() function from the *mysr* module to convert voice commands into a string variable. Then, import the *platform* module, which lets the script automatically identify your operating system and choose the appropriate command for you ❶. If you are using Windows, the script imports the *pyttsx3* module and initiates a text-to-speech engine. Otherwise, the script imports the *os* module so you can use the gtts-cli tool in a subshell.

You then start an infinite loop to take voice inputs. The script takes your voice command and converts it into a string variable called inp ❷. If you say, "Stop listening" into the microphone, the script will say aloud, "You just said stop listening; goodbye!" After that, the script stops. The script uses either the *pyttsx3* module or the gtts-cli tool, depending on your operating system.

If you say anything else into the microphone, the loop will keep running. At each iteration, the script will repeat what you said out loud ❸.

The following is the output from the script after I said, "Hello," "How are you," and "Stop listening" into the microphone sequentially:

```
Python is listening...
You just said hello
Python is listening...
You just said how are you
Python is listening...
You just said stop listening; goodbye!
```

NOTE　*If you pause often while the script stands by, the script may say, "You just said" in a human voice again and again when you are not speaking. To avoid that, you can modify* repeat_me.py *by removing the* You just said *part (❸ in Listing 4-3).*

Customize the Speech

In this section, you'll learn how to customize the speech produced by your text-to-speech module. You can adjust the speed and volume of the speech as well as the identity of the voice in the *pyttsx3* module in Windows. If you are using Mac or Linux, the only thing you can customize is the speed of the voice in the *gTTS* module.

Skip any of the following subsections that don't apply to your operating system.

Retrieve Default Settings in the pyttsx3 Module in Windows

First, you need to see the default values of the parameters for the speed, volume, and identity of the voice in the *pyttsx3* module in Windows.

This script will retrieve the default settings for your speech module. In Spyder, enter the code in Listing 4-4 and save it as *pyttsx3_property.py* in the chapter folder.

```
import pyttsx3

engine = pyttsx3.init()
❶ voices = engine.getProperty('voices')
for voice in voices:
    print(voice)
❷ rate = engine.getProperty("rate")
print("the default speed of the speech is", rate)
vol = engine.getProperty("volume")
print("the default volume of the speech is", vol)
```

Listing 4-4: Retrieving the default settings

At ❶, you use getProperty() to obtain the properties of the voices used in the engine. You then iterate through all the voice objects in the list voices and print out individual voice objects.

You use getProperty() ❷ to obtain the properties of the speed and print the default speed, then do the same for the default volume.

If you run this script in Windows, you'll see the default settings for your speech script, similar to the following output:

```
<Voice id=HKEY_LOCAL_MACHINE\SOFTWARE\Microsoft\Speech\Voices\Tokens\TTS_MS_EN-US_DAVID_11.0
        name=Microsoft David Desktop - English (United States)
        languages=[]
        gender=None
        age=None>
<Voice id=HKEY_LOCAL_MACHINE\SOFTWARE\Microsoft\Speech\Voices\Tokens\TTS_MS_EN-US_ZIRA_11.0
        name=Microsoft Zira Desktop - English (United States)
        languages=[]
        gender=None
        age=None>
the default speed of the speech is 200
the default volume of the speech is 1.0
```

Here you can see the two voices available to the *pyttsx3* module. The first voice, named *David*, has a male voice tone; the second voice, named *Zira*, has a female voice tone. The default voice tone is David—hence the male voice you hear in *test_pyttsx3.py*.

The default speech speed is 200 words per minute. The default volume is set at 1. You'll learn how to adjust the speed, volume, and ID in the *pyttsx3* module in Windows next.

Adjust Speech Properties in the pyttsx3 Module in Windows

This script will change the default settings so you can hear a voice with the speed, volume, and ID that you prefer. Save Listing 4-5 as *pyttsx3_adjust.py*.

```
import pyttsx3
engine = pyttsx3.init()
voice_id = 1
❶ voices = engine.getProperty('voices')
engine.setProperty('voice', voices[voice_id].id)
engine.setProperty('rate', 150)
engine.setProperty('volume', 1.2)
engine.say("This is a test of my speech id, speed, and volume.")
engine.runAndWait()
```

Listing 4-5: Adjusting some settings

Choose the second voice ID, which has a female voice. At ❶, the script obtains the voice objects available in the text-to-speech engine and saves them in a list called voices. Choose the second object in the list voices, which has a female voice tone, by giving the index [1]. The setProperty() function takes two arguments: the property to set and the value to set it to. Set the value to voices[voice_id].id to choose the id value of the female voice object in Windows, which is *HKEY_LOCAL_MACHINE\SOFTWARE\ Microsoft\Speech\Voices\Tokens\TTS_MS_EN-US_ZIRA_11.0*. If you want to change to the male voice in Windows, you can use voices[0].id instead.

Next, you set the speech speed to 150 words per minute. Most of us speak at a rate of about 125 words per minute in everyday conversation. For faster speech, set rate to a number greater than 125, and for slower speech, set it to a number below 125.

Then, the volume is set to 1.2, which is louder than the default value of 1. You can set this to higher or lower than 1 based on your preference and speakers.

Finally, the script converts the text in say() into speech by using the adjusted properties. Try running this script multiple times with different combinations of parameters until you find the best combination for you. You can always come back to this script and make adjustments.

Customize the gTTS Module in Mac or Linux

You can customize the speed, but not the volume or ID, of the voice in *gTTS*, according to the *gTTS* documentation; see, for example, *https://buildmedia .readthedocs.org/media/pdf/gtts/latest/gtts.pdf*. However, *gTTS* can convert text to speech in most major world languages including Spanish, French, German, and so on, which the *pyttsx3* module can't do. You'll use this feature of *gTTS* to build a voice translator in Chapter 16.

This script will change the default speed to slow for the *gTTS* module. In Spyder, enter the following code and save it as *gtts_slow.py* in the chapter folder:

```
import os

os.system('gtts-cli --nocheck --slow "hello, how are you?" | mpg123 -q -')
```

The script is the same as *test_gtts.py* you've created before except that it adds the --slow option. This changes the voice output to slower than normal.

If you run this script in Mac or Linux, you'll hear the computer saying, "Hello, how are you?" slowly.

Since the default setting for the speed is slow=False, and that's what we prefer, we won't customize the *gTTS* module.

Build the Local mysay Module

In Chapter 3, you put all commands related to speech recognition in a local module named *mysr*. You'll do the same here and put all text-to-speech-related commands in a local module.

Create mysay

You'll create a local module *mysay* and save it in the same folder as any script that uses the text-to-speech feature. That way, you can save space in the main script. This module has adjusted the properties for speed, volume, and gender of the speech set in *pyttsx3_adjust.py* if you are using Windows. If you are using Mac or Linux, the local module *mysay* will use the default properties in the *gTTS* module. You can modify these parameters based on your own preferences.

Enter the code in Listing 4-6 and save it as *mysay.py* in your chapter folder.

```
# Import the platform module to identify your OS
import platform

# If you are using Windows, use pyttsx3 for text to speech
❶ if platform.system() == "Windows":
    import pyttsx3
  ❷ try:
        engine = pyttsx3.init()
    except ImportError:
        pass
    except RuntimeError:
        pass
    voices = engine.getProperty('voices')
    engine.setProperty('voice', voices[1].id)
    engine.setProperty('rate', 150)
    engine.setProperty('volume', 1.2)
```

```
def print_say(txt):
    print(txt)
    engine.say(txt)
    engine.runAndWait()

# If you are using Mac or Linux, use gtts for text to speech
❸ if  platform.system() == "Darwin" or platform.system() == "Linux":
    import os

    def print_say(texts):
        print(texts)
        texts = texts.replace('"','')
        texts = texts.replace("'","")
        os.system(f'gtts-cli --nocheck "{texts}" | mpg123 -q -')
```

Listing 4-6: Building the module

You first import the platform module to identify your operating system. If you are using Windows ❶, the *pyttsx3* module is imported. You use exception handling when initiating the text-to-speech engine ❷ so that if you get an ImportError or RuntimeError, the script will keep running rather than crash. You then define print_say(), which prints the text and converts text to speech.

If you are using Mac or Linux ❸, the *os* module is imported to use the gtts-cli tool to run the command in a subshell. You then define a different print_say() function that prints the text and converts text to speech.

NOTE *If you are using Windows, the module* mysay *has adjusted the properties of the speed, volume, and gender of the speech. You can modify these parameters based on your own preferences.*

Import mysay

With *mysay* prepared, you can simply import the module to your script to use the text-to-speech features. Let's revisit the script *repeat_me.py* and modify it to use the *mysay* module. Save the following as *repeat_me1.py*:

```
# Put mysr.py and mysay.py in the same folder as this script
from mysr import voice_to_text
from mysay import print_say

while True:
    print('Python is listening...')
    inp = voice_to_text()
    if inp == "stop listening":
        print_say(f'You just said {inp}; goodbye!')
        break
    else:
        print_say(f'You just said {inp}')
        continue
```

You first import print_say() from *mysay*. You also import voice_to_text() from the *mysr* module created in Chapter 3. You use voice_to_text() to convert your voice command into a variable inp. When you want to covert text to speech, you use print_say().

Run the script and speak into the microphone to test it out. I said, "Hello again," "This one is using a text-to-speech module," and "Stop listening," to the script in that order. Here is the output:

```
Python is listening...
You just said hello again
Python is listening...
You just said this one is using a text-to-speech module
Python is listening...
You just said stop listening; goodbye!
```

TRY IT YOURSELF

Run *repeat_me1.py* and say three phrases into the microphone so that Python repeats after you, phrase by phrase. When it is finished, use the voice command "I am done" to exit the script (you need to modify the script slightly).

Build a Voice-Controlled Calculator

You'll use your text-to-voice and speech-parsing skills to build a calculator that you can speak commands to. The calculator finds the area of a rectangle and tells you the area in a human voice.

This script takes from you the width and length of a rectangle and speaks back its area. Save Listing 4-7 as *area_hs.py* in your chapter folder.

```
# Put mysr.py and mysay.py in the same folder as this script
from mysr import voice_to_text
from mysay import print_say

# Ask the length of the rectangle
❶ print_say('What is the length of the rectangle?')
# Convert the voice input to a variable inp1
inp1 = voice_to_text()
print_say(f'You just said {inp1}.')
# Ask the width of the rectangle
print_say('What is the width of the rectangle?')
# Save the answer as inp2
inp2 = voice_to_text()
print_say(f'You just said {inp2}.')
# Calculate the area
❷ area = float(inp1)*float(inp2)
# Print and speak the result
print_say(f'The area of the rectangle is {area}.')
```

Listing 4-7: Calculating the area of a rectangle

You first import the text-to-speech and speech recognition functions from local modules. The script asks you about the length of the rectangle ❶. Speak a number into the microphone, and the script converts your voice input into text and saves it as the variable inp1. The script then asks you for the width of the rectangle. When you speak your answer, the script saves your voice input in the variable inp2.

Based on your inputs, the script calculates the area of the rectangle ❷ by converting your voice inputs into float variables and multiplying them.

The script will speak the result aloud as well as print the interactions to the screen. Here is one interaction with the script:

```
What is the length of the rectangle?
You just said 5.
What is the width of the rectangle?
You just said 3.
The area of the rectangle is 15.0.
```

Once I told the script that the length of the rectangle was 5 and the width was 3, the script told me that the area was 15.0.

If you say something that isn't a number, the script will not work. It's safest to include the decimal in your response (for example, "five point zero") so the script doesn't accidentally convert your response into a string rather than a number type.

> **TRY IT YOURSELF**
>
> Run *area_hs.py* to determine the area of a rectangle that has a length of 5.3 and width of 1.6.

Read a File Aloud

In this section, you'll learn how to read a file into a script so Python can speak the text aloud.

Listing 4-8 contains the short news article you'll use.

```
Storm Dorian likely to strengthen into hurricane

Thomson Reuters
BY BRENDAN O'BRIEN Aug 25th 2019 3:49PM

Tropical Storm Dorian was likely to strengthen into a hurricane during the
next two days as it churned westward in the Caribbean Sea, putting Puerto
Rico, the Lesser Antilles and the Virgin Islands on alert, forecasters said on
Sunday.
```

The storm, 465 miles (750 km) east-southeast of Barbados, packed 40 mph winds as it headed west at 14 mph. It was forecast to be near the central Lesser Antilles late on Monday or early Tuesday, the National Hurricane Center (NHC) said in a midday advisory on Sunday.

"Right now, it's a tropical storm and we are expecting it to strengthen close to or reaching hurricane intensity as it approaches," NHC meteorologist Michael Brennan told Reuters.

Dorian was expected to turn toward the west-northwest on Monday and continue on that path through Tuesday night, the NHC said.

As of Sunday afternoon, Barbados was under a tropical storm warning while a tropical storm watch was in effect for St. Lucia and St. Vincent and the Grenadines.

The NHC was likely to issue additional watches for portions of the Windward and Leeward Islands on Sunday, Brennan said, noting that Puerto Rico, the Virgin Islands and Hispaniola should monitor Dorian's progress.

"We are approaching the peak of the hurricane season so everybody in the Caribbean and along the U.S. South, Gulf and East Coast needs to be aware and follow these systems," Brennan said. Dorian's winds could weaken as it passes south of Puerto Rico and approaches Hispaniola. Many Caribbean islands are likely to receive 2 to 4 inches (5 to 10 cm) of rain, but some part of the Lesser Antilles islands could get 6 inches, the NHC said.

Listing 4-8: Content for the text file

Including this article as is in a script would clearly be inconvenient, so save it as a text file named *storm.txt* (you can download *storm.txt* with the rest of the book's resources). You can first create a subfolder called *files* in your chapter folder and then save *storm.txt* in the subfolder.

Save Listing 4-9 as *newsfile.py* to have Python read the news article out loud.

```
# Put mysay.py in the same folder as this script
from mysay import print_say
import pathlib

# Open the file, and read the content of the text file
❶ myfile = pathlib.Path.cwd() / 'files' / 'storm.txt'
with open(myfile,'r') as f:
    content = f.read()

# Let Python speak the text in the file
print_say(content)
```

Listing 4-9: Reading out the text file

You first let the script know where to find the news file ❶. You use open() to access *storm.txt* from the subfolder *files*. You then read the content of the file into a string variable called content by using read(). At the end, the script reads the file content out loud in a human voice. Simple!

If you save *storm.txt* in the same folder as the preceding script, you don't need to specify the file path. Python will automatically look in the folder the script is held in when a path is not specified.

TRY IT YOURSELF

Select an online news article and save it as *mynews.txt* on your computer. Modify *newsfile.py* so that the script reads the news article out loud in a human voice.

Summary

In this chapter, you learned how to install the text-to-speech module to make Python talk. You moved crucial text-to-speech features into the module *mysay* to import into scripts.

You have also learned how to have Python repeat what you say. You applied your new skills to a real-world application: using voice inputs to ask Python to calculate the area of a rectangle and tell you the answer in a human voice.

Now that you know how to make Python talk and listen, in Chapter 5 you'll learn how to apply both features to several interesting real-world applications.

End-of-Chapter Exercises

1. If you are using Windows, in *pyttsx3_adjust.py*, modify the code as follows:

    A. The voice is a male voice.

    B. The speed of the speech is 160 words per minute.

    C. The volume is 0.8.

2. Modify the script *area_hs.py* to calculate the area of a triangle when you say the triangle's height and base length.

5

SPEAKING APPLICATIONS

Now that you know how to make Python talk and listen, we'll create several real-world applications that utilize those skills. But before that, you'll create a local package. Since you'll use the *mysr* and *mysay* local modules in every chapter for the reminder of the book, you'll create a Python package to contain all local modules. This way, you don't need to copy and paste these modules to the folders of individual chapters. This also helps keep the code consistent throughout the book. You'll learn how a Python package works and how to create one yourself along the way.

In the first application, you'll build a Guess the Number game that takes voice commands and talks back to you in a human voice.

You'll then learn how to parse text to extract news summaries from National Public Radio (NPR) and have Python read them out to you. You'll also build a script to extract information from Wikipedia based on your voice inquiries and to speak the answers out.

Finally, you'll learn how to traverse files in a folder with your voice, with the aim of building your very own Alexa. You'll be able to say to the script, "Python, play Selena Gomez," and a song by Selena Gomez that's saved on your computer will start playing.

As usual, you can download all the code for all the scripts from *https://www.nostarch.com/make-python-talk/*. Before you begin, set up the folder */mpt/ch05/* for this chapter.

NEW SKILLS

- Learning how Python packages work
- Creating your self-made local Python package
- Parsing the source code of a news website to extract news summaries
- Extracting answers to your queries from Wikipedia and converting them to voice
- Traversing files in a folder on your computer by using the *os* module

---

Create Your Self-Made Local Python Package

In Chapter 3, you built a self-made local module *mysr* to contain all speech recognition–related code. Whenever you need to use the speech-recognition feature, you import voice_to_text() from the module. Similarly, you built a self-made local module *mysay* in Chapter 4 to contain all text-to-speech-related code. You import print_say() from the module whenever you use the text-to-speech feature.

You'll use these two self-made local modules in this chapter and other chapters in this book. To make these modules work, you need to put the module files (namely, *mysr.py* and *mysay.py*) in the same directory as the script that uses these two modules. This means you'd potentially have to copy and paste these files into the directory of almost every chapter in this book. You may wonder: is there a more efficient way to do this?

The answer is yes, and that's what Python packages are for.

Next, you'll first learn what a Python package is and how it works. You'll then learn how to create your self-made local package. Finally, you'll use a Python script to test and import your package.

What's a Python Package?

Many people think that Python modules and Python packages are the same. They're not.

A Python *module* is a single file with the *.py* extension. In contrast, a Python *package* is a collection of Python modules contained in a single directory. The directory must have a file named *__init__.py* to distinguish it from a directory that happens to have *.py* extension files in it.

I'll guide you through the process of creating a local package step-by-step.

Create Your Own Python Package

To create a local Python package, you need to create a separate directory for it and place all related files into it. In this section, you'll create a local package to contain both our speech recognition and text-to-speech module files—namely, *mysr.py* and *mysay.py*.

Create a Package Directory

First, you need to create a directory for the package.

In this book, you use a separate directory for each chapter. For example, all Python scripts and related files in this chapter are placed in the directory */mpt/ch05/*. Since you are creating a package to be used for all chapters in this book, you'll create a directory parallel to all chapters. Specifically, you'll use the directory */mpt/mptpkg/*, where *mptpkg* is the package name. The diagram in Figure 5-1 explains the position of the package relative to the book chapters.

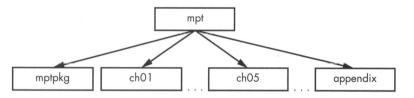

Figure 5-1: The position of the mptpkg *package relative to the chapter folders*

As you can see, the package directory is parallel to the chapter directories, which are all contained in the directory for the book, */mpt*, as in *Make Python Talk*.

Create Necessary Files for Your Package

Next, you need to create and place necessary files in the package.

First, copy and paste the two modules you created in Chapters 3 and 4, *mysr.py* and *mysay.py*, in the package directory */mpt/mptpkg/*. Do not make any changes to the two files.

Then save the following script, *__init__.py*, in the package directory */mpt/mptpkg/* (or you can download it from the book's resources):

```
from .mysr import voice_to_text
from .mysay import print_say
```

The purpose of this file is twofold: it imports voice_to_text() and print_say() so you can use those functions at the package level, and it also tells Python that the directory is a package, not a folder that happens to have Python scripts in it.

Finally, save the following script, *setup.py*, in the book directory */mpt*, one level above the package directory */mpt/mptpkg/*. The script is also available from the book's resources.

```
from setuptools import setup
setup(name='mptpkg',
version='0.1',
description='Install local package for Make Python Talk',
author='Mark Liu',
author_email='mark.liu@uky.edu',
packages=['mptpkg'],
zip_safe=False)
```

The file provides information about the package, such as the package name, author, version, descriptions, and so on.

You'll learn how to install this local package on your computer next.

Install Your Package

Because you'll modify the local package and add more features to it later in the book, it's better to install the package in editable mode.

Open your Anaconda prompt (Windows) or a terminal (Mac or Linux) and activate your virtual environment for this book, *chatting*. Run the following command:

```
pip install -e path-to-mpt
```

Replace *path-to-mpt* with the actual directory path of */mpt*. For example, the book directory */mpt* is *C:\mpt* on my office computer that runs the Windows operating system, so I installed the local package using this command:

```
pip install -e C:\mpt
```

On my Linux machine, the path to the */mpt* directory is */home/mark/Desktop/mpt*, so I installed the local package using this command:

```
pip install -e /home/mark/Desktop/mpt
```

The -e option tells the Python to install the package in editable mode so that you can modify the package anytime you need to.

With that, the local package is installed on your computer.

Test Your Package

Now that you have installed your self-made local package, you'll learn how to import it.

You'll write a Python script to test the package you just created.

Let's revisit the script *repeat_me1.py* from Chapter 4. Enter the following lines of code in your Spyder editor and save it as *repeat_me2.py* in your Chapter 5 directory */mpt/ch05/*:

```
# Import functions from the local package mptpkg
from mptpkg import voice_to_text
from mptpkg import print_say

while True:
    print('Python is listening...')
    inp = voice_to_text()
    if inp == "stop listening":
        print_say(f'you just said {inp}; goodbye!')
        break
    else:
        print_say(f'you just said {inp}')
        continue
```

First, import the functions voice_to_text() and print_say() from the *mptpkg* package directly. Recall that in the script *__init__.py*, you've already imported the two functions from the modules *.mysr* and *.mysay* to the package. As a result, here you can directly import the two functions from the package.

The rest of the script is the same as that in *repeat_me1.py*. It repeats what you say. If you say, "Stop listening," the script stops.

The following is an interaction with *repeat_me2.py*, with my voice input in bold:

```
Python is listening...
you just said how are you
Python is listening...
you just said I am testing a python package
Python is listening...
you just said stop listening; goodbye!
```

As you can see, the script is working properly, which means you've successfully imported functions from the local package.

More on Python Packages

Before you move on, I want to mention a couple of things about Python packages.

First, you can add more modules to your package. Later in this book, you'll add more modules to the existing local package *mptpkg*. You'll use just one local package for the whole book. This will reduce the number of directories and help organize your files.

Second, if you have an interesting package that you want to share with the rest of the world, you can easily do so. You just need to add a few more files, such as the license, a README file, and so on. For a tutorial on how to distribute your Python packages, see, for example, the Python Packaging Authority website, *https://packaging.python.org/tutorials/packaging-projects/*.

Interactive Guess the Number Game

Guess the Number is a popular game in which one player writes down a number and asks the other player to guess it in a limited number of attempts. After each guess, the first player tells whether the guess is correct, too high, or too low.

Various versions of the game are available online and in books, and we'll look at our own version to guess a number between one and nine. Start a new script and save it as *guess_hs.py*; the *hs* stands for *hear and say*.

Because the script is relatively long, I'll break it into three parts and explain them one by one. Listing 5-1 gives the first part.

```
❶ import time
  import sys

  # Import functions from the local package mptpkg
  from mptpkg import voice_to_text
  from mptpkg import print_say

  # Print and announce the rules of the game in a human voice
❷ print_say('''Think of an integer,
         bigger or equal to 1 but smaller or equal to 9,
         and write it on a piece of paper''')
  print_say("You have 5 seconds to write your number down")
  # Wait for five seconds for you to write down the number
  time.sleep(5)
  print_say('''Now let's start. I will guess a number and you can say:
      too high, that is right, or too small''')
  # The script asks in a human voice whether the number is 5
  print_say("Is it 5?")
  # The script is trying to get your response and save it as re1
  # Your response has to be 'too high', 'that is right', or 'too small'
❸ while True:
      re1 = voice_to_text()
      print_say(f"You said {re1}")
      if re1 in ("too high", "that is right", "too small"):
          break
  # If you say "that is right", game over
      if re1 == "that is right":
          print_say("Yay, lucky me!")
          sys.exit
  --snip--
```

Listing 5-1: Part 1 of the Guess the Number game

We start the script by importing needed modules ❶. We import the *time* module so we can pause the script for a period of time. We also import the *sys* module to exit the script when it is finished.

As discussed in the previous section, we import voice_to_text() and print_say() from the local package *mptpkg* to convert voice to text as well as to print out and speak the text message.

The script then speaks and prints out the rules of the game ❷. Since the instructions span several lines, we put them in triple quotation marks to make them more readable.

NOTE *When you have text that spans multiple lines and you want to print it or convert it to speech, use triple quotation marks; for example:*

```
print(''' Line 1 text,
              line 2 text,
              line 3 text''')
```

The script announces that you have five seconds to write down a number then pauses for five seconds by using sleep() to give you time to write your number.

The script then begins to guess; it will ask in a human voice whether the number is five. At ❸, we start an infinite loop to take your voice input. When you speak into the microphone, the computer converts your voice input into a text string variable named re1. The script repeats what you said back to you. Your response needs to be one of three phrases: "too high," "that is right," or "too small." If it isn't, the script will keep asking you for a response until it matches one of the phrases. This gives you a chance to have a correct response before the script moves on to the next step.

If your response is "that is right," the computer will say, "Yay, lucky me!" and exit the script. We'll enter the behavior for the response "too high" next. Listing 5-2 shows the middle part of the *guess_hs.py* script.

```
--snip--
# If you say "too high", the computer keeps guessing
elif re1 == "too high":
    # The computer guesses 3 the second round
    print_say("Is it 3?")
    # The computer is trying to get your response to the second guess
    while True:
        re2 = voice_to_text()
        print_say(f"You said {re2}")
        if re2 in ("too high", "that is right", "too small"):
            break
    # If the second guess is right, game over
    if re2 == "that is right":
        print_say("Yay, lucky me!")
        sys.exit
    # If the second guess is too small, the computer knows it's 4
    elif re2 == "too small":
        print_say("Yay, it is 4!")
        sys.exit
    # If the second guess is too high, the computer guesses the third time
    elif re2 == "too high":
        # The third guess is 1
        print_say("Is it 1?")
        # The computer is getting your response to the third guess
        while True:
            re3 = voice_to_text()
            print_say(f"You said {re3}")
```

```
        if re3 in ("too high", "that is right", "too small"):
            break
    # If the third guess is too small, the computer knows it's 2
    if re3 == "too small":
        print_say("It is 2!")
        sys.exit
    # If the third guess is right, game over
    elif re3 == "that is right":
        print_say("Yay, lucky me!")
        sys.exit
--snip--
```

Listing 5-2: The "too high" behavior

If your response is "too high," the computer will keep guessing, this time a lower number. The second guess from the computer will be three because guessing three reduces the number of attempts the computer needs to find out the answer. The script will detect and catch your response to the second guess.

Here are the options for your response to the second guess: If it's "that is right," the computer will say "Yay, lucky me!" and exit the script. If it's "too small," the computer will know that the number is four and say so. If it's "too high," the computer will make a third guess of one.

Then, the computer captures your response to the third guess. If your response is "too small," the computer will know that the number is two. If your response is "that is right," the computer will say, "Yay, lucky me!" and exit.

Now let's look at the final section of *guess_hs.py*, which handles a "too small" response to the first guess. Listing 5-3 shows the code.

```
--snip--
# If you say "too small", the computer keeps guessing
elif re1 == "too small":
    # The computer guesses 7 the second round
    print_say("Is it 7?")
    # The computer is trying to get your response to the second guess
    while True:
        re2 = voice_to_text()
        print_say(f"You said {re2}")
        if re2 in ("too high", "that is right", "too small"):
            break
    # If the second guess is right, game over
    if re2 == "that is right":
        print_say("Yay, lucky me!")
        sys.exit
    # If the second guess is too high, the computer knows it's 6
    elif re2 == "too high":
        print_say("Yay, it is 6!")
        sys.exit
    # If the second guess is too small, the computer guesses the third time
    elif re2 == "too small":
        # The third guess is 8
```

```
print_say("Is it 8?")
while True:
    re3 = voice_to_text ()
    print_say(f"You said {re3}")
    if re3 in ("too high", "that is right", "too small"):
        break
# If the third guess is too small, the computer knows it's 9
if re3 == "too small":
    print_say("It is 9!")
    sys.exit
# If the third guess is right, game over
elif re3 == "that is right":
    print_say("Yay, lucky me!")
    sys.exit
```

Listing 5-3: The "too small" behavior

The final section of the script is similar to the middle section. If you tell the computer that the first guess of five is "too small," the computer will give you a second guess of seven. The script will then catch your response to the second guess.

If you respond "that is right," the computer will say, "Yay, lucky me!" and exit the script. If you say "too high," the computer will know that the number is six. If your response is "too small," the computer will make a third guess of eight.

The computer then captures your response to the third guess. If your response is "too small," the computer will know that the number is nine. If your response is "that is right," the computer will say, "Yay, lucky me!" and exit the script.

If you have a good internet connection in a fairly quiet environment, you can have close-to-perfect communication with the computer. The internet connection is important because we use the Google Web Speech API to convert voice input into text. The *SpeechRecognition* module has an offline method called recognize_sphinx(), but it makes a lot of mistakes, so we use the online method.

Here's the written output from the script when my number was 8 (my voice input is in bold):

```
Please think of an integer,
bigger or equal to 1 but smaller or equal to 9,
and write on a piece of paper
You have 5 seconds to write it down
Now let's start. I will guess a number and you can say:
too high, that is right, or too small
Is it 5?
You said too small
Is it 7?
You said too small
Is it 8?
You said that is right
Yay, lucky me!
```

The script understood every word I said perfectly. This is, of course, partly because I chose certain words to avoid ambiguity. When building your own projects, you'll want to use voice commands that are unique or put the words in context to get consistently correct results. Since each voice command is usually short, the Python script may have difficulty grasping the context of your voice input and returning the right words.

For example, if you say "too large" into the microphone, the script may return "two large," which is a phrase that does make sense. That is why we use "too high" instead of "too large" in *guess_hs.py*.

Similarly, when I spoke "too low" into the microphone, the script returned "tulo" from time to time. When I use "too small," I get the correct response each time.

TRY IT OUT

Run *guess_hs.py* and play a few rounds. See if Python can understand each of your responses on the first try.

Speaking Newscast

In this project, we'll scrape the NPR News website to collect the latest news summary and have Python read it out loud. This project is split into two scripts: one to scrape and organize the news, another to handle the speech recognition and text-to-speech features. Let's start with the web scraping.

Scrape the News Summary

First, we need to scrape the information from the news site and compile it into a clean and readable format.

Different news sites arrange their content differently, so the methods for scraping are often slightly different. You can refer to Chapter 6 for the basics of web scraping. If you're interested in scraping other news sites, you'll need to adjust this code based on the features of the website. Let's first look at the site and the corresponding source code.

The news we're interested in is on the front page of the NPR News website, shown in Figure 5-2.

One handy feature of this page is the short news summaries. As you can see, the front page lists the latest news with a short summary for each news article.

You want to extract the news title and the teaser of each news article and print them out. To do this, you need to locate the corresponding tags in the HTML program.

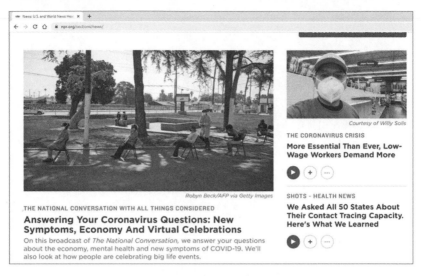

Figure 5-2: News summaries on the NPR News front page

While on the web page, press CTRL-U on your keyboard. The source code for the web page should appear. You can see that it's almost 2,000 lines long. To locate the tags you need, press CTRL-F to open a search box at the top-right corner. Because the title of the first news article starts with "Answering Your Coronavirus Questions," as shown in Figure 5-2, you should enter **Answering Your Coronavirus Questions** and click **Search**. Then skip to the corresponding HTML code, shown in Listing 5-4.

```
--snip--
❶ <div class="item-info">
    <div class="slug-wrap">
    <h3 class="slug">
<a href="https://www.npr.org/series/821003492/the-national-conversation-with-
all-things-considered">The National Conversation With All Things Considered
</a>
</h3>
    </div>
❷ <h2 class="title">
<a href="https://www.npr.org/2020/04/28/847585398/answering-your-coronavirus-
questions-new-symptoms-economy-and-virtual-celebratio" data-
metrics='{"action":"Click Featured Story Headline 1-
3","category":"Aggregation"}' >Answering Your Coronavirus Questions: New
Symptoms, Economy And Virtual Celebrations
</a>
</h2>
❸ <p class="teaser">
<a href="https://www.npr.org/2020/04/28/847585398/answering-your-coronavirus-
questions-new-symptoms-economy-and-virtual-celebratio"><time datetime="2020-
04-28"><span class="date">April 28, 2020 &#149; </span></time>On this
broadcast of <em>The National Conversation, </em>we answer your questions
about the economy, mental health and new symptoms of COVID-19. We'll also
look at how people are celebrating big life events.
```

```
</a>
</p>
</div>
--snip--
```

Listing 5-4: Part of the source code for the NPR News front page

Notice that all the title and teaser information are encapsulated in a parent <div> tag with a class attribute of item-info ❶. Information for the news title is held in a child <h2> tag with a class attribute of title ❷. The information for the teaser is held in a child <p> tag with a class attribute of teaser ❸.

We'll use these patterns to write a Python script to extract the information we need. The script *news.py* will scrape the information and organize all titles and summaries in a clean and concise way. I've added comments in places that need more detailed explanations.

The script will compile the news summary and print it out in text. Enter Listing 5-5 and save it as *news.py*.

```
    # Import needed modules
    import requests
    import bs4

    # Obtain the source code from the NPR news website
❶ res = requests.get('https://www.npr.org/sections/news/')
    res.raise_for_status()
    # Use beautiful soup to parse the code
    soup = bs4.BeautifulSoup(res.text, 'html.parser')
    # Get the div tags that contain titles and teasers
    div_tags = soup.find_all('div',class_="item-info")
    # Index different news
❷ news_index = 1
    # Go into each div tag to retrieve the title and the teaser
❸ for div_tag in div_tags:
        # Print the news index to separate different news
        print(f'News Summary {news_index}')
        # Retrieve and print the h2 tag that contains the title
        h2tag = div_tag.find('h2', class_="title")
        print(h2tag.text)
        # Retrieve and print the p tag that contains the teaser
        ptag = div_tag.find('p', class_="teaser")
        print(ptag.text)
        # Limit to the first 10 news summaries
        news_index += 1
        if news_index>10:
            break
```

Listing 5-5: Python code to scrape the NPR News front page

We start by importing the needed modules *bs4* and *requests* (*bs4* is the newest version of the Beautiful Soup library). Follow the three steps in Chapter 2 for installing these modules if you need to.

At ❶, we obtain the source code for the NPR News front page, which is in HTML format. We then use the *bs4* module to parse HTML files. Because the information we need is encapsulated in <div> tags with a class attribute of item-info, we find all such tags and put them in a list called *div_tags*. To separate different news summaries, we create a variable *news _index* to mark them ❷.

We then go into each individual <div> tag we've collected ❸. First, we print out the news summary index to separate out individual news items. Second, we extract the <h2> tag that contains the news title and print it out. Third, we extract the <p> tag that contains the news summary and print it out. Finally, we stop if the news index exceeds 10 so that we limit the printout to 10 news summaries.

If you run *news.py*, the output will look like Listing 5-6.

```
News Summary 1
Answering Your Coronavirus Questions: New Symptoms, Economy And Virtual Celebrations
April 28, 2020 • On this broadcast of The National Conversation, we answer your questions
about the economy, mental health and new symptoms of COVID-19. We'll also look at how people
are celebrating big life events.
News Summary 2
More Essential Than Ever, Low-Wage Workers Demand More
April 28, 2020 • In this lockdown, low-wage workers have been publicly declared "essential" —
up there with doctors and nurses. But the workers say their pay, benefits and protections
don't reflect it.
News Summary 3
We Asked All 50 States About Their Contact Tracing Capacity. Here's What We Learned
April 28, 2020 • To safely reopen without risking new COVID-19 outbreaks, states need enough
staffing to do the crucial work of contact tracing. We surveyed public health agencies to
find out how much they have.
News Summary 4
Coronavirus Has Now Killed More Americans Than Vietnam War
April 28, 2020 • The number of lives taken by COVID-19 in the U.S. has reached a grim
milestone: More people have died of the disease than the 58,220 Americans who perished in the
Vietnam War.
--snip--
```

Listing 5-6: News summary scraped from the NPR News front page

Now we'll get Python to read the news to us.

Add the Text-to-Speech Features

The next step is to have the text-to-speech module convert the news summary into spoken words. Add Listing 5-7 into a new file and save it as *news_hs.py*.

```
# Import needed modules
import requests
import bs4
import sys

# Import functions from the local package mptpkg
from mptpkg import voice_to_text
```

```
    from mptpkg import print_say
    # Define the news_teaser() function
❶ def news_teaser():
        --snip--
    ❷ print_say(f'News Summary {news_index}')
        h2tag = div_tag.find('h2', class_="title")
        print_say(h2tag.text)
        ptag = div_tag.find('p', class_="teaser")
        print_say(ptag.text)
        --snip--
    # Print and ask you if you like to hear the news summary
    print_say("Would you like to hear the NPR news summary?")
    # Capture your voice command
    inp = voice_to_text().lower()
    # If you answer yes, activate the newscast
    if inp == "yes":
        news_teaser()
    # Otherwise, exit the script
    else:
        sys.exit
```

Listing 5-7: Python code for a voice-activated newscast

We first import the usual modules, and we import voice_to_text() and print_say() from the self-made *mptpkg* package.

We then define a function called news_teaser() ❶, which accomplishes whatever *news.py* does. The only exception is that instead of just printing out the news index, title, and teaser, it both prints and speaks them ❷. We then set the script to ask, "Would you like to hear the NPR news summary?" The voice_to_text() function captures your voice response and converts it into a string variable with all lowercase letters. If you say yes, Python will start broadcasting the news. If you answer anything other than yes, the script will exit.

TRY IT OUT

Run *news_hs.py* and hear news from NPR. To save time, modify the script so that you'll hear only the first 5 news summaries instead of 10.

Voice-Controlled Wikipedia

We'll build a talking Wikipedia in this section. Unlike with the newscaster project, we'll use the *wikipedia* module to get the information we need directly. After that, we'll get the script to understand questions you ask, retrieve the answer, and read it aloud.

Access Wikipedia

Python has a *wikipedia* module that does the work of delving into topics you want to know about, so we don't have to code that part ourselves. The module is not in the Python standard library or the Anaconda navigator. You should install it with pip. Open the Anaconda prompt (in Windows) or a terminal (in Mac or Linux) and run the following command:

```
pip install wikipedia
```

Next, run the following script as *wiki.py*:

```
import wikipedia

my_query = input("What do you want to know?\n")
answer = wikipedia.summary(my_query)
print(answer)
```

After the script is running, in the IPython console in the lower-right panel, enter the name of a topic you want to know about. The script will save your inquiry as the variable *my_query*. The summary() function will produce a summary answer to your question. Finally, the script prints out the answer from Wikipedia.

I entered U.S. China trade war and got the following result:

```
What do you want to know?
U.S. China trade war
China and the United States have been engaged in a trade war through
increasing tariffs and other measures since 2018. Hong Kong economics
professor Lawrence J. Lau argues that a major cause is the growing battle
between China and the U.S. for global economic and technological dominance.
He argues, "It is also a reflection of the rise of populism, isolationism,
nationalism and protectionism almost everywhere in the world, including in the
US."
```

This answer is relatively short. Most searches in Wikipedia will have a much longer result. If you want to limit the length of the responses to, say, the first 200 characters, you can enter [0:200] after answer.

Add Speech Recognition and Text to Speech

We'll now add the speech recognition and text-to-speech features to the script. Enter Listing 5-8 as *wiki_hs.py*.

```
import wikipedia

# Import functions from the local package mptpkg
from mptpkg import voice_to_text
from mptpkg import print_say
```

```
# Ask what you want to know
❶ print_say("What do you want to know?")
# Capture your voice input
❷ my_query = voice_to_text()
print_say (f"you said {my_query}")
# Obtain answer from Wikipedia
ans = wikipedia.summary(my_query)
# Say the answer in a human voice
print_say(ans[0:200])
```

Listing 5-8: Python code for a voice-controlled talking Wikipedia

Once you start the script, a voice asks, "What do you want to know?" ❶. At ❷, the script calls voice_to_text() to convert your voice input into text. Then, the script retrieves the response to your question from Wikipedia, saves it as a string variable *ans*, and converts it to a human voice.

After running the script, if you say to the microphone, "US Federal Reserve Bank," you'll get a result similar to this:

```
What do you want to know?
you said U.S. federal reserve bank
The Federal Reserve System (also known as the Federal Reserve or simply the
Fed) is the central banking system of the United States of America. It was
created on December 23,
1913, with the enactment
```

I've added the [0:200] character limit behind the variable ans, so only the first 200 characters of the result are printed and spoken.

And just like that, you have your own voice-controlled talking Wikipedia. Ask away!

TRY IT OUT

Run *wiki_hs.py* and ask Wikipedia about the city you live in now (or the state if the city is not in Wikipedia). See what the output is like.

Voice-Activated Music Player

Here you'll learn how to get Python to play a certain artist or genre of music just by asking for it with a phrase like "Python, play Selena Gomez." You'll speak the name of the artist you want to listen to, and the script will receive that as keywords and then search for those keywords in a particular folder. To do this, you need to be able to traverse files and folders.

Traverse Files in a Folder

Suppose you have a subfolder *chat* in your chapter folder. If you want to list all files in the subfolder, you can use this *traverse.py* script:

```
import os

with os.scandir("./chat") as files:
    for file in files:
        print(file.name)
```

First, the script imports the *os* module. This module gives the script access to functionalities that are dependent on the operating system, such as accessing all files in a folder.

Next, you put all files in the subfolder *chat* into a list called *files*. The script goes through all items in the list, and prints out the name of each item.

The output from the preceding script is as follows after I run it on my computer:

```
book.xlsx
desk.pdf
storm.txt
graduation.pptx
--snip--
HilaryDuffSparks.mp3
country
classic
lessons.docx
SelenaGomezWolves.mp3
TheHeartWantsWhatItWantsSelenaGomez.mp3
```

As you can see, we can traverse all the files and subfolders in a folder and print out their names. Filenames include the file extension. Subfolders have no extension after the subfolder name. For example, I have two folders, *country* and *classic*, in the folder *chat*. As a result, you see country and classic in the preceding output.

Next, you'll use this feature to select a song you want to play.

Python, Play Selena Gomez

The script in Listing 5-9, *play_selena_gomez.py*, can pick out a song by whatever artist you name (for example, Selena Gomez) and play it. Either save your songs in the subfolder *chat* or replace the file path with a path to somewhere on your computer that you keep music.

```
# Import the required modules
import os
import random
from pygame import mixer
```

```
# Import functions from the local package mptpkg
from mptpkg import voice_to_text
from mptpkg import print_say

# Start an infinite loop to take your voice commands
❶ while True:
    print_say("how may I help you?")
    inp = voice_to_text()
    print_say(f"you just said {inp}")
    # Stop the script if you say 'stop listening'
    if inp == "stop listening":
        print_say("Goodbye! ")
        break
    # If 'play' is in voice command, music mode is activated
❷ elif "play" in inp:
        # Remove the word play from voice command
    ❸ inp = inp.replace('play ','')
        # Separate first and last names
        names = inp.split()
        # Extract the first name
        Firstname = names[0]
        # Extract the last name
        if len(names)>1:
            lastname = names[1]
        # If no last name, use the first name as last name;
        else:
            lastname = firstname
        # Create a list to contain songs
        mysongs = []
        # If either first name or last name in the file name, put in list
        with os.scandir("./chat") as files:
            for file in files:
            ❹ if (firstname in file.name or lastname in file.name) \
and "mp3" in file.name:
                    mysongs.append(file.name)
        # Randomly select one from the list and play
    ❺ mysong = random.choice(mysongs)
        print_say(f"play the song {mysong} for you")
        mixer.init()
        mixer.music.load(f'./chat/{mysong}')
        mixer.music.play()
        break
```

Listing 5-9: Python code to voice activate a song by an artist on your computer

We first import the needed modules. In particular, we import the *os* module to traverse files and the *random* module to randomly select a song from a list the script will build. We use mixer() in the *pygame* module to play the music file.

We then start an infinite loop ❶ to put the script in standby mode to wait for your voice commands. If the script detects the word *play* in your voice command, the music mode is activated ❷. We then replace the word play and the whitespace behind it with an empty string ❸ so that your command "Play Selena Gomez" becomes Selena Gomez. The next command separates the first name and the last name. For artists who are known by just their first names (such as Madonna, Prince, or Cher), we put their first name as a placeholder in the variable lastname.

We then traverse through all files in the subfolder *chat*. If a file has the *mp3* extension and contains either the first or the last name ❹, it will be added to the list *mysongs*. We use choice() from the *random* module to randomly select a song in the list *mysongs* ❺ and load it with mixer.music.load(). After that, we use mixer.music.play() to play it.

As a result, once you say to the script, "Play Selena Gomez," one of the two songs in the subfolder *chat*, *SelenaGomezWolves.mp3* or *TheHeartWantsWhatItWantsSelenaGomez.mp3*, will start playing.

NOTE   *We use the* pygame *module to play music files in this book. Depending on which operating system you are using, other modules, such as* playsound *or* vlc, *can also play music files in Python. Alternatively, you can use* os.system() *to open music files in your computer's default music player, as discussed in Chapter 3.*

TRY IT OUT

Save several songs by your favorite artist, making sure that the filenames contain the artist's first and last name. Then edit and run *play_selena_gomez.py* so that when you say, "Python, play *Firstname Lastname*," one of your songs will start playing.

Python, Play a Country Song

What we'll do now is similar to interacting with the script *play_selena_gomez.py*, but here you'll learn how to access different subfolders by using the *os* module as well as a different way of playing music files.

Suppose you've organized your songs by genre. You put all classical music files in the subfolder *classic*, and all country music files in the folder *country*, and so on. You've placed these subfolders in the folder *chat* you just created.

We want to write a script so that when you say, "Python, play a country song," the script will randomly select a song from the folder *country* and play it. Enter the code in Listing 5-10 and save it as *play_genre.py*.

```
# Import needed modules
import os
import random
from pygame import mixer

# Import functions from the local package mptpkg
from mptpkg import voice_to_text
from mptpkg import print_say
```

```
while True:
    print_say("how may I help you?")
    inp = voice_to_text().lower()
    print_say(f'you just said {inp}')
    if inp == "stop listening":
        print_say('Goodbye!')
        break
    elif "play a" in inp and "song" in inp:
        # Remove 'play a' and 'song' so that only the genre name is left
      ❶ inp = inp.replace('play a ','')
      ❷ inp = inp.replace(' song','')

        # Go to the genre folder and randomly select a song
        with os.scandir(f"./chat/{inp}") as entries:
            mysongs = [entry.name for entry in entries]
        # Use pygame mixer to play the song
      ❸ mysong = random.choice(mysongs)
        print_say(f"play the song {mysong} for you")
        mixer.init()
        mixer.music.load(f"./chat/{inp}/{mysong}")
        mixer.music.play()
        break
```

Listing 5-10: Python code to voice activate a song by genre

Python checks for the terms *play a* and *song* in the voice command and activates the music mode if it finds them. The script then replaces play a ❶ and song ❷ as well as the whitespace behind them with an empty string, leaving only the genre—country, in this case—in the voice command. This is used as the folder for the script to search: in this case, *./chat/country*. Finally, the script randomly selects a song from the folder ❸ and plays it.

Note that we use lower() after voice_to_text() in the script so that the voice command is all lowercase. We do this because the script sometimes converts the voice command into play A Country Song. We can avoid mismatch due to capitalization. On the other hand, the path and filenames are not case sensitive, so even if you have capital letters in your path or filenames, there will not be any mismatch.

TRY IT OUT

Organize your music into various categories. Save a few songs in the subfolder *classic* in the *chat* folder you created. If you say, "Play a classic song," see if a song in the folder will start playing.

Summary

In this chapter, you first learned to create a Python package to contain the local text-to-speech and speech recognition modules. After that, you built several real-world applications that can understand voice commands, react, and speak.

You created a voice-controlled, talking Guess the Number game. In the game, you pick a number between one and nine and interact with the script to let it guess. Then you learned how to parse text to extract a news summary from the NPR website, adding the speech recognition and text-to-speech features to make a voice-controlled newscast.

You learned how to use the *wikipedia* module to obtain answers to your inquiries.

You traversed files in a folder on your computer by using the *os* module, and then created a script that plays a genre or artist when you ask it to.

Now that you know how to make Python talk and listen, you'll apply both features to many other interesting situations throughout the rest of the book so that you can interact with your computer via voice only.

End-of-Chapter Exercises

1. Modify *guess_hs.py* so that the third guess of the script is two instead of one.

2. Change *wiki.py* so that it prints out the first 300 characters of the result from Wikipedia.

3. Modify *play_genre.py* so that the script plays music by using the *os* module and your default music player on your computer, instead of the *pygame* module.

4. Suppose the music files on your computer are not in MP3 format but in WAV format. How can you modify *play_selena_gomez.py* so that the script still works?

WEB SCRAPING PODCASTS, RADIOS, AND VIDEOS

In this chapter, you'll build on the web-scraping basics from Chapter 5. You'll use these skills to voice-activate podcasts, live radio broadcasts, and videos on different websites.

You'll also learn how HyperText Markup Language (HTML) works and how the various types of HTML tags construct web pages. You'll learn how to use Python's Beautiful Soup library to parse HTML files and extract information.

With all these skills, you'll build three apps to do the following:

- Parse the source file of online podcasts, locate an MP3 file, and play the podcast.
- Use voice control to play online live radio.
- Play online videos, such as NBC's *Nightly News with Lester Holt*.

Before you begin, set up the folder */mpt/ch06/* for this chapter. As usual, you can download all the code for all the scripts from *https://www.nostarch.com/make-python-talk/*.

A Primer on Web Scraping

The Beautiful Soup library is designed to extract information from websites. We'll use it often in this book, just as many Python programmers do in the real world.

I'll first discuss the basics of HTML markup and how different types of tags form various blocks on a website. You'll then learn to use the Beautiful Soup library to extract information from websites by parsing their source code.

What Is HTML?

As noted at the start of the chapter, *HTML* stands for *HyperText Markup Language*, the programming language that tells browsers how to construct and display web page content. HTML uses various types of tags to build the structure of web pages.

Anatomy of an HTML Tag

Table 6-1 lists some of the commonly used tags and their main functions.

Table 6-1: Commonly Used HTML Tags

Tag name	Description
<html>	The root-level tag of an HTML document. It encapsulates all other HTML tags.
<head>	The head section of an HTML document that contains metadata about the page.
<title>	The title of the web page, to be displayed on the tab of the browser.
<body>	The body of an HTML document, with all displayed content.
<h1>	A level-1 heading, for example, the title of a news article.
<p>	A paragraph of displayed content.
<div>	A container used for page elements that divide the HTML document into sections.
<a>	A hyperlink to link one page to another.
<li>	A list item.

All tags start with < > and end with </ > so that the browser can identify separate tags. For example, paragraph tags start with <p> and close with </p>.

NOTE *A complete list of all HTML tags and their uses can be found at* https://html.spec .whatwg.org/multipage/.

Let's use <a> to illustrate the components of HTML tags. Here's an example of creating a hyperlink by using an <a> tag:

```
<a class="suprablue" href="http://libraries.uky.edu">Libraries</a>
```

This hyperlink has optional attributes in the opening tag: <a class= "suprablue" href="http://libraries.uky.edu">. The class attribute tells the browser which style to use from the Cascading Style Sheets (CSS), where the class name suprablue is predefined (you'll learn how to define a class in the following section). The href attribute specifies the destination of the hyperlink, *http://libraries.uky.edu/.* The content of the tag that will be displayed on the page is between the opening and closing tags: Libraries.

From HTML Tags to Web Pages

To understand how HTML uses tags to construct a web page, let's look at an extremely simplified example. Enter the script in Listing 6-1 and save it as *UKYexample.html* in your chapter folder, or you can download the file from the book's resources page. All HTML files need the extension *.html* or *.htm.*

```
❶ <html>
     <head>
    <title>Example: University of Kentucky</title>
<style>
.redtext {
  color: red;
}
.leftmargin {
  margin-left: 10px;
}
</style>
  </head>
❷ <body>
    <p>Below are some links:</p>
      <p><a class="redtext" href="http://libraries.uky.edu/">
      University of Kentucky Libraries</a></p>
      <p><a class="leftmargin" href="https://directory.uky.edu/">
      University of Kentucky Directory</a></p>
  </body>
</html>
```

Listing 6-1: HTML code for a simple web page

Before I explain the code, let's see how the actual web page looks. Go to your chapter folder and open *UKYexample.html* with your preferred web browser. I use Google Chrome, and the web page comes out as in Figure 6-1.

Figure 6-1: A simple web page

Now let's link the HTML code to the web page display.

At ❶, we start an opening <html> tag to contain all the code in the script. Then, we have a <title> tag nested in a <head> tag. The <head> tag is usually used to contain metadata, such as the document title or CSS styles. The content of the <title> tag is Example: University of Kentucky, which sets the title of the web page shown in the browser tab at the top-left corner in Figure 6-1.

The content inside the <style> tag is to define two classes: redtext and leftmargin. The first one tells the HTML to display the content in red, while the second tells the HTML to leave a 10-pixel left margin. You can specify multiple styles such as background color, padding, or margins in one class.

At ❷, we start the body HTML that will be displayed on the page. Inside this we have three nested <p> tags. A <p> tag defines a separate paragraph in an HTML document; adding a new <p> tag starts a new paragraph. The first <p> tag contains the message Below are some links:.

We then provide two hyperlinks, each in in an <a> tag nested in a <p> tag. We put each <a> tag in a separate <p> tag so the links are displayed as two different paragraphs instead of side by side on the same line. If you click the first link, it will bring you to the University of Kentucky Libraries. If you click the second link, you'll be directed to the University of Kentucky Directory. The first tag has a class attribute of redtext, displaying the text in red, as defined in the <style> tag previously. Similarly, the second tag has a class attribute of leftmargin, and as a result, a 10-pixel margin precedes the text University of Kentucky Library.

Extract Information with Beautiful Soup

Now that you understand how a few basic HTML tags work, you'll use the Beautiful Soup library to parse the HTML code and extract the information you want. I'll first discuss how to parse a locally saved HTML file. Then you'll learn how to extract information from a live web page.

Let's revisit the simple example *UKYexample.html* saved in your chapter folder. Suppose you want to extract some web addresses from a web page. You can use Listing 6-2, *parse_local.py*, to accomplish the task.

```
# Import the Beautiful Soup library
from bs4 import BeautifulSoup
# Open the local HTML file as a text file
❶ textfile = open("UKYexample.html", encoding='utf8')
# Use the findAll() function to locate all <p> tags
soup = BeautifulSoup(textfile, "html.parser")
ptags = soup.findAll("p")
# Print out <p> tags
print(ptags)
# Find the <a> tag nested in the third <p> tag
❷ atag = ptags[2].find('a')
print(atag)
# Print the web address of the hyperlink
print(atag['href'])
# Print the content of the <a> tag
print(atag.text)
```

Listing 6-2: Parsing a local HTML file

First, we import BeautifulSoup() from the *bs4* module, the latest version of Beautiful Soup. At ❶, we open the local HTML file as a text file by using the built-in Python function open(). We then use findAll() to locate all <p> tags in the HTML file, and we put them in the list ptags.

NOTE   *Listing 6-2 assumes you've put the file* UKYexample.html *in the same folder as the script* parse_local.py. *If the file is elsewhere, you must specify its path at* ❶.

There are three <p> tags in the list ptags:

```
[<p>Below are some links:</p>,
<p><a class="redtext" href="http://libraries.uky.edu/">
University of Kentucky Libraries</a></p>,
<p><a class="leftmargin" href="https://directory.uky.edu/">
University of Kentucky Directory</a></p>]
```

Let's use the third tag as an example. At ❷, we locate the <a> tag nested in the third <p> tag. We then print out the href attribute of the <a> tag:

```
https://directory.uky.edu/
```

Finally, we print out the content of the <a> tag:

```
University of Kentucky Directory
```

The output for the whole script is as follows:

```
[<p>Below are some links:</p>,
<p><a class="redtext" href="http://libraries.uky.edu/">
```

```
University of Kentucky Libraries</a></p>,
<p><a class="leftmargin" href="https://directory.uky.edu/">
University of Kentucky Directory</a></p>]
<a class="leftmargin" href="https://directory.uky.edu/">
University of Kentucky Directory</a>
https://directory.uky.edu/
University of Kentucky Directory
```

Scrape Live Web Pages

Now let's scrape a live web page. The HTML markup for a live web page is much more complicated than our simple static version and might be thousands of lines long, so you'll need to learn to quickly locate the lines of code you want.

Suppose you want to extract the contact information from the University of Kentucky Libraries website. Go to *http://libraries.uky.edu/.* Then scroll to the bottom of the page and you'll see the contact information for various areas, as shown in Figure 6-2.

Circulation:	(859) 218-1881
	lib.circdesk@email.uky.edu
Reference:	(859) 218-2048
	refdesk@uky.edu
Interlibrary Loan:	(859) 218-1880
	ILLBorrowing@uky.edu
All Other Questions & Comments:	WebAdmin@lsv.uky.edu

Figure 6-2: Information you want from a live web page

You want to extract the department name, phone number, and email address for each of the three departments shown in Figure 6-2: Circulation, Reference, and Interlibrary Loan. First you need to locate the corresponding tags in the HTML document.

While on the web page, press CTRL-U on your keyboard (or right-click and choose **View ▸ Source**). The source code for the web page should appear. You can see that it's more than 2,000 lines long. To locate the tags you need, press CTRL-F to access a search box at the top-right corner. Enter `Circulation` and click **Search** to skip to the corresponding HTML code, shown in Listing 6-3.

```
--snip--
❶ <div class="sf-middle">
        ❷ <div class="dashing-li">
        <span class="contact_area">Circulation:</span>
        <span class="contact_methods">
            <div class="contact_phone"><a class="suprablue"
            href="tel:8592181881">(859) 218-1881</a></div>
            <div class="contact_email"><a class="suprablue"
            href="mailto:lib.circdesk@email.uky.edu">
```

```
                    lib.circdesk@email.uky.edu</a></div>
             </span>
        </div>
❸ <div class="dashing-li">
        <span class="contact_area">Reference:</span>
        <span class="contact_methods">
            <div class="contact_phone"><a class="suprablue"
            href="tel:8592182048">(859) 218-2048</a></div>
            <div class="contact_email"><a class="suprablue"
            href="mailto:refdesk@uky.edu">refdesk@uky.edu</a></div>
        </span>
    </div>
❹ <div class="dashing-li">
        <span class="contact_area">Interlibrary Loan:</span>
        <span class="contact_methods">
            <div class="contact_phone"><a class="suprablue"
            href="tel:8592181880">(859) 218-1880</div>
            <div class="contact_email"><a class="suprablue"
            href="mailto:ILLBorrowing@uky.edu">
            ILLBorrowing@uky.edu</a></div>
        </span>
    </div>
    <div class="dashing-li-last">
        <span class="featured_area">All Other Questions & Comments:
        </span>
        <span class="featured_email"><a class="suprablue"
        href="mailto:webadmin@lsv.uky.edu">
        WebAdmin@lsv.uky.edu</a></span>
    </div>
  </div>
--snip--
```

Listing 6-3: Part of the source code for a live web page

Notice that all the information is encapsulated in a parent <div> tag
with class attribute of sf-middle ❶. Information for the Circulation department (name, phone number, and email address) is held in a child <div>
tag with class attribute of dashing-li ❷. The information for the other two
areas, Reference ❸ and Interlibrary Loan ❹, is held in two other child
<div> tags within the parent tag. Within each child tag, subtags each contain a
piece of the following information: department name, phone number, and
email address.

These patterns are important to notice when writing a Python script to
extract the information you need. Next, I'll explain how to use these patterns to extract the information from the HTML file.

Download *scrape_live_web.py* from the book's resources page and save
it in your chapter folder. The first part of the script is shown in Listing 6-4,
which locates the <div> tags for each of the three areas.

```
from bs4 import BeautifulSoup
import requests
# Provide the web address of the live web
url = 'http://libraries.uky.edu'
```

```
# Obtain information from the live web
❶ page = requests.get(url)
# Parse the page to obtain the parent div tag
soup = BeautifulSoup(page.text, "html.parser")
div = soup.find('div', class_="sf-middle")
# Locate the three child div tags
❷ contacts = div.find_all("div", class_="dashing-li")
# Print out the first child div tag to examine it
print(contacts[0])
--snip--
```

Listing 6-4: Python code to scrape a live web page

We import the *requests* module to obtain the source code from the live web page. The address of the web page is defined in the variable url. At ❶, we use get() to fetch the HTML code. Then, we find the <div> tag with the class value of sf-middle and use it as the parent tag.

WARNING *Be careful not to miss the trailing underscore in class_="sf-middle" or class_= "dashing-li". We must use the trailing underscore because the name class is a Python keyword and cannot be used as a variable name. See Chapter 1 for Python rules.*

At ❷, we locate the three child <div> tags with the class value of dashing-li and put them in the list contacts, because each child <div> tag contains all the contact information for one department. Each element in the list corresponds to one of the departments. For example, the first element contains all the information for the Circulation department, and we print it out in Listing 6-5.

```
<div class="dashing-li">
<span class="contact_area">Circulation:</span>
<span class="contact_methods">
<div class="contact_phone"><a class="suprablue" href="tel:8592181881">
(859) 218-1881</a></div>
<div class="contact_email"><a class="suprablue"
href="mailto:lib.circdesk@email.uky.edu">lib.circdesk@email.uky.edu
</a></div>
</span>
</div>
```

Listing 6-5: Source code for the Circulation department on the live web page

The second part of *scrape_live_web.py* will print out the detailed information for each of the three areas. It is shown in Listing 6-6.

```
--snip--
# Obtain information from each child tag
for contact in contacts:
    # Obtain the area name
    area = contact.find('span', class_="contact_area")
    print(area.text)
```

```
# Obtain the phone and email
atags = contact.find_all('a', href = True)
for atag in atags:
    print(atag.text)
```

Listing 6-6: Python code to print out the scraped information

We go into each element in the list contacts. To print out the department name, we locate the <span> tag with the class attribute of contact_area. The content of the tag is the department name. The two <a> tags contain the phone number and the email address of each department, and we also print them out. The output is shown here:

```
Circulation:
(859) 218-1881
lib.circdesk@email.uky.edu
Reference:
(859) 218-2048
refdesk@uky.edu
Interlibrary Loan:
(859) 218-1880
ILLBorrowing@uky.edu
```

NOTE *The Beautiful Soup library often provides more than one way of accomplishing the same task. For example, findAll() and find_all() work the same, and find('span', class_="contact_area") and find('span', {"class":"contact_area"}) produce the same result. Many Python modules or libraries have different versions over time, and the old functions are carried over to newer versions to maintain backward compatibility.*

Voice-Activated Podcasts

In this project, our goal is to write a script that enables you to say, "Python, tell me the latest news," and the script will broadcast a brief from an NPR news podcast. You'll first learn how to extract the MP3 file associated with the podcast and play it, and then you'll add the speech recognition feature to the script so that you can voice-activate it. Because the news brief is about five minutes long, you'll also learn how to stop the podcast via voice control while the news is playing.

Extract and Play Podcasts

First, find a website with a newscast you like. For this, we'll use *NPR News Now* because it's free and updated every hour, 24/7. The web address is *https://www.npr.org/podcasts/500005/npr-news-now/*.

Go to the site, and you should see something like Figure 6-3.

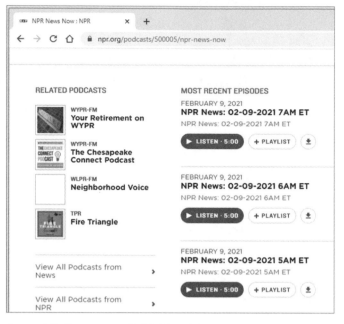

Figure 6-3: Front page of NPR News Now

As you can see, the latest news brief for me was updated at 7 AM ET on Feb 9, 2021. Below it, you can also see news briefs from 6 AM, 5 AM, and so on.

To locate the MP3 file that contains the news briefs, right-click anywhere on the page and, from the menu that appears, select the **View page source** option (or press CTRL-U). You should see the source code, as in Figure 6-4.

Figure 6-4: Source code for NPR News Now

You'll notice that the MP3 files are contained in <a> tags. We need to use the Beautiful Soup library to extract all <a> tags that contain MP3 files and then extract the link from the first tag, which will contain the latest news brief. If you wanted to, you could listen to previous news briefs as well; for example, the second and the third tags contain the news briefs from 6 AM and 5 AM in Figure 6-3.

Next, we need to extract the link, remove unwanted components, and use the *webbrowser* module to open the URL of the MP3 file so that the podcast can start playing. The script *npr_news.py*, in Listing 6-7, shows how to accomplish this.

```
# Import needed modules
import requests
import bs4
import webbrowser

# Locate the website for the NPR news brief
url = 'https://www.npr.org/podcasts/500005/npr-news-now'
# Convert the source code to a soup string
response = requests.get(url)
❶ soup = bs4.BeautifulSoup(response.text, 'html.parser')
# Locate the tag that contains the mp3 files
❷ casts = soup.findAll('a', {'class': 'audio-module-listen'})
print(casts)
# Obtain the weblink for the mp3 file related to the latest news brief
❸ cast = casts[0]['href']
print(cast)
# Remove the unwanted components in the link
❹ pos = cast.find('?')
print(cast[0:pos])
# Extract the mp3 file link, and play the file
mymp3 = cast[0:pos]
webbrowser.open(mymp3)
```

Listing 6-7: A script to play online podcasts

We first use get() from the *requests* module to obtain the source code of the *NPR News Now* website and save it in the variable response. At ❶, we use the Beautiful Soup library to parse the text and the html.parser option to specify that the source code is in HTML. We saw in Figure 6-4 that the MP3 files are held in <a> tags with a class attribute of audio-module-listen. Therefore, at ❷ we use findAll() from Beautiful Soup to get all those tags and put them in the list casts. Listing 6-8 shows the content of casts.

```
[<a class="audio-module-listen"
href="https://play.podtrac.com/500005/edge1.pod.npr.org/anon.npr-
mp3/npr/newscasts/2021/02/09/newscast070736.mp3?dl=1&amp;
siteplayer=true&amp;size=4500000&amp;awCollectionId=500005&amp;
awEpisodeId=965747474&amp;dl=1">
<b class="audio-module-listen-inner">
<b class="audio-module-listen-icon icn-play"></b>
<b class="audio-module-listen-text">
<b class="audio-module-cta">Listen</b>
<b class="audio-module-listen-duration">
<span>· </span>
<span>5:00</span>
</b>
</b>
</b>
</a>, <a class="audio-module-listen"
```

```
href="https://play.podtrac.com/500005/edge1.pod.npr.org/anon.npr-
mp3/npr/newscasts/2021/02/09/newscast060736.mp3?dl=1&amp;
siteplayer=true&amp;size=4500000&amp;awCollectionId=500005&amp;
awEpisodeId=965731320&amp;dl=1">
<b class="audio-module-listen-inner">
<b class="audio-module-listen-icon icn-play"></b>
<b class="audio-module-listen-text">
<b class="audio-module-cta">Listen</b>
<b class="audio-module-listen-duration">
<span>· </span>
<span>5:00</span>
</b>
</b>
</b>
</a>, <a class="audio-module-listen"
href="https://play.podtrac.com/500005/edge1.pod.npr.org/anon.npr-
mp3/npr/newscasts/2021/02/09/newscast050736.mp3?dl=1&amp;
siteplayer=true&amp;size=4500000&amp;awCollectionId=500005&amp;
awEpisodeId=965721223&amp;dl=1">
--snip--
</a>]
```

Listing 6-8: All <a> tags with a class attribute of audio-module-listen

As you can see, multiple <a> tags contain MP3 files. At ❸, we extract the first <a> tag in the list and obtains the href attribute of the tag (the link to the MP3 file), saving it to cast. The link is as follows:

```
https://play.podtrac.com/500005/edge1.pod.npr.org/anon.npr-
mp3/npr/newscasts/2021/02/09/newscast070736.mp3?dl=1&siteplayer=true&size=450
0000&awCollectionId=500005&awEpisodeId=965747474&dl=1
```

We trim the link so that it ends with the *.mp3* extension. To do that, we use the fact that the ? character is right after *.mp3* in the link and then use the string method find() to locate the position of ? in the link ❹. We then trim the link accordingly and print it out. The trimmed link is as follows:

```
https://play.podtrac.com/500005/edge1.pod.npr.org/anon.npr-
mp3/npr/newscasts/2021/02/09/newscast070736.mp3
```

Finally, we extract the link to the online MP3 file and use open() in the *webbrowser* module to open and play the MP3 file.

If you run the script, you should hear the latest NPR news brief playing in your default web browser.

Voice-Activate Podcasts

Next, we'll add speech recognition to the script so you can voice-activate the podcast. Further, since the podcast is about five minutes long, being able to stop it with your voice is useful. To achieve that, we need to install the *pygame* module because it allows the Python script to stop the audio file while the audio is playing. The *webbrowser* module does not have that functionality.

Installing *pygame* is straightforward in Windows. Execute this line of code in an Anaconda prompt with your virtual environment activated:

```
pip install pygame
```

Then follow the instructions.

If you are using Mac, recent versions of macOS require the installation of Pygame 2. To install it, execute this line of code in a terminal with your virtual environment activated:

```
pip install pygame==2.0.0
```

Then follow the instructions.

If you are using Linux, execute the following three lines of code in a terminal with your virtual environment activated:

```
sudo apt-get install python3-pip python3-dev
sudo pip3 install pygame
pip install pygame
```

See Appendix A at the end of this book for further detail. If the installation is not successful, you can use the *vlc* module as an alternative.

The script *news_brief_hs.py* in Listing 6-9 shows how to use voice control to activate the *NPR News Now* podcast and stop it whenever you want.

```
from io import BytesIO

import requests
import bs4
from pygame import mixer

# Import functions from the local package
from mptpkg import voice_to_text, print_say

❶ def news_brief():
    # Locate the website for the NPR news brief
    url = 'https://www.npr.org/podcasts/500005/npr-news-now'
    # Convert the source code to a soup string
    response = requests.get(url)
    soup = bs4.BeautifulSoup(response.text, 'html.parser')
    # Locate the tag that contains the mp3 files
    casts = soup.findAll('a', {'class': 'audio-module-listen'})
    # Obtain the web link for the mp3 file
    cast = casts[0]['href']
    # Remove the unwanted components in the link
    mp3 = cast.find("?")
    mymp3 = cast[0:mp3]
    # Play the mp3 using the pygame module
    mymp3 = requests.get(mymp3)
    Voice = BytesIO()
    voice.write(mymp3.content)
    voice.seek(0)
    mixer.init()
```

```
    mixer.music.load(voice)
    mixer.music.play()
❷ while True:
    print_say('Python is listening…')
    inp = voice_to_text().lower()
    print_say(f'you just said: {inp}')
    if inp == "stop listening":
        print_say('Goodbye!')
        break
    # If "news" in your voice command, play news brief
❸ elif "news" in inp:
        news_brief()
        # Python listens in the background
        while True:
            background = voice_to_text().lower()
            # Stops playing if you say "stop playing"
            if "stop playing" in background:
                mixer.music.stop()
                break
        continue
```

Listing 6-9: Python script to voice-activate NPR News Now

We import needed modules first. In particular, we import `BytesIO()` from the *io* module to create a temporary file to contain the news brief audio file. This prevents crashes that could occur if the script had to overwrite the file when you rerun it.

We define `news_brief()` ❶. This function accomplishes what we did in *npr_news.py* with a few exceptions. We download the MP3 file and save it to the temporary file *voice*. After that, we use the *pygame* module to play the latest news brief from *NPR News Now*.

At ❷, we start an infinite loop. At each iteration, the script captures your voice. When the word *news* is in your voice command ❸, the script will call `news_brief()` and start playing the latest NPR news brief. While the news is playing, the script is constantly listening to your voice command in the background. When you say, "Stop playing," anytime while or after the news plays, the loop will break and go back to the main menu. If you want to end the script, simply say, "Stop listening."

TRY IT YOURSELF

Wait Wait . . . Don't Tell Me! is a weekly radio show, and recent episodes are available as podcasts at *https://www.npr.org/programs/wait-wait-dont-tell-me/*. Its source code is similar to that of *NPR News Now*. Create a script similar to *new_brief_hs.py* to voice-activate the latest episode of the online broadcast.

Voice-Activated Radio Player

Our goal in this project is to write a script to play online live radio using voice control. When you say, "Python, play online radio," the script will go to the website and click the Play button so that the live radio starts playing on your computer.

We'll be using the *selenium* module to automate web browser interaction from Python. We'll then add voice control to the script to achieve voice activation.

Install the selenium Module

The *selenium* module is not in the Python standard library, so first we'll install it. Open your Anaconda prompt (Windows) or a terminal (Mac or Linux), activate your virtual environment, and execute this command:

```
conda install selenium
```

Follow the onscreen instructions to finish the installation.

Control Web Pages

The *selenium* module allows you to automate web browser interactions with Python.

Online Radio Box (*https://onlineradiobox.com/us/*) will serve as our radio station platform. You can change this to any online radio station you like, such as Magic 106.7 or NPR online radio stations.

Go to the website and you should see a screen similar to that shown in Figure 6-5.

Figure 6-5: Front page of Online Radio Box

When the web page loads, live radio is not playing. You need to use *selenium* to interact with the web browser to click the Play button (the triangle-shaped white button at the bottom in Figure 6-5).

Now you'll learn how to locate the XPath of the Play button on the website. *XPath* is short for *Extensible Markup Language (XML) path*. It is the syntax for finding an element on the web page by using an XML path expression.

NOTE   *We use the Chrome browser because it supports all major operating systems. Websites for other browsers and other operating systems are on the Selenium website (https://www.selenium.dev/).*

Here are the steps to find the XPath of the Play button:

1. Open the web page of Online Radio Box, shown in Figure 6-5, using the Chrome browser.

2. Put your mouse cursor on the Play button (do not click). Then right-click and choose **Inspect** from the pop-up menu. The source code will show at the right side of the web page, as shown in Figure 6-6.

3. Right-click the highlighted line of code at the right side of the page and select **Copy ▶ XPath**.

4. Paste the XPath in a blank file to be used later. In this example, the XPath for the Play button is //*[@id="b_top_play"].

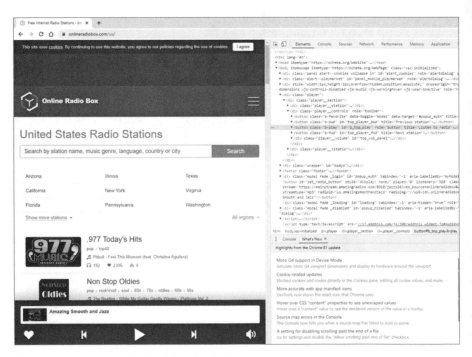

Figure 6-6: Locate the XPath of the Play button

Next, you need to download the web driver for a specific browser. If you'd like to learn more about the Selenium project, an abundance of information is on its website.

Follow the instructions at *https://chromedriver.chromium.org/downloads/* and download the executable file appropriate to your operating system. In Windows, this is *chromedriver_win32.zip*; extract the ZIP file and place the executable file in the chapter folder. On Unix-based operating systems, the executable file is called *chromedriver*. On Windows, the executable file is *chromedriver.exe*.

WARNING   *The XPath of a link may change constantly on many sites. You may have to get the most updated XPath before you run a script.*

As the final step, save *play_live_radio.py* in your chapter folder and run it. The script, also available at the book's resources page, is shown in Listing 6-10.

```
# Put your web driver in the same folder as this script
from selenium import web driver
browser = webdriver.Chrome(executable_path='./chromedriver')
browser.get("https://onlineradiobox.com/us/")
button = browser.find_element_by_xpath('//*[@id="b_top_play"]')
button.click()
```

Listing 6-10: Python code to automate online live radio

NOTE   *For Windows, it's important to put* chromedriver.exe *in the same folder as* play_ live_radio.py *and have Chrome installed on your computer. On Linux with Firefox, the Gecko web driver needs to be on the system path. Otherwise, the* selenium *module will not be able to automate the web browser. You can find further installation details on the Chromium website or on sites such as Stack Overflow.*

We first import webdriver() from the *selenium* module. First, the script launches the web browser. Then, the get() function brings us to the live radio site based on the web address provided. We then define the Play button as a variable button, using the XPath that we've generated . Finally, we use click() in the *selenium* module to activate the Play button on the website. Consequently, if everything is installed and configured correctly, when you run the script, the web browser will open and the online live radio will start playing.

It's educational to run the script line by line by using the F9 key. You will see that after the first line is run, the Chrome browser opens on your computer, and after the second, the browser brings you to the Online Radio Box site. With the final two lines, the Play button is being activated. You will then hear the live radio playing.

Voice-Activate Live Radio

We'll add speech recognition and text-to-speech functionality to the script so you can voice-activate the online live radio. The script *voice_live_radio.py* in Listing 6-11 shows you how to accomplish that.

```
# Put web driver in the same folder as this script
# Import the web driver function from selenium
from selenium import webdriver
from selenium.webdriver.chrome.options import Options

# Import functions from the local package
from mptpkg import voice_to_text, print_say

❶ def live_radio():
    global button
    chrome_options = Options()
    chrome_options.add_argument("−headless")
    browser = webdriver.Chrome\
    (executable_path = './chromedriver',chrome_options = chrome_options)
    browser.get("https://onlineradiobox.com/us/")
    button = browser.find_element_by_xpath('//*[@id="b_top_play"]')
    button.click()

❷ while True:
        print_say("how may I help you?")
    ❸ inp = voice_to_text().lower()
        print_say(f'you just said {inp}')
    ❹ if inp == "stop listening":
            print_say('Goodbye!')
            break
    ❺ elif "radio" in inp:
            print_say('OK, play live radio online for you!')
            live_radio()
            while True:
                background = voice_to_text().lower()
                if "stop playing" in background:
                    button.click()
                    break
                else:
                    continue
```

Listing 6-11: Python code to voice-activate online live radio

We first import all needed modules. Since we need the speech recognition and text-to-speech features, we import voice_to_text() from the local mptpkg package to convert speech to text. We also import print_say() from the local mptpkg package to convert text to human speech.

We then define live_radio() to accomplish what *play_live_radio.py* does with a few modifications ❶. When the function is activated, the script will go to the online live radio station and click the Play button so that live radio starts playing. We use the headless option so you won't see a web browser pop up. We also make the variable button a global variable so we can use the variable later in the script.

At ❷, an infinite loop begins. At each iteration, the script asks, "How may I help you?" After you speak into the microphone, `voice_to_text()` converts your speech to text and saves it as the string variable inp. The `lower()` function converts all characters to lowercase to avoid mismatch due to letter capitalization ❸.

When you say, "Stop listening," the `if` branch of the code is activated ❹. The script prints Goodbye, the loop breaks, and the script ends. When the word *radio* is in your voice command, the `elif` branch of the code is activated ❺. As a result, `live_radio()` is called, and the online live radio starts playing. While the radio is playing, the script is quietly listening to you in the background. If you say, "Stop playing" anytime when the radio is playing, the button will click again and the radio will change from Play to Stop. After that, the script exits the radio mode and returns to the main menu.

TRY IT YOURSELF

Magic 106.7 FM is a radio station in Boston (*https://www.radio.com/magic1067/listen/*). Write a script similar to *voice_live_radio.py* to voice-activate the live radio on this site.

Voice-Activated Videos

You can apply the method you learned in the preceding section to voice-activate prerecorded online videos or even online live TV.

NBC's *Nightly News with Lester Holt* provides prerecorded videos at *https://www.nbcnews.com/nightly-news-full-episodes/*, shown in Figure 6-7.

Figure 6-7: Front page of NBC's Nightly News

We'll use Python to interact with the web browser to click the Play button that activates the online video. You can see a triangle-shaped Play button on the video frame. Follow the steps in "Control Web Pages" on page 125 to find the XPath of the button.

The script *voice_online_video.py* in Listing 6-12 shows how to voice-activate the online video.

```
# Import functions from the local package
from mptpkg import voice_to_text, print_say

# Import the web driver function from selenium
from selenium import webdriver
def online_video():
    browser = webdriver.Chrome(executable_path='./chromedriver')
    browser.get("https://www.nbcnews.com/nightly-news-full-episodes")
    button = browser.find_element_by_xpath\
('//*[@id="content"]/div[6]/div/div[3]/div/\
❶ section[2]/div[2]/div/div[1]/article/div[1]/h2/a[2]/span')
    button.click()
❷ while True:
    print_say("how may I help you?")
    inp = voice_to_text().lower()
    print_say(f'you just said {inp}')
    if inp == "stop listening":
        print('Goodbye!')
        break
    elif "video" in inp:
        print_say('OK, play online video for you!')
        online_video()
        break
```

Listing 6-12: A script to voice-activate online video

The logic is the same as when dealing with live radio. We first define online_video() to be called later. When the function is activated, the script will go to the site, locate the XPath of the Play button ❶, and click it so the video will start playing.

An infinite loop starts at ❷. At each iteration, the script asks, "How may I help you?" After you speak into the microphone, voice_to_text() converts your speech to text and saves it as an all-lowercase string variable inp.

When you say, "Stop listening," the if branch of the code is activated. The script prints Goodbye!, the loop breaks, and the script ends. When the word *video* is in your voice command, the elif branch of the code is activated. As a result, online_video() is called, and the online video starts playing.

TRY IT YOURSELF

Vimeo provides a music video by Katy Perry at *https://vimeo.com/160883302/*. Write a script to voice-activate the online music video (try the XPath `//*[@ id="160883302"]/div[7]/div[3]/button` if you have trouble locating it).

Summary

In this chapter, you learned the basics of web scraping: how HTML works, including the different types and uses of HTML tags, and how to use the Beautiful Soup library to parse HTML files and scrape the information you need.

Armed with these techniques, you learned how to parse a source file of the podcast *NPR News Now* and locate its MP3 file. You then used the *webbrowser* module to play the online MP3. You also learned how to voice activate online podcasts, using the *pygame* module to play the audio file so that you can stop it anytime via voice commands.

You then learned to voice activate an Online Radio Box station. Specifically, you learned how to use the Selenium web driver to interact with a web browser. You directed Python to click the Play button to activate the live radio broadcast. You also learned to use voice control to accomplish these tasks.

Finally, you applied the same idea to online videos, such as NBC's *Nightly News with Lester Holt*.

End-of-Chapter Exercises

1. Modify *parse_local.py* to print out the class attribute value and the web address of the `<a>` tag for the University of Kentucky Libraries.

2. Modify *scrape_live_web.py* to print out the information for the site area All Other Questions & Comments, as shown in Figure 6-2.

3. This URL points to a podcast by Gwyneth Paltrow and Oprah Winfrey: *https://goop.com/the-goop-podcast/gwyneth-x-oprah-power-perception-soul-purpose/*. Write a script to voice activate the online podcast.

7

BUILDING A VIRTUAL PERSONAL ASSISTANT

In this and the next chapter, you'll learn how to create your own virtual personal assistant (VPA), similar to Amazon's Alexa. You'll first have an overview of your VPA and its functionalities. You'll then import all needed modules at once so you can start to run your VPA right away. You'll create a script to make your VPA stand by 24/7 without disturbing you. Whenever you need assistance, you can say, "Hello Python" to wake it up, and when you want it to stand by again, you can use a voice command to put it in standby mode.

After that, you'll examine various functionalities to add to your VPA. The first two are a timer and an alarm clock.

The third functionality enables your VPA to tell jokes. When you say, "Tell me a joke," the script will randomly select a joke from a list and speak it out loud to you.

The fourth functionality sends email. If you say, "Send Jessica an email," the script will activate the email feature, retrieve Jessica's email address from your recipient list, and ask you for the subject line and content, which you can dictate before telling the VPA to send.

In Chapter 8, you'll learn how to make your VPA capable of answering (almost) any question. Before you begin, set up the folder */mpt/ch07/* for this chapter. As always, all scripts in this chapter are available at the book's resources page, *https://www.nostarch.com/make-python-talk/*.

NEW SKILLS

- Creating a standby mode to silently wait for your commands 24/7
- Using the time-out option in the speech recognition module to make it more responsive
- Setting a timer or an alarm clock
- Voice-activating a joke-telling functionality
- Asking Python to send an email by using the *smtplib* module

---

An Overview of Your VPA

Before you learn about the functionalities of your VPA, let's explore its structure. You'll start by downloading needed files and installing a third-party module.

Download VPA Files

Let's download the needed files. Go to the book's resources website *https://www.nostarch.com/make-python-talk/* and download the following files from the */mpt/mptpkg/* directory: *mywakeup.py, mytimer.py, myalarm.py, myjoke.py,* and *myemail.py*. Put them in the same directory on your computer where you place your self-made local package files. Refer to Chapter 5 for instructions. I'll explain the purpose of these files later in this chapter.

NOTE *The files* mywakeup.py, mytimer.py, *and so on are local module files to be put in the local package* mptpkg. *As a result, they should be placed in the package folder /* mpt/mptpkg/ *instead of the chapter folder* /mpt/ch07/.

Next, open the script *__init__.py* in the package directory */mpt/mptpkg/* on your computer. As you may recall from Chapter 5, you've already placed the following two lines of code in it:

```
from .mysr import voice_to_text
from .mysay import print_say
```

Add the five lines of code in Listing 7-1 to the end of __init__.py.

```
from .mywakeup import wakeup
from .mytimer import timer
from .myalarm import alarm
from .myjoke import joke
from .myemail import email
```

Listing 7-1: Importing functions from local modules to the local package

This code imports the five functions wakeup(), timer(), alarm(), joke(), and email() from the five modules to the local package so you can later import them at the package level. More on this point soon.

Next, go to the book's resources website and download *vpa.py* from the chapter directory */mpt/ch07/*. Save it on your computer where you place this chapter's Python scripts. The code for *vpa.py* is shown in Listing 7-2.

```
# Import functions from the local package
from mptpkg import voice_to_text, print_say, wakeup, timer, alarm, joke, email

# Put the script in standby
❶ while True:
    # Capture your voice command quietly in standby
    wake_up = wakeup()
    # You can wake up the VPA by saying "Hello Python"
    while wake_up == "Activated":
        print_say("How may I help you?")
        inp = voice_to_text().lower()
        print_say(f'You just said {inp}.')
        if "back" in inp and "stand" in inp:
            print_say('OK, back to standby; let me know if you need help!')
            break
        # Activate the timer
      ❷ elif "timer for" in inp and ("hour" in inp or "minute" in inp):
            timer(inp)
            continue
        # Activate the alarm clock
        elif "alarm for" in inp and ("a.m." in inp or "p.m." in inp):
            alarm(inp)
            continue
        # Activate the joke-telling functionality
        elif "joke" in inp and "tell" in inp:
            joke()
            continue
        # Activate the email-sending functionality
        elif "send" in inp and "email" in inp:
            email()
            continue
        else:
            continue
    # End the script by including "stop" in your voice command
```

```
    if wake_up == "ToQuit":
        print_say("OK, exit the script; goodbye!")
        break
```

Listing 7-2: Python code for a VPA

We first import the seven functions (voice_to_text(), print_say(), wakeup(), and so on) from the local package *mptpkg*. The code in Listing 7-1 already imported the five functions (wakeup(), timer(), and so on) from the local modules to *mptpkg*, so here we import the functions at the package level directly.

We start the script by creating an infinite loop ❶. At each iteration, the VPA listens to your voice command quietly in the background. You can say, "Hello Python" to wake up the VPA. After it wakes up, the VPA asks, "How may I help you?" and takes your voice command. You can activate one of the four functionalities of the VPA ❷: setting a timer, setting an alarm clock, telling a joke, or sending an email.

You can put the VPA back on standby when you are finished by including "back" and "standby" in your voice input. While the script is in standby, you can terminate the script by saying, "Stop the script" or "Stop listening."

Before running *vpa.py*, you need to install a third-party module.

Install the arrow Module

We'll first install the *arrow* module to tell the time and date for the timer and alarm clock functionalities in the VPA.

The Python standard library has several modules that can tell the time and date, including the well-known *time* and *datetime*. However, they are not very user-friendly, with complicated formatting. Further, you need to use several modules in the Python standard library to achieve what we try to accomplish in this chapter. As a result, we'll use the third-party module *arrow*, which offers a more convenient way to deal with times.

You can install *arrow* in your Anaconda prompt (Windows) or a terminal (Mac or Linux) by using the following command, with the virtual environment *chatting* activated:

```
conda install arrow
```

Manage the Standby Mode

Here you'll set up the standby mode for your VPA. At the end of this section, you'll be able to activate the VPA by saying, "Hello Python." The VPA will respond, "How may I help you?"

If you then say, "Go back to standby," the script will return to standby mode and keep quiet. While it's in standby, you can even choose to end the script by including *stop* in your voice command.

Create the Local Module mywakeup

First, you'll set the script to recognize certain commands. Open *mywakeup.py* you just downloaded in your Spyder editor. This script is based on *mysr.py* from Chapter 3, with some significant modifications. Listing 7-3 highlights the differences.

```
import speech_recognition as sr

speech = sr.Recognizer()
# Define a wakeup() function to determine the status of the VPA
❶ def wakeup():
    wakeup = "StandBy"
    voice_input = ""
    with sr.Microphone() as source:
        speech.adjust_for_ambient_noise(source)
        try:
        ❷   audio = speech.listen(source,timeout=3)
            voice_input = speech.recognize_google(audio).lower()
        except sr.UnknownValueError:
            pass
        except sr.RequestError:
            pass
        except sr.WaitTimeoutError:
            pass
    if "hello" in voice_input and "python" in voice_input:
        wakeup = "Activated"
    elif "stop" in voice_input:
        wakeup = "ToQuit"
    return wakeup
```

Listing 7-3: Python code for the mywakeup *module*

We first import speech_recognition and define wakeup() ❶. We create a variable wakeup and set the default value as StandBy. We then capture the voice input from the microphone.

Here I did a little tweaking to make the script more responsive: the timeout=3 option in the listen() method tells the script to time out every three seconds and analyze the voice input ❷, meaning it checks for a voice command every three seconds. Without this option, the script may wait too long to respond, and you may have to say, "Hello Python" a couple of times before you catch the script's attention.

We convert all text to lowercase to avoid mismatch due to capitalization. We also use exception handling to prevent the script from crashing.

When a voice command is captured, the script checks whether *hello* and *Python* are in the voice input. If yes, the variable wakeup changes its value to Activated. Similarly, if you say, "Stop listening" or "Stop the script," the variable wakeup changes to ToQuit. When the function is called, it will return whatever value is stored in the variable wakeup.

Set Some Responses

Now that you know how the *mywakeup* module works, let's learn how to manage standby mode.

Run *vpa.py* in your Spyder editor. You'll notice that when the script is running, nothing happens. However, your VPA is quietly listening in the background. You can activate the VPA by saying, "Hello Python." Once the job is done, you can put it back to standby.

The following output is from one interaction with the script, with my voice input in bold:

```
hello Python
How may I help you?
go back to standby
You just said go back to standby.
OK, back to standby; let me know if you need help!
hello Python
How may I help you?
go back to standby
You just said go back to standby.
OK, back to standby; let me know if you need help!
stop listening
OK, exit the script; goodbye!
```

As you can see, I activated the VPA and then put it back to standby. I activated the VPA and then returned it to standby a second time. After that, I said, "Stop listening" to end the script.

Run the script several times to ensure that you can voice-activate the VPA, put it on standby, and end the script. Next, we'll examine the individual functionalities of the VPA one by one.

Ask Your VPA to Set a Timer

Let's explore the first feature: setting a timer. To do that, you'll first learn how to tell time in Python. We'll use the *arrow* module to tell time in Python and then create a timer that takes written commands. Finally, we'll create a timer() function in the local module *mytimer* that we'll import into the VPA script; this will allow us to set a timer by using voice commands.

Tell the Time with Python

Let's first learn how to tell time with Python.

The following script, *get_time.py*, shows how to retrieve the current time for your time zone in different formats. This is just an example so you can familiarize yourself with the *arrow* module; it's not part of the VPA script.

```
import arrow

# Current time in HH:MM:SS format
❶ current_time = arrow.now().format('H:m:s')
```

```
  print('the current time is', current_time)
❷ current_time12 = arrow.now().format('hh:mm:ss A')
  print('the current time is', current_time12)
  # We can also print out hour, minute, and second individually
❸ print("the current hour is",arrow.now().format('H'))
  print("the current minute is",arrow.now().format('m'))
  print("the current second is",arrow.now().format('s'))
```

We first import the *arrow* module. Its now() function gives you the current local date and time, but you need to use format() to let the script know the format and level of detail of that information.

Table 7-1 lists some commonly used formats and the meanings associated with the format() function in *arrow*. For example, the uppercase HH and H generate the current hour value in a 24-hour clock, with and without a leading 0, respectively, whereas hh and h do the same in a 12-hour clock.

NOTE   *For a complete list of all formats and their meanings associated with* format() *in the* arrow *module, go to* https://arrow.readthedocs.io/en/latest/.

At ❶, we retrieve the current time in H:m:s format on a 24-hour clock and then print it out. At ❷, we obtain the time on a 12-hour clock, followed by AM or PM, in the format hh:mm:ss. Finally we print out just the hour value of the current time ❸. You can do the same for the minute value or the second value.

If you run this script, you'll have output similar to the following:

```
the current time is 8:35:46
the current time is 08:35:46,AM
the current hour is 8
the current minute is 35
the current second is 46
```

Table 7-1: Some Commonly Used Formats for the format() Method of the *arrow* Module

Format code	Meaning
dddd	Full weekday name
ddd	Abbreviated weekday name
MMM	Abbreviated month name
MMMM	Full month name
YYYY	Year in normal form (for example, 2021)
HH	Hour (24-hour clock) as a decimal number with leading zero
hh	Hour (12-hour clock) as a decimal number with leading zero
A	AM or PM
mm	Minute as a decimal number with leading zero
ss	Second as a decimal number with leading zero

You can also use the *arrow* module to get today's date and weekday information, shown here in the *get_date.py* script:

```
import arrow

# Get today's date
❶ today_date = arrow.now()

# Print today's date in different formats
❷ print("today is", today_date.format('MMMM DD, YYYY'))
  print("today is", today_date.format('MMM D, YYYY'))
  print("today is", today_date.format('MM/DD/YYYY'))
  # Print today's weekday in different formats
❸ print("today is", today_date.format('dddd'))
  print("today is", today_date.format('ddd'))
```

At ❶, we use now() to generate the current date and time and save it in a string variable today_date. At ❷, we print out the date in the format of January 01, 2021, with an abbreviated form of the month name, and in numbers using the pattern MM/DD/YYYY. At ❸, we print out the day of the week and then again in abbreviated form.

This script generates output similar to the following:

```
today is March 01, 2021
today is Mar 01, 2021
today is 03/01/2021
today is Monday
today is Mon
```

Now that you know how to tell time in Python, you'll learn how to set a timer.

Build a Timer

We'll use our new *arrow* module skills with the sleep() function from the *time* module to build a timer that takes written commands. You won't use this in your VPA script, but you'll learn the skills needed to build a timer that takes voice commands.

We'll restrict the input to take hours only, minutes only, or hours and minutes (the script won't take seconds). So you can set the timer to go off in 2 hours, or in 1 hour 30 minutes, or in 20 minutes—but not in 1 hour 30 minutes 20 seconds.

Before we go into the details of the script, let's understand the logic behind it. Your written command should be in the form of set a timer for 1 hour 20 minutes, set a timer for 2 hours, or set a timer for 25 minutes. The script then saves your written command in the string variable inp.

The string method find() returns a value of -1 if the characters you're looking for are not in the string. We'll use this feature to extract the hour and minute values in inp.

There are three cases:

- The value of inp.find("hour") is not -1, while the value of inp.find("minute") is -1. This means minute is not in the variable inp but hour is. You've set the timer in the form of set a timer for 2 hours. We extract the hour value between timer for and hour and set the minute value to 0.

- The value of inp.find("hour") is -1, and the value of inp.find("minute") is not -1. This means minute is in the variable inp but not hour. You've set the timer in the form of set a timer for 25 minutes. We extract the minute value between timer for and minute and set the hour value to 0.

- Neither the value of inp.find("hour") nor the value of inp.find("minute") is -1. This means both hour and minute are in the variable inp. You've set the timer in the form of set a timer for 1 hour 20 minutes. We extract the hour value between timer for and hour and the minute value between hour and minute.

We'll add that amount of time to the current time to determine when the timer should go off. We then check the time every 0.5 seconds to make sure we don't miss when the timer should go off. When the time reaches the preset time, the timer goes off.

The timer is set in *timer.py* in Listing 7-4.

```
import time
import arrow

# Tell you the format to set the timer
print('''set your timer; you can set it to the number of hours,
    number of minutes,
    or a combination of both ''')
# Set the timer
❶ inp = input("How long do you want to set your timer for?\n")
# Find the positions of "timer for" and "hour" and "minute"
pos1 = inp.find("timer for")
pos2 = inp.find("hour")
pos3 = inp.find("minute")
# Handle the case "set a timer for hours only"
❷ if pos3 == -1:
    Addhour = inp[pos1+len("timer for"):pos2]
    Addminute = 0
# Handle the case "set a timer for minutes only"
❸ elif pos2 == -1:
    addhour=0
    addminute = inp[pos1+len("timer for"):pos3]
# Handle the case for "set a timer for hours and minutes"
❹ else:
    Addhour = inp[pos1+len("timer for"):pos2]
    Addminute = inp[pos2+len("hour"):pos3]
# Current hour, minute, and second
startHH = arrow.now().format('H')
startmm = arrow.now().format('m')
```

```
    startss = arrow.now().format('s')
    # Obtain the time for the timer to go off
    newHH = int(startHH)+int(addhour)
    newmm = int(startmm)+int(adminute)
❺ if newmm>59:
        newmm -= 60
        newHH += 1
    newHH = newHH%24
    end_time = str(newHH)+":"+str(newmm)+":"+startss
    print("Your timer will go off at "+end_time)
    while True:
        timenow = arrow.now().format('H:m:s')
        if timenow == end_time:
            print("Your timer has gone off!")
            break
        time.sleep(0.5)
```

Listing 7-4: The script to set a timer

We first print out the instructions. At ❶, the script takes the user's written input specifying how long to set the timer, then saves this to the variable inp.

WARNING *In* timer.py, *we use* int() *to convert the number of minutes or hours to an integer. Therefore, your input must be a natural number such as 2, 5, or 10. You can't use a decimal number such as 2.5 hours or 8.6 minutes because* int() *can't convert those to an integer.*

We then check whether the input included hour and minute. If minute is not in the input ❷, we set the value of adminute to 0 and set the value of addhour to whatever number is between timer for and hour. We use similar methods to handle cases when hour is not in the written command ❸ or when both hour and minute are in the written command ❹.

The function now() from the *arrow* module obtains the current time in hour, minute, and second values. We add the values of adminute and addhour to the current time to obtain the time when the timer should go off. At ❺, we adjust for the cases when the minute value exceeds 59 or the hour value exceeds 23. We then set the time the alarm should go off in the H:m:s format.

We start an infinite while loop to check the current time every 0.5 seconds. When the current time reaches the alarm time, we set off the alarm. The script prints Your timer has gone off! and the script ends.

WARNING *The script* timer.py *is written to build up your skill set. It won't be used in the final VPA script, so we don't use exception handling. As a result, the script is easy to break.*

Here's an example interaction with *timer.py*, with user input in bold:

```
set your timer; you can set it to the number of hours,
    number of minutes,
    or a combination of both
```

How long do you want to set your timer for?
set a timer for 1 minute
Your timer will go off at 21:9:15
Your timer has gone off!

TRY IT OUT

Run *timer.py* and set the timer to go off in two minutes.

Create the mytimer Module

Now we'll create a timer() function that's similar to the *timer.py* script, but we'll use a voice command instead of a written one.

Open the file *mytimer.py* you just downloaded from the book's resources website and open it in your Spyder editor. The module will define the function timer() that your VPA will use, shown in Listing 7-5.

```
import time

import arrow

from mptpkg import print_say

def timer(v_inp):
    # Find the positions of "timer for" and "hour" and "minute"
    pos1= v_inp.find("timer for")
    pos2= v_inp.find("hour")
--snip--
    print_say("Your timer will go off at "+end_time)
--snip--
            print_say("Your timer has gone off!")
--snip--
```

Listing 7-5: The script for the local mytimer *module*

Set the Timer

Now you'll test the first functionality of your VPA. Let's zoom in to the part where you can activate the timer in your VPA script:

```
--snip--
from mptpkg import timer
--snip--
        # Activate the timer
        elif "timer for" in inp and ("hour" in inp or "minute" in inp):
            timer(inp)
            continue
--snip--
```

First, we've imported the `timer()` function to the script. Second, the `elif` branch between the `if` branch and `else` branch in the inner while loop is where you can set a timer.

If you run *vpa.py*, it will start in standby mode. You can wake it up by saying, "Hello Python." Then you can set a timer by saying, "Set a timer for 1 hour 20 minutes" or "Set a timer for 2 hours."

The following output is from one interaction with the script, with my voice input in bold:

```
hello Python
How may I help you?
set a timer for 1 minute
You just said set a timer for 1 minute
Your timer will go off at 21:37:46
Your timer has gone off!
How may I help you?
--snip--
```

As you can see, I first activate the VPA and then set a timer for one minute. The VPA tells me, "Your timer will go off at 21:37:46." After one minute, the timer goes off.

TRY IT OUT

Run *VPA.py*, wake the VPA up, and set the timer to go off in two minutes. After the timer goes off, ask the VPA to go back to standby.

Ask Your VPA to Set an Alarm Clock

Now you'll learn how to ask your VPA to set an alarm clock. You'll first use written commands to set the alarm clock. You'll then create a *myalarm* module, in which you define an `alarm()` function. Finally, you'll import `alarm()` to the VPA script to set the alarm clock by using voice commands.

Build an Alarm Clock

Building an alarm clock is similar to setting a timer, except that we specify the time the alarm should go off rather than saying it should go off a certain time from now. You can either specify an hour value alone, such as 8 PM, or an hour and minute value, such as 7:25 AM.

The script will take written commands for now. The script *alarm_clock.py* is shown in Listing 7-6.

```
import time

import arrow
```

```
        # Tell you the format to set the timer
        print('''set your alarm clock\nyou can use the format of:\n
              \tset an alarm for 7 a.m., or
              \tset an alarm for 2:15 p.m.''')
        # Set the alarm
❶ inp = input("What time would you like to set your alarm for?\n")
        # Find the positions of the four indicators
❶ p1 = inp.find("alarm for")
  p2 = inp.find("a.m.")
  p3 = inp.find("p.m.")
  p4 = inp.find(":")
        # Handle the four different cases
❷ if p2 != -1 and p4 != -1:
      inp=inp[p1+len("alarm for")+1:p2]+"AM"
  elif p3 != -1 and p4 != -1:
      inp=inp[p1+len("alarm for")+1:p3]+"PM"
  elif p2 != -1 and p4 == -1:
      inp=inp[p1+len("alarm for")+1:p2-1]+":00 AM"
  elif p3 != -1 and p4 == -1:
      inp=inp[p1+len("alarm for")+1:p3-1]+":00 PM"
  print(f"OK, your alarm will go off at {inp}!")
❸ while True:
      # Obtain time and change it to "7:25 AM" format
      tm = arrow.now().format('h:mm A')
      time.sleep(5)
      # If the clock reaches alarm time, the alarm clock goes off
      if inp == tm:
          print("Your alarm has gone off!")
          break
```

Listing 7-6: The script to set an alarm clock

First, the script captures our written input and saves it as the string variable inp. We then look for the positions of the four indicators: alarm for, a.m., p.m., and : ❶. If you include the colon in your input, the script knows to check for a minute value.

Depending on what you pass at ❷, one of four scenarios results:

- You input a.m. and specify hour and minute values. We extract the preset time value between set alarm for and a.m., convert it to a string, and add AM at the end. For example, if you input set an alarm for 7:34 a.m., the returned string value is 7:34 AM.

- You input p.m. and specify the hour and minute value. We extract the preset time value, convert it to a string, and add PM at the end. For example, if you input set an alarm for 2:55 p.m., the returned string value is 2:55 PM.

- You input a.m. but specify only an hour value. We extract the preset time value, convert it to a string, and add :00 AM at the end. For example, if you input set an alarm for 7 a.m., the returned string value is 7:00 AM.

- You input p.m. but specify only an hour value. We extract the preset time value, convert it to a string, and add :00 PM at the end. For example, if you input set an alarm for 3 p.m., the returned string value is 3:00 PM.

Once we've extracted the time when the alarm should go off, we start an infinite loop ❸. At each iteration, we check the current time every five seconds in the 7:25 AM format.

Finally, we check whether the time we set for the alarm clock matches the current time. If the times match, the alarm clock goes off, and the script prints Your alarm has gone off!.

Run the script and use it to set an alarm clock for yourself. Try all four cases: with and without the minute value, with either a.m. or p.m. at the end. Next, we'll create an alarm clock module based on this script.

Create the Alarm Clock Module

Now we'll create the alarm() function that will use the *alarm_clock.py* code. This code will take voice input instead of written input and give both voice and text output.

Open *myalarm.py*, which you just downloaded from the book's resources website, and open it in your Spyder editor. The script will define the function alarm() that your VPA will use, shown in Listing 7-7.

```
import time

import arrow

from mptpkg import print_say

# Define the Alarm() function
def alarm(v_inp):
    # Find the positions of the four indicators
    p1 = v_inp.find("alarm for")
--snip--
```

Listing 7-7: The script for the local myalarm *module*

Set an Alarm

Now you can ask your VPA to set an alarm clock for you. Let's zoom in on the part of *vpa.py* that can set an alarm clock:

```
--snip--
from mptpkg import alarm
--snip--
        # Activate the alarm clock
        elif "alarm for" in inp and ("a.m." in inp or "p.m." in inp):
            alarm(inp)
            continue
--snip--
```

First, we've imported the alarm() function in the local *myalarm* module to the script from the self-made package *mptpkg*. Second, an elif branch is in the inner while loop, where you can activate the alarm clock by including *alarm for* and either *a.m.* or *p.m.* in your voice command.

Run *vpa.py*. You can set an alarm clock after waking up your VPA. The following output is from one interaction with the script, with my voice input in bold:

```
hello Python
How may I help you?
set an alarm for 8:38 a.m.
You just said set an alarm for 8:38 a.m.
OK, your alarm will go off at 8:38 AM!
Your alarm has gone off!
How may I help you?
--snip--
```

TRY IT OUT

Run *vpa.py*, wake up your VPA, and set an alarm clock to go off in one minute.

Ask Your VPA to Tell a Joke

In this section, you'll learn how to ask your VPA to tell a joke. You'll find a good joke list to pull from, then create a joke module and import it to your main script so that your VPA can tell you jokes in a human voice.

Create Your Joke List

You can create a joke list from many resources. I'm using the Quick, Funny Jokes! website (*https://www.quickfunnyjokes.com/math.html*).

I selected 15 jokes and saved them in a file called *jokes.txt* in the chapter folder */mpt/ch07/* on my computer. You can use as many jokes as you like, as long as you also save them in a separate text file as we are doing here. Here are my 15 jokes:

```
There are three kinds of people in the world—those who can count and those who
can't.

Without geometry, life is pointless.

Write the expression for the volume of a thick-crust pizza with height "a" and
radius "z".

Two random variables were talking in a bar. They thought they were being
discrete, but I heard their chatter continuously.

3 out of 2 people have trouble with fractions.

Parallel lines have so much in common . . . it's a shame they'll never meet.

Math is like love; a simple idea, but it can get complicated.
```

Dear Math, please grow up and solve your own problems; I'm tired of solving them for you.

Dear Algebra, Please stop asking us to find your X. She's never coming back, and don't ask Y.

Old mathematicians never die; they just lose some of their functions.

I strongly dislike the subject of math; however, I am partial to fractions.

Zenophobia is the irrational fear of convergent sequences.

Philosophy is a game with objectives and no rules. Mathematics is a game with rules and no objectives.

Classification of mathematical problems as linear and nonlinear is like classification of the universe as bananas and non-bananas.

A circle is just a round straight line with a hole in the middle.

Next, you'll learn in detail how to create the joke-telling module.

Create a Joke Module

In this section, you'll create a joke() function. When the function is called, it will go to the file *jokes.txt* on your computer, access its content, and break it into individual jokes and put them in a list. It will then randomly select a joke from the list and read it out loud to you.

We'll import the script *myjoke.py*, shown in Listing 7-8, as a local module in your VPA.

```
❶ import random

from mptpkg import print_say

# Define the joke() function
❷ def joke():
    # Read the content from the file jokes.txt
    with open('../ch07/jokes.txt','r') as f:
        content = f.read()
    # Split the content at double line breaks
  ❸ jokelist = content.split('\n\n')
    # Randomly select a joke from the list
    joke = random.choice(jokelist)
    print_say(joke)
```

Listing 7-8: The script to create a joke module

First, we import the *random* module, which we'll use to randomly select a joke from the list. At ❶, we start the definition of joke().

We then read the content from *jokes.txt* and put the content in the string variable content ❷. Note that since we put *jokes.txt* in a different directory from the module script *myjoke.py*, we need to specify the path of the file, and ../ch07/ tells Python that the file is in a parallel folder called *mptpkg*. This way, we can use the joke-telling functionality in other chapters as well, which we will do in Chapter 17.

We know that individual jokes are separated by double line breaks, so we use split() to separate the content of the file into individual strings and put them in the list jokelist ❸. We then randomly select a joke by using choice() from the *random* module. Finally, the script prints out and speaks aloud the selected joke.

Tell a Joke

Now you'll import the joke module you just created to your VPA so that it can tell you jokes in a human voice. Let's zoom in on the part of *vpa.py* that can tell a joke:

```
--snip--
from mptpkg import joke
--snip--
        # Activate the joke-telling functionality
        elif "joke" in inp and "tell" in inp:
            joke()
            continue
--snip--
```

We first import the joke() function in our newly made *myjoke* module from the local *mptpkg* package. In the inner while loop section of the VPA code is an elif branch, in which we tell the VPA that if *tell* and *joke* are in your voice command, the joke-telling functionality is activated.

Here's the outcome from one interaction with the script *vpa.py*, with my input in bold:

```
hello Python
How may I help you?
tell me a joke
You just said tell me a joke
I strongly dislike the subject of math; however, I am partial to fractions.
How may I help you?
--snip--
```

TRY IT OUT

The HuffPost website has a list of motivational quotes: *https://www.huffpost .com/entry/100-motivational-quotes-t_b_4505356/*. Create a quote module to provide you with uplifting quotes, similar to the joke module you created.

Send Hands-Free Email

In this section, we'll examine the functionality of sending email 100 percent hands-free. You'll first learn how to send an email by using written commands in Python; this will give you the skill set to create an email module that takes voice commands. After that, you'll import the email module to your VPA so you can send email with your voice.

Send Email with Written Commands

Before moving on, you need to prepare a few things.

First, you need an email account from which to send email via Python. This example uses my Gmail account, *ukmarkliu@gmail.com*, which you should replace with your own email address.

Gmail and many other email providers require you to apply for a separate application password, which is different from your regular email password. For example, the Google Account Help page shows how to set up your Gmail app password; see *https://support.google.com/accounts/answer/185833/*.

Sending email in Python requires a few steps. You'll first need to connect to your email provider's Simple Mail Transfer Protocol (SMTP) server. SMTP is an internet standard for sending email. Once the connection is established, you'll need to log in using your email address and password. You'll then provide the recipient's email address, the subject line, and the email content. Finally, you'll ask Python to send the actual email.

The *smtplib* module is in the Python standard library, so no installation is needed. You also need at least one email as the recipient's address. You can use another one of your own email addresses or ask for a friend's.

The script *emails.py* can take your written commands and send out email using Python, as shown in Listing 7-9.

```
import smtplib

# Build a dictionary of names and emails
emails = {'mark':'mark.liu@uky.edu',
          'sarah':'Sarah email address here',
          'chris':'Chris email address here'}
# Different email providers have different domain names and port numbers
❶ mysmt = smtplib.SMTP('smtp.gmail.com', 587)
mysmt.ehlo()
mysmt.starttls()
# Use your own login info; you may need an app password
mysmt.login('ukmarkliu@gmail.com', '{Your password here}')
# Ask for the name of the recipient
❷ name = input('Who do you want to send the email to?\n')
email = emails[name]
print(f"You just said {name}.")
# Ask for the subject line
subline = input('What is the subject line?\n')
print(f"You just said {subline}.")
# Ask for the email content
content = input('What is the email content?\n')
print(f"You just said {content}.")
```

```
# Send the actual email
❸ mysmt.sendmail('ukmarkliu@gmail.com', email,
                f'Subject: {subline}.\nHello, {content}.')
{}
print('Ok, email sent')
mysmt.quit()
```

Listing 7-9: The script to send an email using Python

We import the *smtplib* module and create a dictionary *emails* to match names with email addresses. This way, when you type in a person's name, the script will retrieve the corresponding email from the dictionary.

At ❶, we connect to the Gmail SMTP. If you aren't using Gmail, you'll need to search for the domain name and port number of your email provider. No change is needed if you are using Gmail.

We then start the communication with your email server and the Transport Layer Security (TLS) encryption. The TLS encryption is needed by the script for security reasons. Once the connection is established, you need to log in using your email address and password, so make sure to replace *ukmarkliu@gmail.com* with your own email address. I've blocked out my Gmail password in the code.

The script then requests several pieces of information in order to send the email ❷. It first requests the name of the recipient, which you must already have stored in the dictionary emails for the script to retrieve. With the name, the script retrieves the email from the dictionary. It will then also ask you for the email subject line and email content, which you enter in the IPython console at the lower-right corner of your computer screen.

At ❸, we send out the email with sendmail(), which takes three inputs: your email address; the recipient's email address; and the subject line and the email content, separated by the line break escape character \n.

Once done, the script will confirm that the email has been sent. Try this script yourself and make sure that you can send email using Python.

Next, we'll create the module to send email using Python and then add it to your VPA.

Create the Email Module

We first need to create the script *myemail.py* to use as a local module in your VPA. In the module, we define an email() function. Once called, it will connect to your email server and ask you for voice inputs—the recipient's name, the subject line, and the email content—before sending out the actual email.

The content of *myemail.py* is similar to that of *emails.py*, with a few differences: the script will ask you for input using voice as well as printed messages, and you need to use voice input instead of written input. The differences are highlighted in Listing 7-10.

```
--snip--
from mptpkg import voice_to_text, print_say
```

```
# Define the email() function
def email():
    # Build a dictionary of names and emails
--snip--
    # Voice input the name of the recipient
    print_say('Who do you want to send the email to?')
    name = voice_to_text().lower()
    email = emails[name]
    print_say(f"You just said {name}.")
    # Voice input the subject line
    print_say('What is the subject line?')
    subline = voice_to_text()
    print_say(f"You just said {subline}.")
    # Voice input the email content
    print_say('What is the email content?')
    content = voice_to_text()
    print_say(f"You just said {content}.")
    # Send the actual email
    mysmt.sendmail('ukmarkliu@gmail.com', email,
                    f'Subject: {subline}.\nHello, {content}.')
    {}
    print_say('Ok, email sent.')
    mysmt.quit()
```

Listing 7-10: The script to create a local myemail module

As you can see, you need to import voice_to_text() from your local
mptpkg package to capture your voice input to dictate the recipient's name,
email subject line, and content. You also need print_say() from your local
mptpkg package to print and speak messages.

Now the module is ready to be imported to the VPA script.

Add the Email Functionality

Next, you need to import email() from *myemail.py* into your VPA so that you
can send email 100 percent hands-free. Let's zoom in to the part of *vpa.py*
that can send an email:

```
--snip--
from mptpkg import email
--snip--
        # Activate the email-sending functionality
        elif "email" in inp and "send" in inp:
            email()
            continue
--snip--
```

We import the email() function in the local *myemail* module from the
local *mptpkg* package. There's an elif branch in which you can activate the
email-sending feature.

Here's an example interaction with *vpa.py*, with my voice input in bold. All output is printed as well as spoken out loud.

```
hello Python
How may I help you?
send an email
You just said send an email
Who do you want to send the email to?
mark
You just said mark.
What is the subject line?
this is from python
You just said this is from python.
What is the email content?
this email is sent using the Python programming language
You just said this email is sent using the Python programming language
Ok, email sent
How may I help you?
--snip--
```

First, you should wake up your VPA. After you say, "Send an email," the email feature is activated. The VPA then asks you for the recipient's name—I gave my own name, and my University of Kentucky (UKY) email address was matched to it. It also asks for the subject line and email content. Once the information is collected, the email is sent, and the script exits the email functionality.

Figure 7-1 shows the email I received as a result in my UKY email account.

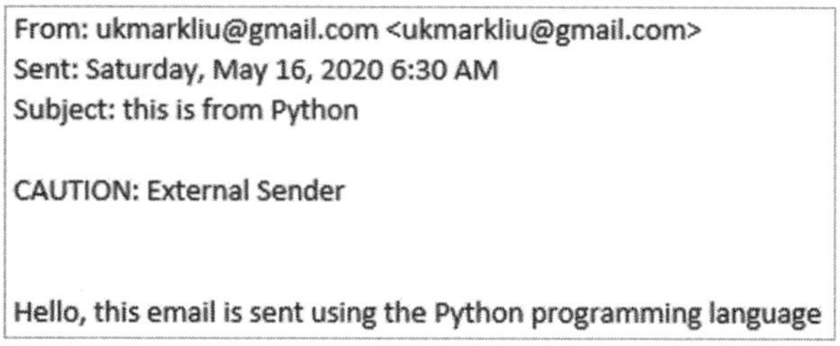

From: ukmarkliu@gmail.com <ukmarkliu@gmail.com>
Sent: Saturday, May 16, 2020 6:30 AM
Subject: this is from Python

CAUTION: External Sender

Hello, this email is sent using the Python programming language

Figure 7-1: An email sent using a Python script 100 percent hands-free

TRY IT OUT

Put your own email account and password in *myemail.py*. Then place a legitimate email in the dictionary emails. Wake up your VPA and ask it to send an email to one of your friends.

Summary

In this chapter, you learned how to create a VPA that can set an alarm and timer, tell jokes, and even send email hands-free! You wake your VPA with "Hello Python" and then give it an instruction to activate one of the four functionalities. This chapter taught you how to create a new feature, make it into a local module, and use it in your main script.

In the next chapter, you'll learn how to use the WolframAlpha API to tap into the vast knowledge space on the website so that your VPA will be able to answer (almost) any question.

End-of-Chapter Exercises

1. Write a script to print out a message and speak aloud today's date and time, formatted as "Today is September 8, 2021, and the time now is 09:03:07 AM."

2. Modify *mywakeup.py* so that the only way to end the script *vpa.py* is by saying, "Quit the script."

8

KNOW-IT-ALL VPA

The VPA we created in Chapter 7 can set a timer or an alarm clock for you, tell you jokes, or send your email. Now we'll upgrade it so you can ask it about nearly anything—including daily news and weather, gas prices, and travel information—and tap into its nearly unlimited knowledge of science, math, history, and society.

In this chapter, you'll access the storehouse of information in the computational engine WolframAlpha and use Wikipedia as a backup if WolframAlpha can't provide an answer. If neither site can answer, your VPA will tell you, "I am still learning, and I don't know the answer to that yet." Your VPA will be complete and capable of answering almost any question.

Before you begin, set up the folder */mpt/ch08/* for this chapter. As always, all scripts in this chapter are available at the book's resources page.

NEW SKILLS

- Using APIs with your Python code
- Exploring areas of knowledge in WolframAlpha
- Using `try` and `except` to use one source as the backup of another source
- Creating a know-it-all functionality for your VPA

Get Answers from WolframAlpha

WolframAlpha is a computational knowledge engine that provides an online service for factual queries, with a focus on numerical and computational capabilities, especially in the areas of science and technology. In this section, you'll learn how to get answers from WolframAlpha through its API and then write a Python script to retrieve information.

Apply for an API Key

The first step is to apply for an API key. WolframAlpha gives you up to 2,000 noncommercial API calls per month at no charge. Go to *https://account.wolfram.com/login/create/* and complete the steps to create an account, as shown in Figure 8-1.

NOTE *The WolframAlpha website is subject to change. What you see, and the API application process, may be slightly different from the instructions here. Please follow the instructions you find at the website.*

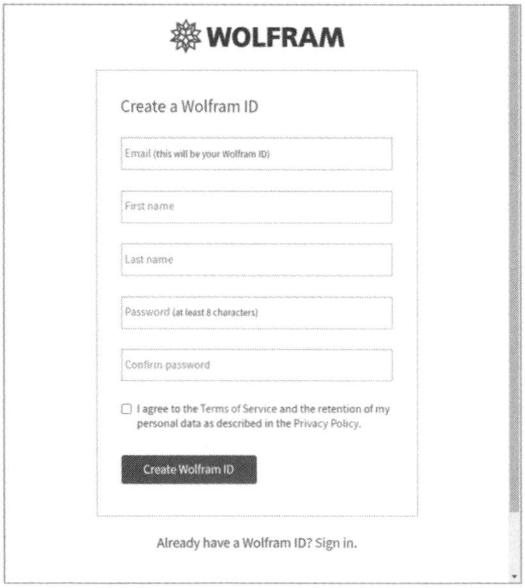

Figure 8-1: Create your free Wolfram ID.

Click **Create Wolfram ID** and then log in. The Wolfram ID itself gives you only browser access, so you need to get an AppID to gain query access using Python. Apply for an API at *https://products.wolframalpha.com/api/* and click **Get API Access** in the bottom left, as shown in Figure 8-2.

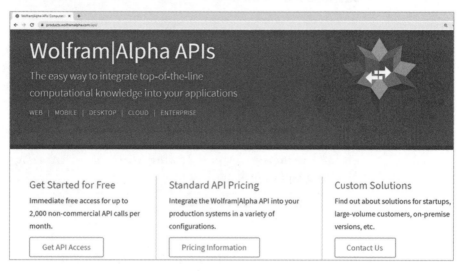

Figure 8-2: Apply for an API at WolframAlpha.

A small dialog should pop up, as shown in Figure 8-3.

Figure 8-3: The Get a New AppID window at WolframAlpha

Fill in the Application name and Description information, then click **Get AppID**. For example, you might enter `Virtual assistant` as the application name and `Learn to build my own virtual personal assistant in Python` in the description field.

After that, your AppID should appear in a pop-up window. You need to click **OK** to activate the AppID. The key will be a long, unique string of characters to distinguish you from other users, something like `HG*************YQ` (I've blocked out the middle characters). Save your AppID in a safe place; you'll need it later.

NOTE *Don't simply copy and try to use your AppID in Python before clicking the OK button on the pop-up window. Your AppID is not activated unless you click the OK button.*

Retrieve Information

Once you have your WolframAlpha API, you can use a Python script to send queries and obtain answers from WolframAlpha. You must first install the third-party *wolframalpha* module on your computer. Go to your Anaconda prompt (Windows) or a terminal (Mac or Linux) and activate the virtual *chatting* environment; then run the following at the command line:

```
pip install wolframalpha
```

Follow the instructions to finish the installation.

The *wolfram.py* script in Listing 8-1 retrieves information from WolframAlpha by using text input.

```
# Import the wolframalpha module
import wolframalpha

# Enter your own WolframAlpha APIkey below
APIkey = "{your WolframAlpha APIkey}"
wolf = wolframalpha.Client(APIkey)
# Enter your query
❶ inp = input("What do you want to know from WolframAlpha?\n")
# Send your query to WolframAlpha and get a response
❷ response = wolf.query(inp)
# Retrieve the text from the response
res = next(response.results).text
# Print out the response
print(res)
```

Listing 8-1: Python code for the script wolfram.py

We first import the *wolframalpha* module. Enter the API key you retrieved earlier as the value of the APIkey variable. Without it, the script won't work.

We then create the client with your AppID. At ❶, the script asks the user for a query to send to WolframAlpha, which the user will enter in the IPython console at the lower-right panel of the Spyder IDE.

At ❷, we send the query to WolframAlpha and retrieve the result object, saving it in the variable response. The result object contains a collection of results in a generator object. *Generator functions* are a convenient shortcut to building iterators, sometimes used to avoid keeping large amounts of data in short-term memory (RAM). You can learn more about generators from authoritative online sources (for example, *https://wiki.python.org/moin/ Generators*). This is why we use the built-in function next() to iterate through different answer groups from WolframAlpha in the result object and obtain the text part of the answer. For a detailed description of how the querying process works with the *wolframalpha* module, see *https://pypi.org/project/wolframalpha/*. Finally, the extracted text is printed out.

Here's a simple exchange with *wolfram.py*, with my text input in bold:

```
What do you want to know from WolframAlpha?
How many states are in the USA?
50
```

As you can see, WolframAlpha has given me a correct and succinct answer.

Explore Different Areas of Knowledge

WolframAlpha can provide information on a variety of topics, so we'll put *wolfram.py* through its paces with questions about weather, general knowledge, science, and math before adding the API to your VPA.

Real-Time Information

WolframAlpha provides real-time information, such as the current temperature in your area. Here's one interaction with the script *wolfram.py*, with my written input in bold:

```
What do you want to know from WolframAlpha?
What is the temperature outside right now?
87 °F
(2 hours 21 minutes ago)
```

The script tells you the temperature in Fahrenheit and the length of time that has passed since the information was obtained. WolframAlpha gets your local information by looking at the location associated with your IP address. If you have an active virtual private network (VPN), your local information will be for the location of your VPN provider.

You can also obtain a weather forecast for a specific day in a certain location like so:

```
What do you want to know from WolframAlpha?
What is the weather forecast for Chicago in 2 days?
between 70 °F and 74 °F
rain (very early morning) | clear (all day)
```

You can check other real-time information such as local gas price or US inflation rate:

```
What do you want to know from WolframAlpha?
What is the current gas price?
$2.548/gal (US dollars per gallon) (Monday, February 8, 2021)
```

General Questions

You can ask general knowledge questions, such as how many teaspoons are in a cup, how to convert Fahrenheit to Celsius, the regional sales tax rate, a state capital, and so on:

```
What do you want to know from WolframAlpha?
How many yards are in a mile?
1760 yards

What do you want to know from WolframAlpha?
What's the capital of West Virginia?
Charleston, West Virginia, United States

What do you want to know from WolframAlpha?
What is the calorie expenditure walking an hour at 5 miles per hour?
energy expenditure | 366 Cal (dietary calories)
fat burned | 0.1 lb (pounds)
oxygen consumption | 19.3 gallons
metabolic equivalent | 4.8 metabolic equivalents
(estimates based on CDC standards)

What do you want to know from WolframAlpha?
What is the speed of light?
2.998×10^8 m/s (meters per second)
```

WolframAlpha has gathered information from various sources such as the CIA's *The World Fact Book* and *The United States Geological Survey*, so it has comprehensive historical data. You can ask questions about events, people, or facts, such as when the vehicle airbag was invented:

```
What do you want to know from WolframAlpha?
When was the airbag invented
1941
```

You can even use WolframAlpha as a dictionary by using *define*, like so:

```
What do you want to know from WolframAlpha?
Define obliterate
1 | verb | mark for deletion, rub off, or erase
```

2 | verb | make undecipherable or imperceptible by obscuring or concealing
3 | verb | remove completely from recognition or memory
4 | verb | do away with completely, without leaving a trace
5 | adjective | reduced to nothingness
(5 meanings)

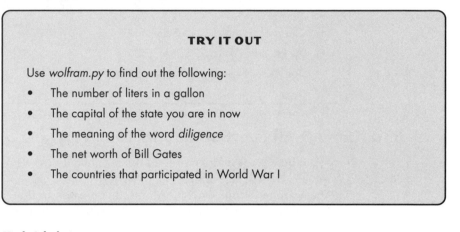

TRY IT OUT

Use *wolfram.py* to find out the following:

- The number of liters in a gallon
- The capital of the state you are in now
- The meaning of the word *diligence*
- The net worth of Bill Gates
- The countries that participated in World War I

Math Calculations

WolframAlpha can answer your questions in the fields of mathematics, science, and technology, ranging from elementary math to calculus to differential equations.

For example, if you want to convert 125 to binary, you can use *wolfram.py* as follows:

```
What do you want to know from WolframAlpha?
convert 125 to binary
1111101_2
```

The 2 at the end of the output indicates that the response is in binary format. Wolfram Alpha can also answer your personal finance questions on topics such as mortgage payments, credit card calculations, and state taxes. For example, to calculate your monthly mortgage payment, you just need to provide three pieces of information—loan amount, interest rate, and loan term—and you'll get the answer:

```
What do you want to know from WolframAlpha?
mortgage $150,000 6.5% 30 years
monthly payment | $948
```

Using the keyword mortgage, you tell the script the loan amount $150,000, the interest rate 6.5%, and the term 30 years. Know that the formatting of your query doesn't really matter—you don't need a comma in the number and you could provide the arguments in any order, and the script should understand.

Add a Know-It-All Functionality to Your VPA

Our goal here is to add a know-it-all functionality to the VPA you created in Chapter 7. We will rely mainly on WolframAlpha to answer your questions, but there are questions WolframAlpha can't answer. In that case, we'll search in Wikipedia. If Wikipedia can't provide an answer either, the VPA will let you know that it doesn't have an answer.

To make use of the next script, be sure to install the following package with your virtual environment activated:

```
pip install wikipedia
```

What WolframAlpha Cannot Answer

Even though WolframAlpha has a vast knowledge base, it doesn't know the answers to all questions. Wikipedia can provide more answers than Wolfram Alpha in certain areas, especially for general reference questions. For example, if you enter **University of Kentucky** as a query in *wolfram.py*, the script will raise a StopIteration exception. This is because next() cannot find a result in any answer group.

On the other hand, if you run the script *wiki.py* from Chapter 5 and enter **University of Kentucky** as a query, you'll get the following output:

```
The University of Kentucky (UK) is a public university in Lexington,
Kentucky. Founded in 1865 by John Bryan Bowman as the Agricultural and
Mechanical College of Kentucky
--snip--
```

Wikipedia can't answer all your questions, either. For example, if you enter **how many people live outside the earth** as a query in *wiki.py*, the API will raise a PageError exception that causes this version of the script to abruptly end with an error status.

We'll improve our VPA by writing a script that queries WolframAlpha first and, if no results are found, will query Wikipedia. If you can't get an answer there, the script will print out the message I am still learning. I don't know the answer to your question yet. We'll handle the errors raised by these external APIs by enclosing the calls in a try block and handling the exceptions in an except block.

Go to the book's resources page, download *know_all.py*, and save it in your chapter folder. This script is shown in Listing 8-2.

```python
import wolframalpha
import wikipedia

# You must put your WolframApha APIkey below
❶ APIkey = "{your WolframAlpha appID here}"
wolf = wolframalpha.Client(APIkey)

while True:
    # Put your question here
    Inp = input("What do you want to know?\n")
    # Stop the loop if you type in "done"
    if inp == "done":
        break
    # Look for answer in Wolfram Alpha
    res = wolf.query(inp)
    # Use try and except to handle errors
    try:
        print(next(res.results).text)
    except:
    # If no answer, try Wikipedia
        try:
            ans = wikipedia.summary(inp)
            print(ans[0:200])
        except:
        # If still no answer
            print('I am still learning. I don\'t know the answer to your question yet')
```

Listing 8-2: Python code for the script know_all.py

We first import the two modules *wolframalpha* and *wikipedia*. At ❶, you should put your own WolframAlpha AppID in the script for it to work. We then put the script in an infinite while loop. At each iteration, it takes your text input as a query. If you key in the word done, the while loop stops and the script ends.

The script sends the query first to WolframAlpha. We use try and except to handle any errors that the API from WolframAlpha might raise. If Wolfram Alpha doesn't return an answer, the script directs the same query to Wikipedia. If there's no answer found from Wikipedia, the script prints I am still learning. I don't know the answer to your question yet.

Now, if you run the script *know_all.py* and enter **University of Kentucky** and **How many people live outside the earth?** as the two queries, you'll get the following output:

```
What do you want to know?
University of Kentucky
The University of Kentucky (UK) is a public university in Lexington, Kentucky.
```

```
Founded in 1865 by John Bryan Bowman as the Agricultural and Mechanical
College of Kentucky, the university is one of the

What do you want to know?
How many people live outside the earth?

I am still learning. I don't know the answer to your question yet

What do you want to know?
done
```

As you can see, the script never crashes, and it provides a result for the
first query but not the second.

TRY IT OUT

Try asking three questions by using the two scripts *wiki.py* and *wolfram.py*: one
with an answer in WolframAlpha, one with an answer in Wikipedia but not
WolframAlpha, and one with an answer in neither. Run the script *know_all.py*,
enter the three questions as queries, and see what happens.

Create the myknowall Module

Now we'll create the know_all() function that will use the script *myknowall.py*,
but this time will take voice commands instead of written commands and will
both print and speak the response instead of just printing out messages.

Download *myknowall.py* from the book's resources and save it in your
local package folder */mpt/mptpkg/*. Since we'll use this as one of the local
modules in the local package, be sure to save it in the local package folder
instead of the chapter folder. The script will define the function know_all()
that your VPA will use, shown in an abbreviated format in Listing 8-3.

```
--snip--
# Import the print_say() function from the local package
from mptpkg import print_say
--snip--
def know_all(v_inp):
    #look for answer in Wolfram Alpha
    res = wolf.query(v_inp)
--snip--
        print_say('I am still learning. I don\'t know the answer to your
question yet')
```

Listing 8-3: The script for the local myknowall *module*

The content of know_all() is similar to the script *know_all.py* except that
the input and output include voice.

A VPA That Can Answer (Almost) Any Question for You

Now you'll make your VPA capable of answering (almost) any question, using the *know_all.py* module.

First, open the script *__init__.py* in the package directory */mpt/mptpkg/* on your computer. Add the following line of code at the end of the file and save the change:

```
from .myknowall import know_all
```

This code imports know_all() from the *myknowall* module to the local package so you can later import it at the package level.

Next, open *vpa.py* from the previous chapter, add the following to the script, and save it as *vpa.py* in this chapter's folder. You'll need to delete the original else branch in the inner while loop and replace it with the following:

```
# Import the know_all() function from the local package
from mptpkg import know_all
--snip--
        # Activate the Know-It-All functionality
        else:
            if len(inp)>6:
                know_all(inp)
            continue
--snip--
```

We import know_all() from the local *mptpkg* package and replace the original else branch. In *vpa.py* in Chapter 7, if none of the four functionalities is activated, the script goes to the next iteration. In the new script *vpa.py*, if none of the four functionalities is activated, the know-it-all functionality is activated, and by default the script searches for answers in WolframAlpha and Wikipedia.

Note here that we've added a condition if len(inp)>6 before we call know_all(). Without the condition, if you don't say anything for a long period of time, the script treats the input as an empty string. As a result, you'll keep hearing the answer I am still learning. I don't know the answer to your question yet. With the condition, if you don't say anything, the script goes to the next iteration without doing anything because the length of an empty string is 0.

Run *vpa.py* and wake it up by saying, "Hello Python." After that, you can ask any question you want. Here's the output from an example interaction with the script, with my voice input in bold:

```
hello Python
how may I help you?
who was us president in 1981
you just said who was us president in 1981
Jimmy Carter (from January 20, 1977 to January 20, 1981)
Ronald Reagan (from January 20, 1981 to January 20, 1989)

how may I help you?
coronavirus
```

```
you just said coronavirus
Coronaviruses are a group of related RNA viruses that cause diseases in
mammals and birds. In humans, these viruses cause respiratory tract infections
that can range from mild to lethal. Mild illness
--snip--
```

As you can see, after activating the VPA, I first asked who the US presi-
dent was in 1981. The answer includes two presidents, because the transi-
tion of power was in January 1981. After that, I asked about the coronavirus.
The VPA provided a detailed answer to the question.

NOTE   *The condition if* `len(inp)>6` *means your query must contain at least seven charac-*
ters. You can change the cutoff value in the condition from 6 to a smaller number
such as 5 or 3 if you want `know_all()` *to be called even if you send a short query such*
as "wolf" or "Python."

TRY IT OUT

Run *vpa.py*, wake it up, and ask via voice the same three questions you used in
the preceding Try It Out on page 164, and see what happens.

Summary

In this chapter, you upgraded the VPA from Chapter 7 so you can ask it just
about anything—including for up-to-date information about weather, gas
prices, and travel conditions, as well as nearly unlimited facts about science,
math, history, and society.

You learned to apply for an API and gain access to the vast knowledge
base in the computational engine WolframAlpha, and you can use Wikipedia
as a backup when WolframAlpha can't provide an answer. If neither site can
answer, your VPA tells you as much. With that, your VPA is complete and
capable of answering almost any question for you. Using APIs like this is an
incredibly powerful skill.

In the next couple of chapters, you'll learn how to create your own
voice-controlled graphical games that can speak to you.

PART III

INTERACTIVE GAMES

9

GRAPHICS AND ANIMATION WITH THE *TURTLE* MODULE

Our goal in the next few chapters is to build voice-controlled graphical games such as tic-tac-toe, Connect Four, and guess-the-word. You'll do all these with the *turtle* module.

In this chapter, you won't be working with voice interactivity. Instead you'll learn the *turtle* module's basic commands that will let you set up a turtle screen, draw shapes, and create animations. This functionality will be the basis for all the games you'll be building.

Before you begin, set up the folder */mpt/ch09/* for this chapter. As always, all scripts in this chapter are available at the book's resources page, *https://www.nostarch.com/make-python-talk/*.

Basic Commands

The *turtle* module allows us to use a robotic turtle to draw shapes and create animations on a canvas. The turtle mimics the way people draw on a physical canvas, but we use commands to move the turtle and create the drawings.

For its underlying graphics, the *turtle* module uses the *tkinter* module, which is Python's de facto standard graphical user interface (GUI) package. Both *turtle* and *tkinter* are in the Python standard library, so there's no need to install them.

Turtle graphics were invented in the 1960s, three decades before the Python language. The *turtle* module allows Python programmers to take advantage of many features of turtle graphics. The first is their simplicity: *turtle* is easier to learn than other game modules such as *pygame* or *tkinter*. The *turtle* module is also intuitive, making it easy to create pictures and shapes by manipulating the drawing pen on a canvas (that is, the screen).

The *turtle* module is also better suited to voice activation. Unlike other game modules, which constantly run through a game loop too fast to capture voice commands, *turtle* scripts don't need a game loop. This makes voice-controlled games possible.

Create a turtle Screen

To use *turtle*, you need to create a turtle screen to contain all objects in the script. The following script shows you a simple example of the turtle screen. Enter the following lines of code in Spyder and save the script as *set_up _screen.py*:

```
import turtle as t

❶ t.Screen()
  t.setup(600,500,100,200)
  t.bgcolor('SpringGreen3')
❷ t.title('Setting Up a Screen with Turtle Graphics')
  t.done()
  t.bye()
```

We import the *turtle* module and give it a short alias name, t. This is one situation where a short alias module name is beneficial, since we'll be calling multiple functions from the module, and often. Therefore, we want to use only t., instead of turtle., in front of all the functions.

At ❶, we create a screen by using Screen(), which doesn't require arguments. We then use setup() to specify the size and location of the screen. The four parameters are screen width, screen height, horizontal distance from the top left of your computer screen, and vertical distance from the top left of your computer screen, in that order. Our screen will be 600 pixels wide and 500 pixels tall, 100 pixels from the left edge of the computer screen, and 200 pixels from the top edge.

Next, we give the turtle screen a background color by using bgcolor(). The *turtle* module provides a wide range of colors, including brown, black, gray, white, yellow, gold, orange, red, purple, navy, blue, lightblue, darkblue, cyan, turquoise, lightgreen, green, and darkgreen.

NOTE *For a more comprehensive list of colors in the* turtle *and* tkinter *modules, see* https://www.tcl.tk/man/tcl8.4/TkCmd/colors.htm.

At ❷, we give a title to the screen, which you'll see at the top beside the turtle graphics symbol (Figure 9-1).

The done() command tells the script to start the event, which is how objects on the screen could be animated. The bye() command tells the script to exit *turtle* when you click the X symbol.

The screen should look something like Figure 9-1.

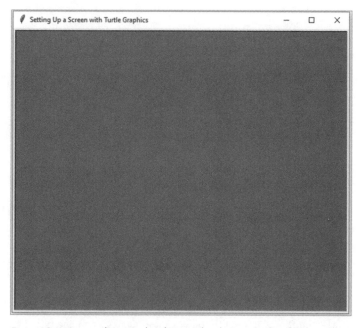

Figure 9-1: Set up the size, background color, and title of the screen.

A turtle screen uses a *Cartesian* coordinate system, with the center coordinate (x = 0, y = 0). The x-value increases from left to right, and the y-value increases from bottom to top, just like the two-dimensional plane you learned in high school mathematics.

NOTE   *In* turtle, *the point (x = 0, y = 0) is at the center of the screen. This is different from most other graphical modules such as* pygame *or* tkinter, *which have the point (x = 0, y = 0) at the top-left corner.*

Create Movements

In earlier days, the turtle cursor was literally a picture of a turtle moving around on the screen. Now, instead of a literal turtle, you see a small arrowhead as the default cursor. The turtle has three attributes: location, direction, and a pen. You can adjust the color and width of the pen, and you can decide whether to put the pen down on the plane so the turtle's path is marked when it moves or lift it up so the movement isn't tracked.

Let's see an actual drawing before looking at the various movements in the module. Enter the code shown in Listing 9-1 in a Spyder editor and save it as *show_turtle.py* in your chapter folder.

```
import turtle as t

t.Screen()
t.setup(600,500,100,200)
t.bgcolor('SpringGreen')
t.title('Show Turtle')
❶ t.shape('turtle')
t.forward(200)
t.right(90)
t.up()
t.forward(100)
t.done()
t.bye()
```

Listing 9-1: Showing the turtle in the turtle module

At ❶, we change the shape of the cursor back to the original turtle shape, as you can see in Figure 9-2. If you run the script, you can see that the turtle starts at position (x = 0, y = 0) and faces right. It moves forward 200 pixels with the default down pen position, so this movement draws a line on the canvas. We turn the turtle right 90 degrees and lift up the pen before moving forward 100 pixels. This time, no line is drawn on the canvas since the drawing pen is not touching the canvas.

TRY IT YOURSELF

Use the F9 key to run the code in *show_turtle.py* one line at a time. See the changes in cursor shape, pen position, and cursor movements on the screen.

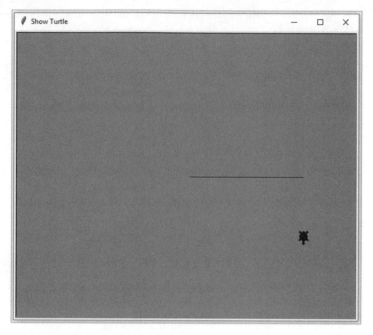

Figure 9-2: The turtle moves on the canvas to make a drawing.

Now we'll discuss in detail some basic movements in the *turtle* module that are useful for our projects.

The forward() and backward() Functions

The forward() function tells the turtle to move forward the specified number of pixels on the screen. The backward() function does the same backward. Enter the code shown in Listing 9-2 in a Spyder editor and save it as *forward _backward.py* in your chapter folder.

```
import turtle as t

t.Screen()
t.setup(600,500,100,200)
t.bgcolor('blue')
t.title('Movements in Turtle Graphics')
❶ t.forward(200)
❷ t.backward(300)
t.done()
t.bye()
```

Listing 9-2: Basic movement functions in the turtle *module*

We set up the screen with a different background color and a title. At ❶, the turtle moves forward 200 pixels. The default starting position of the turtle is at (x = 0, y = 0), facing to the right, so moving forward 200 pixels leads the turtle to the point (x = 200, y = 0).

At ❷, the turtle moves from the point (x = 200, y = 0) backward 300 pixels, ending up at (x = –100, y = 0).

TURTLE ADJUSTMENTS IN SPYDER

When you run *turtle* scripts in Spyder, the turtle scripts crash with a Terminator error after multiple runs in the same IPython console instance. This is a known problem for *turtle* scripts in Spyder. To avoid the crash and the error message, we'll use try and except for the remainder of the book, starting in the script *left_right.py*.

The left() and right() Functions

The left() or right() function changes the direction the turtle is facing. As the argument, we give the degree of the angle to move by. For example, 90 degrees turns the turtle perpendicular to the original direction. A degree value of 360 turns the turtle in a full circle so it's still going in the original direction.

The script *left_right.py* in Listing 9-3 shows how the left() and right() functions work.

```
  import turtle as t

  t.Screen()
  t.setup(600,500,100,200)
  t.bgcolor('light blue')
  t.title('Python Turtle Graphics')
❶ t.pensize(5)
❷ t.right(30)
  t.forward(200)
  t.left(30)
  t.backward(400)
  t.left(90)
❸ t.pencolor('red')
  t.forward(200)
  t.done()
  try:
      t.bye()
  except Terminator:
      print('exit turtle')
```

Listing 9-3: Python code for left_right.py

The pensize() function specifies the thickness of the line the turtle is drawing ❶. The default value is 1 pixel. Here we set the pen size to 5 pixels. At ❷, we tell the turtle to turn right 30 degrees. Then, we move the turtle forward 200 pixels. We then turn the turtle left 30 degrees and move backward 400 pixels.

The pencolor() function changes the color of the drawing pen to red ❸. The default is black. After this step, the lines will be red instead of black.

Run the script and you should see a screen similar to Figure 9-3.

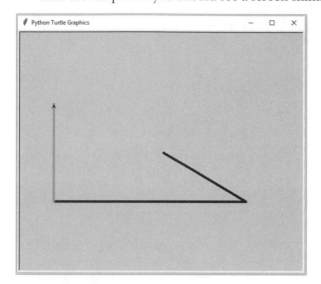

Figure 9-3: The left() and right() functions in the turtle module

---

TRY IT OUT

Run *left_right.py* and then add more activity: change the pen color to green, make a 90-degree right turn, and move forward 250 pixels.

The goto() Function

The goto() function tells the turtle to go to the specified point on the screen. Together with up() and down(), it can create straight lines and dashed lines. The up() function means the turtle pen is not touching the canvas and so doesn't draw as it moves. The down() function puts the pen on the canvas and creates drawings.

If the turtle pen is in the down position, goto() will create a straight line between the current position and the specified position. However, if the turtle pen is in the up position, goto() will create nothing on the screen, but merely moving the turtle from the current position to the specified position. Dashed lines can be created by drawing a sequence of short lines with spaces in between.

Enter the script *create_lines.py* in Listing 9-4.

```
import turtle as t

t.Screen()
t.setup(600,500,100,200)
```

```
    t.bgcolor('lightgreen')
    t.title('Python Turtle Graphics')
    t.pensize(6)
❶  t.goto(200,100)
❷  t.up()
    t.pencolor('blue')
❸  for i in range(8):
        t.goto(-200+50*i,-150)
        t.down()
        t.goto(-200+50*i+30,-150)
        t.up()
❹  t.hideturtle()
    t.done()
    try:
        t.bye()
    except t.Terminator:
        print('exit turtle')
```

Listing 9-4: Python code for create_lines.py

At ❶, we tell the turtle to go to (x = 200, y = 100). By default, the turtle is in the down position and the starting position is (x = 0, y = 0), so goto(200,100) draws a line between the two points (0, 0) and (200, 100), as you can see in Figure 9-4.

At ❷, the script tells the turtle to lift up the pen so that no line is drawn on the screen when the turtle goes to another point. We then change the pen color to blue. At ❸, we start a for loop. In each iteration, the turtle goes to a point, puts down the pen, and goes to another point 30 pixels to the right. This leaves a 30-pixel-long dash, done eight times with gaps between.

The hideturtle() function hides the turtle so that the black arrow cursor is not shown on the screen ❹.

Run the script and you should see a screen similar to Figure 9-4.

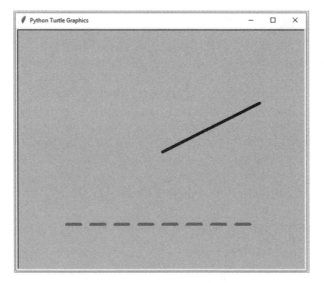

Figure 9-4: Use the goto() *function to create lines using the* turtle *module.*

Basic Shapes

The *turtle* module has several built-in shapes, including the commonly used dot() function that creates a dot. You'll also learn how to create basic shapes such as a triangle, a square, and gridlines.

Use the dot() Function

The dot() function creates a dot with the specified diameter and color. For example, the command dot(30,'red') creates a red dot with a diameter of 30 pixels. We'll use this in our tic-tac-toe and Connect Four games to create game pieces.

Listing 9-5, *dots.py*, shows how the dot() function works.

```
import turtle as t

t.Screen()
t.setup(600,500,100,200)
t.bgcolor('lightgreen')
t.title('Python Turtle Graphics')
❶ t.up()
t.goto(150,100)
t.dot(120,'red')
t.goto(-150,100)
t.dot(135,'yellow')
❷ t.goto(150,-100)
t.dot(125,'blue')
t.goto(-150,-100)
t.dot(140,'green')
t.hideturtle()
t.done()
try:
    t.bye()
except t.Terminator:
    print('exit turtle')
```

Listing 9-5: Python code for dots.py

First we lift up the pen ❶. Then we go to the point (150, 100). We tell the turtle to put a red dot centered on the point (150, 100) and with a diameter of 120 pixels.

Next, we move the turtle to (–150, 100) and draw a yellow dot with a diameter of 135 pixels. Note that you don't need to use up() again since the pen is already lifted up. With the pen up, the turtle can still draw dots.

Starting from ❷, the turtle goes to (150, –100) and draws a blue dot with a diameter of 125 pixels. Then it goes to (–150, –100) and draws a green dot with a diameter of 140 pixels. Figure 9-5 shows the outcome.

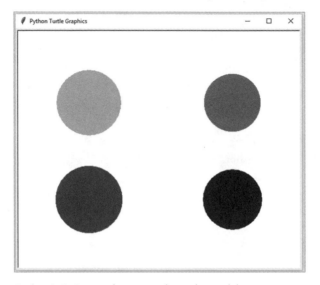

Figure 9-5: Create dots using the turtle module.

Draw Your Own Shapes

You can also draw your own shapes using the *turtle* module. We'll look at some basic shapes here.

Triangles

The easiest way to create a triangle is by using goto(). Listing 9-6, *triangle.py*, draws a triangle with the corners at (–50, –50), (50, –50), and (0, 100).

```
from turtle import *

Screen()
setup(600,500,100,200)
bgcolor('springgreen3')
title('Python Turtle Graphics')
hideturtle()
tracer(False)
❶ pencolor('blue')
pensize(5)
up()
goto(-50,-50)
down()
```

```
goto(50,-50)
goto(0,100)
goto(-50,-50)
update()
done()
try:
    bye()
except Terminator:
    pass
```

Listing 9-6: Python code for triangle.py

The tracer() function tells the script whether to trace the movements of the turtle. The default value is tracer(True), which means the script shows you the movement of the turtle step-by-step. When the turtle pen draws something, you'll see the drawing, one stroke after another. Here, we use tracer(False), so the final drawing is printed, but the script doesn't show the intermediate steps.

We change the pen's color to blue ❶ and its size to 5. We lift up the pen and go to point (–50, –50) then put down the pen and go to point (50, –50). This forms the first leg of the triangle. With the pen down, we ask the turtle to go to point (0, 100), which forms the second leg. The base is drawn when we send the pen back to point (–50, –50) to complete the triangle.

Note that since we've used the command tracer(False) to not display each drawing step (thus saving time), we need to put update() at the end of the script to show the completed picture, as shown in Figure 9-6.

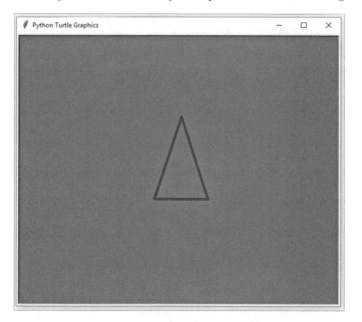

Figure 9-6: Draw a triangle using the turtle *module.*

Rectangles

We can draw rectangles by using goto(), as we did for triangles, but we can also use forward() and left(). In many situations, you can achieve the same goal by using either the goto() function or the forward() and left() functions. If you know the coordinates of the destination, goto() is easier, and if you know the distances between two points, the directional functions are easier.

Here, we'll use forward() and left(). You'll achieve the same results by using goto() in the "End-of-Chapter Exercises" on page 187.

We'll draw a rectangle with the points (0, 0), (200, 0), (200, 100), and (0, 100). Enter the script *rectangle.py* shown in Listing 9-7.

```
import turtle as t

# Set up the screen
t.Screen()
t.setup(600,500,100,200)
t.bgcolor('green')
t.title('Python Turtle Graphics')
t.hideturtle()
t.tracer(False)
❶ t.pensize(6)
# Draw the first side
❷ t.forward(200)
t.left(90)
# Draw the second side
t.forward(100)
t.left(90)
# Draw the third side
t.forward(200)
t.left(90)
# Finish the rectangle
t.forward(100)
t.update()
t.done()
try:
    t.bye()
except t.Terminator:
    print('exit turtle')
```

Listing 9-7: Python code for rectangle.py

We first set up the screen. At ❶, we set the pen size to 6. We don't specify the pen color, so the default color of black will be used. At ❷, the turtle moves forward 200 pixels from the initial position of (0, 0) to form the first side of the rectangle.

Next, the turtle turns left 90 degrees so that it faces up. Then it moves forward 100 pixels to form the second side. We then make the turtle turn left 90 degrees so that it faces west, and move it forward 200 pixels for the third side. The last side of the rectangle is formed similarly.

The output is shown in Figure 9-7.

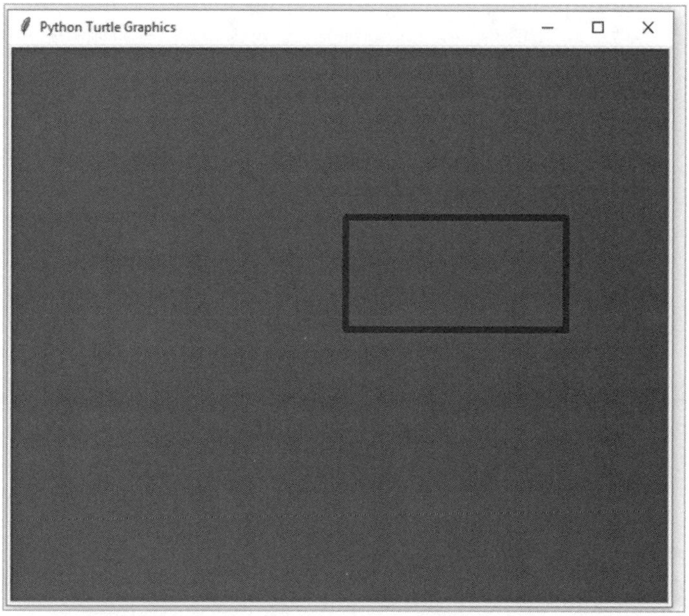

Figure 9-7: Draw a rectangle using the turtle *module.*

We'll use this rectangle-drawing skill to create a board for our upcoming games.

Draw Grid Lines

Games such as tic-tac-toe and Connect Four use a grid. We can make a grid simply by drawing squares. Here we'll draw a game board with six rows and seven columns; the horizontal lines will be thinner and lighter than the vertical ones to match what we'll do in the Connect Four game. Enter the code from *grid_lines.py* in Listing 9-8.

```
import turtle as t

# Set up the screen
t.Screen()
```

```
t.setup(810,710, 10, 70)
t.hideturtle()
t.tracer(False)
t.bgcolor('lightgreen')
# Draw the vertical lines to create 7 columns
❶ t.pensize(5)
for i in range(-350,400,100):
    t.up()
    t.goto(i, -298)
    t.down()
    t.goto(i, 303)
    t.up()
# Draw the horizontal lines to separate the screen in 6 rows
❷ t.pensize(1)
t.color('gray')
for i in range(-300,400,101):
    t.up()
    t.goto(-350,i)
    t.down()
    t.goto(350,i)
    t.up()
t.done()
try:
    t.bye()
except t.Terminator:
    print('exit turtle')
```

Listing 9-8: Python code for grid_lines.py

We first set up the screen. Since we plan to draw a game board with six rows and seven columns, we set the screen size to 810 pixels wide and 710 pixels tall. This way, we can make each cell a square that's 100 by 100 pixels, with a 55-pixel margin around the board. It's important to think about your screen size so you can calculate the coordinates of various points.

We draw eight thick vertical lines with a pen size of 5 ❶ to divide the screen into seven columns. The function range(-350,400,100) produces eight values: -350, -250, ..., 350.

After that, we draw seven thin, gray, horizontal lines to form six rows ❷. If you run the script, you'll see a screen similar to Figure 9-8.

We'll use this board in Chapter 11 for our games.

Animation

In this section, you'll learn to create animation by using clear() and update() to clear the current image and replace it with the next, producing animation frames.

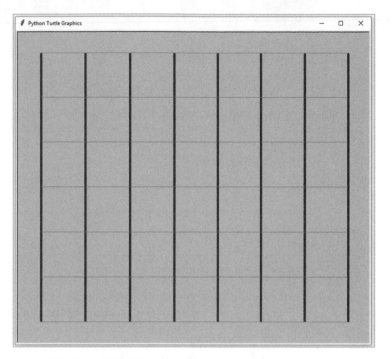

Figure 9-8: Draw grid lines to form a six-by-seven game board

How Animation Works

The clear() function erases everything the turtle has drawn on the screen. You can then redraw objects and use update() to put them onscreen. If you do this repeatedly, the rapid replacement of images will create an animation effect.

We'll explore animation by making a simple clock, shown in *turtle_clock.py* in Listing 9-9.

```
import turtle as t
import time

import arrow

# Set up the screen
t.setup(800,600, 10, 70)
t.tracer(False)
t.bgcolor('lightgreen')
t.hideturtle()
# Put the script in an infinite loop
❶ while True:
    # Clear the screen
    t.clear()
    # Obtain the current time
    current_time = arrow.now().format('hh:mm:ss A')
```

```
            t.color('blue')
            t.up()
            t.goto(-300,50)
            # Write the first line of text
❷        t.write('The Current Time Is\n',font=('Arial',50,'normal'))
            t.color('red')
            t.goto(-300,-100)
            # Write what time it is
❸        t.write(current_time,font=('Arial',80,'normal'))
            time.sleep(1)
            # Put everything on screen
            t.update()
t.done()
try:
    t.bye()
except t.Terminator:
    print('exit turtle')
```

Listing 9-9: Python code for turtle_clock.py

We import the modules and set up the screen. At ❶, we start an infinite loop. In each iteration, the script first erases everything onscreen by using clear(). We then obtain the current time by using the *arrow* module and store the value in the variable current_time.

The write() function from the *turtle* module writes text onscreen. It takes the text to be displayed as the first argument and the font to use as the second argument. At ❷, we write The Current Time Is to the screen in blue. At ❸, the script writes the current time in red.

The script then pauses for one second and makes sure that all the new drawings are updated by using update(). If you run the script, you'll notice that the time changes every second (Figure 9-9).

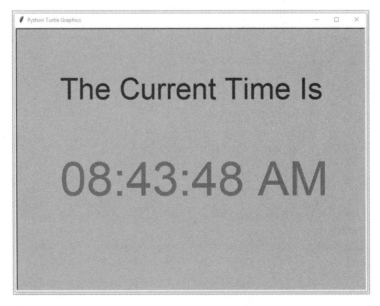

Figure 9-9: Create animation in the turtle *module.*

We'll use this method frequently to create animations in various games.

Use Multiple Turtles

Now we'll look at using two turtles simultaneously—the equivalent of using two pens. In Chapter 12, when we create a guess-the-word game, we'll use one turtle to create a gold coin on the game board and another to count the number of chances the player has left. Whenever the player misses a letter, we'll erase the previous number and change it to the new number. If we used only one turtle, everything, including the coin image, would be wiped. If we use a second turtle, we can keep everything else onscreen and change only whatever the second turtle draws.

In Listing 9-10, *two_turtles.py*, we'll use one turtle to draw a square and another to write something below it.

```
import turtle as t

# Set up the screen
t.setup(810,710, 10, 70)
t.tracer(False)
t.hideturtle()
t.bgcolor('lightgreen')
t.color('blue')
t.pensize(5)
❶ t.up()
t.goto(-200,-100)
t.down()
t.forward(400)
t.left(90)
t.forward(400)
t.left(90)
t.forward(400)
t.left(90)
t.forward(400)
# Create a second turtle
❷ msg = t.Turtle()
msg.hideturtle()
msg.up()
msg.color('red')
msg.goto(-300,-200)
msg.write('this is written by the second turtle',font=('Arial',30,'normal'))
t.update()
t.done()
```

```
try:
    t.bye()
except t.Terminator:
    print('exit turtle')
```

Listing 9-10: Python code for two_turtles.py

We import the *turtle* module and set up a screen with a size of 810 by 710 pixels. Starting at ❶, we draw a blue square in the middle of the screen, similar to the way we drew a rectangle but with all sides the same length.

At ❷, we create a second turtle with Turtle() and name it msg. We tell the script to hide the second turtle

The second turtle msg lifts up the pen, changes the color to red, goes to (−300, −200), and writes the message this is written by the second turtle. The update() function refreshes the screen to draw everything created by the two turtles, shown in Figure 9-10.

this is written by the second turtle

Figure 9-10: A screen created with two turtles

TRY IT OUT

Run *two_turtles.py* and then modify it to add a third turtle. Use the new turtle to write a message at the bottom of the screen.

Summary

In this chapter, you learned the basics of the *turtle* module. You first learned how to set up a turtle screen and then learned basic movements like going forward or backward and turning left or right. You created various shapes by using both the built-in function and basic movement commands.

Finally, you learned to create animation effects in the *turtle* module by using the clear() and update() functions. In the next few chapters, you'll learn how to use these skills to create voice-controlled graphical games.

End-of-Chapter Exercises

1. Modify *set_up_screen.py* so that the screen size is 500 pixels wide and 400 pixels tall, the background color is blue, and the title is Modified Screen.

2. Modify *forward_backward.py* so that the turtle first moves backward 100 pixels and then moves forward 250 pixels.

3. Modify *dots.py* to have only two light green dots with diameters of 60 at points (–100, –100) and (100, 100).

4. Modify *triangle.py* so that the three sides of the triangle are red with a thickness of 3.

5. Replicate the result in *rectangle.py* by using goto(). You aren't allowed to use the functions forward(), backward(), left(), or right().

10

TIC-TAC-TOE

In this chapter, you'll build a voice-controlled tic-tac-toe game to put all your new skills into practice. You'll draw a game board with blue and white game pieces, disallow invalid moves, and detect if a player has won. You'll then add the speech recognition and text-to-speech functionality and set the game so you play with your own computer.

As usual, all scripts in this chapter are available at the book's resources page at *https://www.nostarch.com/make-python-talk/*. Before you begin, set up the folder */mpt/ch10/* for this chapter.

Game Rules

Tic-tac-toe is probably one of the most well-known games in the world, but just to be sure, I'll go over the rules before we create our game board. In tic-tac-toe, two players take turns marking a cell with an X or O in a three-by-three grid. The first player to connect three Xs or Os in a row horizontally, vertically, or diagonally wins. If no one connects three before all the cells are full, the game is tied. Instead of X and O, we'll use blue and white dots as game pieces.

Draw the Game Board

We'll draw a three-by-three grid on the screen and assign a number to each cell so we can tell the script where to place each game piece. Open your Spyder editor, copy the code in Listing 10-1, and save the script as *ttt_board.py* in your chapter folder.

```
import turtle as t

# Set up the screen
t.setup(600,600,10,70)
t.tracer(False)
t.bgcolor("red")
t.hideturtle()
t.title("Tic-Tac-Toe in Turtle Graphics")
# Draw horizontal lines and vertical lines to form grid
t.pensize(5)
❶ for i in (-100,100):
    t.up()
    t.goto(i,-300)
    t.down()
    t.goto(i,300)
    t.up()
    t.goto(-300,i)
    t.down()
```

```
        t.goto(300,i)
        t.up()
    # Create a dictionary to map cell numbers to cell center coordinates
❷ cellcenter = {'1':(-200,-200), '2':(0,-200), '3':(200,-200),
               '4':(-200,0), '5':(0,0), '6':(200,0),
               '7':(-200,200), '8':(0,200), '9':(200,200)}
    # Go to the center of each cell, write down the cell number
❸ for cell, center in list(cellcenter.items()):
        t.goto(center)
        t.write(cell,font = ('Arial',20,'normal'))
    t.done()
    try:
        t.bye()
    except t.Terminator:
        print('exit turtle')
```

Listing 10-1: Drawing the tic-tac-toe game board

We import all functions in the *turtle* module and set the screen to 600 by 600 pixels. Because we have a three-by-three grid, each cell is 200 by 200 pixels. We set the background color to red and set the title as Tic-Tac-Toe in Turtle Graphics.

With the command for i in (-100, 100), we iterate the variable i through the range −100 to 100 ❶. As a result, the for loop produces two horizontal lines and two vertical lines. The two horizontal lines are between points (−300, −100) and (300, −100) and points (−300, 100) and (300, 100). The two vertical lines are between points (−100, −300) and (−100, 300) and points (100, −300) and (100, 300). These lines evenly divide the screen into nine cells.

We then create a dictionary cellcenter to map each cell number to the x- and y-coordinates of the center of the corresponding cell ❷. For example, the lower-left cell is cell number 1, and the coordinates of its center are (x = −200, y = −200). We do this for all nine cells in the dictionary, using the cell number as the key and the coordinates as the value.

At ❸, we use the for loop to iterate through nine pairs of values to write the cell number at the cell's center. The command list(cellcenter.items()) produces a list of the nine key-and-value pairs from cellcenter, which should look like this:

```
[('1', (-200, -200)), ('2', (0, -200)), ('3', (200, -200)), ('4', (-200, 0)),
('5', (0, 0)), ('6', (200, 0)), ('7', (-200, 200)), ('8', (0, 200)), ('9',
(200, 200))]
```

At each iteration of the for loop, the turtle goes to the center of the cell and writes the cell number there. Run the script and you should see a screen similar to Figure 10-1.

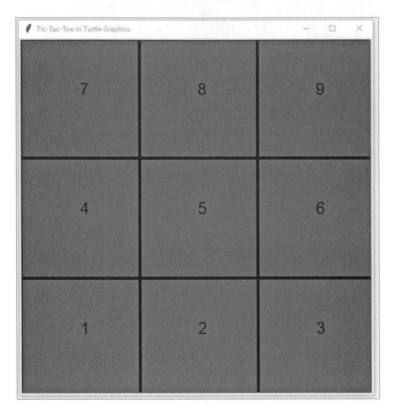

Figure 10-1: The board for tic-tac-toe

Create the Game Pieces

Now we'll add code to place game pieces in the cells. You'll first learn how mouse clicks work in the *turtle* module and then use them to place the pieces.

How Mouse Clicks Work in turtle

When you left-click on the turtle screen, the x- and y-coordinates of the point you clicked are displayed onscreen. Listing 10-2, *mouse_click.py*, handles a simple mouse click. This is just for example purposes; we won't use this code in the final script but will use the same principles.

```
import turtle as t

# Set up the screen
t.setup(620,620,360,100)
t.title("How Mouse-Clicks Work in Turtle Graphics")
# Define get_xy() to print the coordinates of the point you click
❶ def get_xy(x,y):
      print(f'(x, y) is ({x}, {y})')
# Hide the turtle so that you don't see the arrowhead
t.hideturtle()
# Bind the mouse click to the get_xy() function
❷ t.onscreenclick(get_xy)
```

```
❸ t.listen()
  t.done()
  try:
      t.bye()
  except t.Terminator:
      print('exit turtle')
```

Listing 10-2: How mouse clicks work in the turtle *module*

As usual, we import the *turtle* module and set up the screen. At ❶, we define the function get_xy(), which prints out the x- and y-coordinates of your click. We also hide the turtle so you don't see the cursor moving around the screen. At ❷, we bind the onscreen mouse click to the get_xy() function by using the *turtle* function onscreenclick(), which returns the x- and y-coordinates of the click. As a result, onscreenclick(get_xy) supplies the x- and y-coordinates of your mouse click to get_xy() as its two inputs. At ❸, we use listen() to detect events like mouse clicks and keyboard presses.

Run *mouse_click.py*, randomly click the screen several times, and you should see something like this:

```
(x, y) is (-46.0, 109.0)
(x, y) is (14.0, -9.0)
(x, y) is (-185.0, -19.0)
(x, y) is (-95.0, 109.0)
(x, y) is (13.0, -81.0)
```

For each of my five clicks, onscreenclick() captured the x- and y-coordinates of the point and provided the two values to get_xy(), which printed out the corresponding x- and y-values.

Convert Mouse Clicks to Cell Numbers

Next, we'll combine the board creation and click detection scripts so that when you click a cell, the script prints out the cell number. In Figure 10-2, I've marked the row and column numbers on the game board along with the x- and y-coordinates of the gridlines.

Open *ttt_board.py*, add the code in Listing 10-3 at the bottom (above t.done()) and save the new script as *cell_number.py* in your chapter folder. This script is just an example; we won't use it in the final code but will use something similar.

```
--snip--
for cell, center in list(cellcenter.items()):
    t.goto(center)
    t.write(cell,font = ('Arial',20,'normal'))
# Define a function cell_number() to print out the cell number
❶ def cell_number(x,y):
    if -300<x<300 and -300<y<300:
        # Calculate the column number based on x value
      ❷ col = int((x+500)//200)
        print('column number is ', col)
        # Calculate the row number based on y value
```

```
        row = int((y+500)//200)
        print('row number is ', row)
        # Calculate the cell number based on col and row
    ❸ cellnumber = col+(row-1)*3
        print('cell number is ', cellnumber)
    else:
        print('you have clicked outside the game board')
# Hide turtle so that you don't see the arrowhead
t.hideturtle()
# bind the mouse click to the cell_number() function
onscreenclick(cell_number)
t.listen()
--snip--
```

Listing 10-3: Converting mouse clicks to cell numbers

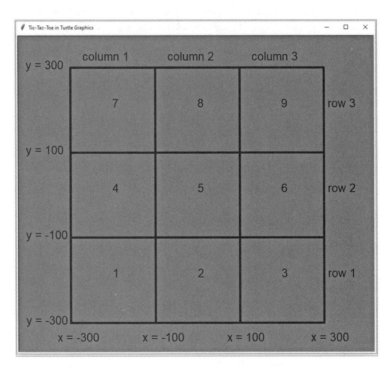

Figure 10-2: Mark the row and column numbers on the game board.

At ❶, we define cell_number(), which will convert the x- and y-coordinates of the mouse click to the cell number. Inside the function, we restrict the x- and y-coordinates of the point you click to the range of the board. If you click outside the range, the script will print you have clicked outside the game board.

At ❷, we convert the x-coordinate of the click to the column number. Points in column 1 have x-coordinates between −300 and −100, and points in column 2 have x-coordinates between −100 and 100, so we use the formula col = int((x+500)//200) to get the full range of pixel coordinates in the column so we can convert the x-coordinate to the column number. We use the same method to convert the y-coordinate to the row number.

We then calculate the cell number by using the formula cellnumber = col+(row-1)*3 because the cell numbers increase from left to right and then from bottom to top ❸. Finally, we bind the onscreen click to cell_number().

Run *cell_number.py*. Here's the output from one exchange with the script:

```
column number is  3
row number is  2
cell number is  6
column number is  1
row number is  3
cell number is  7
column number is  2
row number is  1
cell number is  2
```

Each time you click a cell, the script prints out the column number, row number, and cell number.

TRY IT OUT

Run *cell_number.py* and click each cell to make sure the numbers match those in Figure 10-2.

Place Game Pieces

Next, we'll place the game pieces on the board. When you first click any of the nine cells, a blue piece will appear at the center of the cell. When you click again, the piece will be white, then blue, and so on.

Open *ttt_board.py*, add the code in Listing 10-4, and save the new script as *mark_cell.py* in your chapter folder. Make sure you don't add this code snippet to *cell_number.py*!

```
--snip--
for cell, center in list(cellcenter.items()):
    t.goto(center)
    t.write(cell,font = ('Arial',20,'normal'))
# The blue player moves first
turn = "blue"
# Define a function mark_cell() to place a dot in the cell
❶ def mark_cell(x,y):
    # Make the variable turn a global variable
```

```
❷ global turn
  # Calculate the cell number based on x and y values
  if -300<x<300 and -300<y<300:
      col = int((x+500)//200)
      row = int((y+500)//200)
      # The cell number is a string variable
    ❸ cellnumber = str(col + (row - 1)*3)
  else:
      print('you have clicked outside the game board')

  # Go to the corresponding cell and place a dot of the player's color
  t.up()
❹ t.goto(cellcenter[cellnumber])
  t.dot(180,turn)
  t.update()
  # give the turn to the other player
  if turn == "blue":
      turn = "white"
  else:
      turn = "blue"

# Hide the turtle so that you don't see the arrowhead
t.hideturtle()
# Bind the mouse click to the mark_cell() function
t.onscreenclick(Mark_cell)
t.listen()
--snip--
```

Listing 10-4: Placing game pieces on the board

We draw the board and then define the variable turn that will keep track of whose turn it is. We first assign the value blue to the variable so that the blue player moves first.

At ❶, we define mark_cell(), which places a piece in the cell you click. At ❷, we declare the global variable turn. Python provides the global keyword, which allows turn to be used both inside and outside mark_cell(). Without making the variable global, you'd get the error message UnboundLocalError: local variable 'turn' referenced before assignment each time you clicked the board.

NOTE   *Python has two types of variables:* global variables, *which can be reached anywhere in the script, and* local variables, *which live only inside a function and can't be reached outside the function. By declaring a global variable, you make it reachable everywhere in the script. In* mark_cell.py, *the variable* turn *is created outside the function* mark_cell(), *but because* turn *will be modified in* mark_cell(), *we need to make it accessible in the global namespace as well. Otherwise, the change in the value of* turn *will not be carried outside the function.*

We then convert the x- and y-coordinates of the click to the cell number on the game board ❸. Within the same line, we also convert the cell number from an integer to a string to match the variable type used in the dictionary cellcenter.

At ❹, we get the coordinates for the center of the clicked cell from cellcenter and tell the turtle to go there. The turtle places a dot 180 pixels wide and the color of the value stored in turn. After that, the turn is over, and we assign the turn to the other player. Finally, we bind mark_cell() to the mouse-click event.

Run the script and you'll be able to click the board and mark the cell. The color of the dot will alternate between blue and white, as in Figure 10-3.

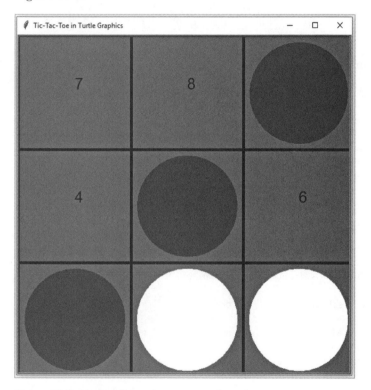

Figure 10-3: Mark cells on the tic-tac-toe board.

The script is now a playable game! However, we need to implement three new rules to make it follow the rules of tic-tac-toe:

- If a cell is already occupied, you cannot mark it again.
- If a player marks three cells in a straight line—either horizontally, vertically, or diagonally—the player wins, and the game should stop.
- If all nine cells are occupied, the game should stop, and a tie should be called if no player wins.

Determine Valid Moves, Wins, and Ties

Next, we'll implement those rules, allowing only valid moves and declaring wins (or ties). Download *ttt_click.py* from the book's resources and save it in your chapter folder or alter *mark_cell.py* with the differences highlighted in Listing 10-5.

```
from tkinter import messagebox
--snip--
# The blue player moves first
turn = "blue"
# Count how many rounds played
rounds = 1 ❶
# Create a list of valid moves
validinputs = list(cellcenter.keys())
# Create a dictionary of moves made by each player
occupied = {"blue":[],"white":[]}
# Determine if a player has won the game
def win_game(): ❷
    win = False
    if '1' in occupied[turn] and '2' in occupied[turn] and '3' in occupied[turn]:
        win = True
    if '4' in occupied[turn] and '5' in occupied[turn] and '6' in occupied[turn]:
        win = True
    if '7' in occupied[turn] and '8' in occupied[turn] and '9' in occupied[turn]:
        win = True
    if '1' in occupied[turn] and '4' in occupied[turn] and '7' in occupied[turn]:
        win = True
    if '2' in occupied[turn] and '5' in occupied[turn] and '8' in occupied[turn]:
        win = True
    if '3' in occupied[turn] and '6' in occupied[turn] and '9' in occupied[turn]:
        win = True
    if '1' in occupied[turn] and '5' in occupied[turn] and '9' in occupied[turn]:
        win = True
    if '3' in occupied[turn] and '5' in occupied[turn] and '7' in occupied[turn]:
        win = True
    return win
# Define a function mark_cell() to place a dot in the cell
def mark_cell(x,y):
    # Declare global variables
    global turn, rounds, validinputs ❸
```

```
# Calculate the cell number based on x and y values
if -300<x<300 and -300<y<300:
    col = int((x+500)//200)
    row = int((y+500)//200)
    # The cell number is a string variable
    cellnumber = str(col + (row - 1)*3)
else:
    print('you have clicked outside the game board')
# Check if the move is a valid one
if cellnumber in validinputs: ❹
    # Go to the corresponding cell and place a dot of the player's color
    t.up()
    t.goto(cellcenter[cellnumber])
    t.dot(180,turn)
    t.update()
    # Add the move to the occupied list for the player
    occupied[turn].append(cellnumber) ❺
    # Disallow the move in future rounds
    validinputs.remove(cellnumber)
    # Check if the player has won the game
    if win_game() == True: ❻
        # If a player wins, invalid all moves, end the game
        validinputs = []
        messagebox.showinfo("End Game",f"Congrats player {turn}, you won!")
    # If all cells are occupied and no winner, it's a tie
    elif rounds == 9: ❼
        messagebox.showinfo("Tie Game","Game over, it's a tie!")
    # Counting rounds
    rounds += 1
    # Give the turn to the other player
    if turn == "blue":
        turn = "white"
    else:
        turn = "blue"
# If the move is not a valid move, remind the player
else:
    messagebox.showerror("Error","Sorry, that's an invalid move!")
# Bind the mouse click to the mark_cell() function
t.onscreenclick(mark_cell)
--snip--
```

Listing 10-5: Allow only valid moves and declare wins and ties.

Our first change is to import the *messagebox* module from the *tkinter* package; this module displays a message box for a win, tie, or invalid move.

Starting at ❶, we create a variable rounds, a list validinputs, and a dictionary occupied. The variable rounds keeps track of the number of turns taken, which is the number of cells that have been marked. When the number of rounds reaches nine and no player wins (which is often the case in tic-tac-toe), we'll declare a tie game.

We use validinputs to determine whether a move is valid. If a cell is marked by a player, we'll remove it from the list of valid moves.

The dictionary occupied keeps track of each player's moves. At the beginning of the game, the keys blue and white both have an empty list as their value. When a player occupies a cell, the cell number will be added to that player's list. For example, if the blue player has occupied cells 1, 5, and 9 and the white player has occupied cells 3 and 7, occupied will become {"blue" :["1","5","9"],"white":["3","7"]}. We'll use this later to determine whether a player has won the game.

At ❷, we define win_game(), which checks whether a player has won the game. There are eight ways a player can win, which we explicitly check for:

- Cells 1, 2, and 3 have been occupied by the same player.
- Cells 4, 5, and 6 have been occupied by the same player.
- Cells 7, 8, and 9 have been occupied by the same player.
- Cells 1, 4, and 7 have been occupied by the same player.
- Cells 2, 5, and 8 have been occupied by the same player.
- Cells 3, 6, and 9 have been occupied by the same player.
- Cells 1, 5, and 9 have been occupied by the same player.
- Cells 3, 5, and 7 have been occupied by the same player.

The function win_game() creates the variable win and assigns False as a default value. The function checks the dictionary occupied for the list of cells occupied by the player who currently has the turn, checking all eight win cases listed earlier. If one of the cases matches, the value win changes to True. When win_game() is called, it returns the value stored in the variable win.

We've made significant changes to mark_cell(). At ❸, we declare three global variables; all must be declared global because they will be modified inside the function. At ❹, we check whether the cell number most recently clicked is in the list validinputs; if it is, a dot is placed in the cell, and the cell number is added to the player's list of occupied cells ❺. The cell is then removed from validinputs so that players can't mark the same cell in future rounds.

At ❻, we call win_game() and see whether the current player has won the game. If yes, we change validinputs to an empty list so no further moves can be made. A message box will pop up to say, Congrats player blue, you won! or Congrats player white, you won!, using showinfo() from the *messagebox* module (Figure 10-4).

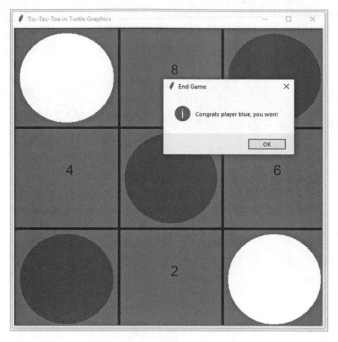

Figure 10-4: A win for blue!

If the player hasn't won, the script checks whether the number of rounds has reached nine ❼. If yes, the script declares a tie game, displaying Game over, it's a tie! (Figure 10-5).

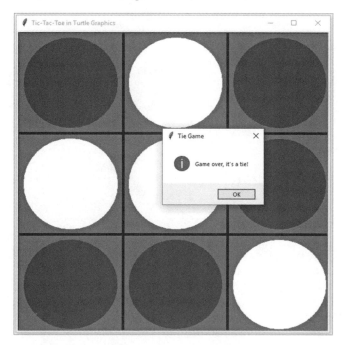

Figure 10-5: A tied game

If the game doesn't end, we increase the number of rounds by one and assign the turn to the other player. During the game, if a player clicks an invalid cell, we'll display Sorry, that's an invalid move! (Figure 10-6).

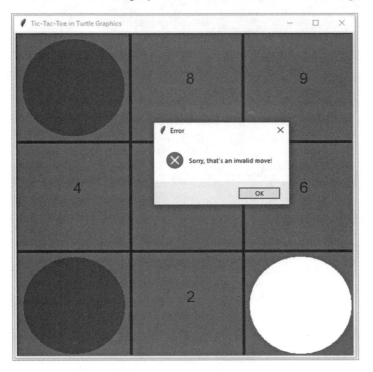

Figure 10-6: An invalid move

TRY IT OUT

Run *ttt_click.py* and play a few games, generating the following three instances: you make an invalid move, a player wins the game, and the game is tied.

Voice-Controlled Version

Now we're ready to add the voice control and speech functionality. One significant change is that we'll now make your opponent your computer. We'll build on the latest *ttt_click.py* file. After you make a move as the blue player, the computer will randomly select a move as the white player until the game ends.

NOTE *If you want to play a voice-controlled game with two players, go to the book's resources page and download ttt_hs_2players.py. We discuss only the one-player version here to save space. In our ultimate VPA in Chapter 17, you'll see a generalized version of the game in which you can choose to play against a computer or a human and whether you want to play first or second.*

Download *ttt_hs.py* from the book's resources or make the changes shown in Listing 10-6.

```python
import turtle as t
from random import choice
from tkinter import messagebox

# Import functions from the local package
from mptpkg import voice_to_text, print_say
--snip--
    if '3' in occupied[turn] and '5' in occupied[turn] and '7' in
occupied[turn]:
        win = True
    return win
# Start an infinite loop to take voice inputs
❶ while True:
    # Ask for your move
    print_say(f"Player {turn}, what's your move?")
    # Capture your voice input
    inp = voice_to_text()
    print(f"You said {inp}.")
    inp = inp.replace('number ','')
    inp = inp.replace('one','1')
    inp = inp.replace('two','2')
    inp = inp.replace('three','3')
    inp = inp.replace('four','4')
    inp = inp.replace('five','5')
    inp = inp.replace('six','6')
    inp = inp.replace('seven','7')
    inp = inp.replace('eight','8')
    inp = inp.replace('nine','9')
    if inp in validinputs:
        # Go to the corresponding cell and place a dot of the player's color
        t.up()
        t.goto(cellcenter[inp])
        t.dot(180,turn)
        t.update()
        # Add the move to the occupied list for the player
        occupied[turn].append(inp)
        # Disallow the move in future rounds
        validinputs.remove(inp)
        # Check if the player has won the game
      ❷ if win_game() == True:
            # If a player wins, invalid all moves, end the game
            validinputs = []
            print_say(f"Congrats player {turn}, you won!")
            messagebox.showinfo\
            ("End Game",f"Congrats player {turn}, you won!")
            break

        # If all cells are occupied and no winner, game is a tie
        elif rounds == 9:
            print_say("Game over, it's a tie!")
            messagebox.showinfo("Tie Game","Game over, it's a tie!")
            break
```

```python
        # Counting rounds
        rounds += 1
        # Give the turn to the other player
        if turn == "blue":
            turn = "white"
        else:
            turn = "blue"

        # The computer makes a random move
❸       inp = choice(validinputs)
        print_say(f'The computer occupies cell {inp}.')
        t.up()
        t.goto(cellcenter[inp])
        t.dot(180,turn)
        t.update()
        occupied[turn].append(inp)
        validinputs.remove(inp)
        if win_game() == True:
            validinputs = []
            print_say(f"Congrats player {turn}, you won!")
            messagebox.showinfo\
            ("End Game",f"Congrats player {turn}, you won!")
            break
        elif rounds == 9:
            print_say("Game over, it's a tie!")
            messagebox.showinfo("Tie Game","Game over, it's a tie!")

            break
        rounds += 1
        if turn == "blue":
            turn = "white"
        else:
            turn = "blue"

    # If the move is not a valid move, remind the player
    else:
        print_say("Sorry, that's an invalid move!")
t.done()
--snip--
```

Listing 10-6: Adding speech and voice-control functionality

We import the functions we'll need: the choice() function from the *random* module to let the computer randomly select a move and our print_say() and voice_to_text() functions from the custom package *mptpkg*.

At ❶, we start an infinite while loop. At each iteration, the script asks for your move out loud. You speak into the microphone to make your move, and the script captures your voice command, storing the response in the variable inp.

Here we did a little tweaking to make voice_to_text() more responsive to your voice commands. When your voice input is just one word, such as "One" or "Two," it's hard for the software to put the word in context and respond. On the other hand, if you say "Number one" or "Number two," the software can easily pick up your meaning. The script simply replaces the "number" part of the voice command with an empty string so that only the number is left in inp. Sometimes voice_to_text() returns the number in word form such as one or two, instead of in numeric form, such as 1 or 2. We therefore also change all the word forms to numerical forms. This way, you can say "number one" or "one" to the microphone, and inp will always be in the form you want: 1.

If your choice is in validinputs, the script performs the sequence of actions to make the move: place a dot in the corresponding cell, add the cell number to your list of occupied cells, and remove the occupied cell number from the list of valid inputs.

The script then checks if you've won or tied the game ❷ and responds out loud appropriately.

Once your turn is over, the computer randomly selects a move from validinputs to play against you ❸. The script checks whether the computer has won or tied the game. If your voice command is not a valid move, the script speaks an alert.

Here's one interaction with the game:

```
Player blue, what's your move?
You said 7.
The computer occupies cell 3.
Player blue, what's your move?
You said 8.
The computer occupies cell 1.
Player blue, what's your move?
You said 9.
Congrats player blue, you won!
```

I've managed to win in just three moves!

TRY IT OUT

Run *ttt_hs.py* and try to beat the computer.

Summary

In this chapter, you learned to build a voice-controlled graphical tic-tac-toe game that talks in a human voice. Along the way, you learned a few new skills.

You learned how mouse clicks work in the *turtle* module. With that knowledge, we marked cells on the game board with mouse clicks.

You learned how to determine whether a player has won tic-tac-toe based on the explicit game rules. This is at the heart of game creation. You listed all cases when a player can win the game, then added code to check all cases and see whether there is a winner.

You also added the speech recognition and text-to-speech features to a game, making a few tweaks to make sure the script can understand your input. By combining these skills, you'll be able to create your own voice-controlled games.

End-of-Chapter Exercises

1. Modify *ttt_board.py* so that the cell number appears in 15-point font at the lower-left corner of each cell (80 pixels from the center of the cell, both horizontally and vertically).

2. Modify *mouse_click.py* so that each time you click the screen, the script prints out the additional message x + y is, followed by the actual value of the x- and y-coordinates of the clicked point.

3. Modify *cell_number.py* so that each time you click the screen, the script prints you clicked the point (x, y) before printing the column, row, and cell numbers, where x and y are the actual coordinates. For example, if you click the point (x = –100, y = 50), the message should say you clicked the point (-100, 50).

4. Modify *mark_cell.py* so that the white player moves first.

5. Modify *ttt_click.py* so that a player wins only by marking three cells in a row horizontally or vertically, but not diagonally.

11

CONNECT FOUR

In this chapter, you'll build a voice-controlled Connect Four game. As with tic-tac-toe in Chapter 10, you'll first draw the board and set the yellow and red game pieces to alternate turns. You'll animate the effect of a disc falling from the top of a column to the lowest available row to make the game more visually engaging. You'll disallow invalid moves, detect if a player has won, and detect if all 42 cells have been occupied with no winner, meaning the game is tied.

In Chapter 10, you learned how to check whether a player has won the game by laying out all winning scenarios and checking whether the current game board matches one of the scenarios. We'll apply that same strategy here. You'll also learn how to use exception handling to prevent crashing during the process of checking and how to prevent negative indexing errors.

Once the game is set up, we'll add the speech recognition and text-to-speech features so you can play the game with your voice alone.

To start, set up the folder */mpt/ch11/* for this chapter. All scripts in this chapter are available through the book's resources page at *https://www.nostarch.com/make-python-talk/*.

NEW SKILLS

- Creating animations using *turtle*
- Using exception handling to check for winning cases
- Handling negative indexing in Python
- Mapping a list of lists to coordinates in a two-dimensional space

---

Game Rules

Connect Four is a well-known board game, but I'll go over the rules to clarify the logic in the upcoming code. In Connect Four, two players take turns dropping discs into one of seven columns, from the top. One player has red discs and the other yellow. The seven columns are on a six-row, vertically suspended grid. When a disc is dropped into a column, it will fall to the lowest available space in that column. Discs cannot move from one column to another.

The first player who forms a direct line—either horizontally, vertically, or diagonally—with four of their game pieces wins. If all 42 slots have been filled and nobody has won, the game is tied. We'll use a red dot and a yellow dot to represent the discs.

Draw the Game Board

We first draw a grid with six rows and seven columns. We'll number the columns at the top of the screen to make it easier to play.

Open your Spyder editor and enter the code from Listing 11-1. Save the script as *conn_board.py* in your chapter folder.

```
import turtle as t

# Set up the screen
❶ t.setup(700,600,10,70)
t.hideturtle()
t.tracer(False)
t.bgcolor("lightgreen")
t.title("Connect Four in Turtle Graphics")
# Draw six thick vertical lines
```

```
❷ t.pensize(5)
  for i in range(-250,350,100):
      t.up()
      t.goto(i,-350)
      t.down()
      t.goto(i,350)
      t.up()
  # Draw five thin gray horizontal lines to form grid
❸ t.pensize(1)
  t.pencolor("grey")
  for i in range(-200,300,100):
      t.up()
      t.goto(-350,i)
      t.down()
      t.goto(350,i)
      t.up()
  # Write column numbers on the board
❹ colnum = 1
  for x in range(-300,350,100):
      t.goto(x,270)
      t.write(colnum,font = ('Arial',20,'normal'))
      colnum += 1
  t.done()
  try:
      t.bye()
  except t.Terminator:
      print('exit turtle')
```

Listing 11-1: Drawing the Connect Four game board

We first import all functions in the *turtle* module, and then we set up the screen as 700 by 600 pixels ❶. That lets us make each cell 100 by 100 pixels to keep things simple. We set the background color to light green and the title to Connect Four in Turtle Graphics.

We then draw six thick vertical lines to divide the screen into seven columns. At ❷, we set the pen width to 5 pixels. The command line for i in range(-250,350,100) tells the variable i to iterate through the following six values: –250, –150, –50, 50, 150, and 250. These are the x-coordinates of the six vertical lines. The y-coordinates of the two endpoints of the six vertical lines are all –350 and 350. Similarly, we draw five thin, gray horizontal lines to divide the screen into six rows, starting at ❸, with a pen size of 1 pixel and color of gray so that the lines appear thin and light. This all gives us an even grid with seven columns and six rows.

Next, we number the columns to let players know where to place the discs. We first create a variable colnum and assign a value 1 to it ❹. We then iterate through the x-coordinates of the center of the seven columns and write the corresponding column number by adding one to the value of colnum.

Run the script and you should see a screen like Figure 11-1.

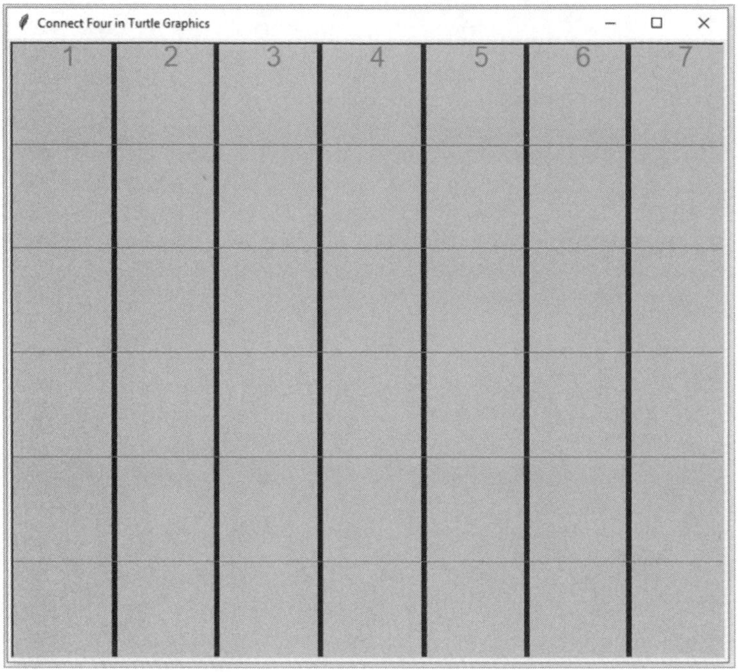

Figure 11-1: The board for the Connect Four game

The Mouse-Click Version

Now you have a game board. Let's drop some discs into the columns. In this section, you'll learn how to use mouse clicks to place a disc in a column and let it fall to the lowest available cell. After that, you'll detect invalid moves, wins, and ties.

Drop a Disc

Here, you'll use mouse clicks to place a disc in a column of your choice. The column number in which the disc will appear is determined by where you click. The row number depends on the number of discs already in that column.

When you first click a column, a red dot will be placed in the lowest available cell. The colors will alternate with each click.

Open *conn_board.py* and add the code in Listing 11-2. Then save the new script as *show_disc.py* in your chapter folder.

```
--snip--
# Write column numbers on the board
colnum = 1
for x in range(-300, 350, 100):
    t.goto(x,270)
    t.write(colnum,font = ('Arial',20,'normal'))
    colnum += 1
# The red player moves first
❶ turn = "red"
# The x-coordinates of the center of the 7 columns
```

```
❷ xs = [-300,-200,-100,0,100,200,300]
# The y-coordinates of the center of the 6 rows
ys = [-250,-150,-50,50,150,250]
# Keep track of the occupied cells
occupied = [list(),list(),list(),list(),list(),list(),list()]
# Define a function conn() to place a disc in a cell
❸ def conn(x,y):
    # Make the variable turn a global variable
    global turn
    # Calculate the column number based on x- and y-values
    if -350<x<350 and -300<y<300:
        col = int((x+450)//100)
    else:
        print('You have clicked outside the game board!')
    # Calculate the lowest available row number in that column
    row = len(occupied[col-1])+1
    # Go to the cell and place a dot of the player's color
    t.up()
    t.goto(xs[col-1],ys[row-1])
    t.dot(80,turn)
    # Add the move to the occupied list to keep track
    occupied[col-1].append(turn)
    # Give the turn to the other player
    if turn == "red":
        turn = "yellow"
    else:
        turn = "red"
# Bind the mouse click to the conn() function
t.onscreenclick(conn)
t.listen()
t.done()
--snip--
```

Listing 11-2: Dropping discs on the game board

The red player goes first, so after the game board is drawn, we define the variable turn and assign the value red to it ❶. Starting at ❷, we define three lists. The list xs contains values corresponding to the x-coordinates of the middle points of the seven columns. The list ys has six values corresponding to the y-coordinates of the middle points of the six rows. Later, we'll use these lists to determine the x- and y-coordinates of the center of all 42 cells.

The list occupied is a list of lists. It starts as a list of seven empty lists, each representing a column. When you place a disc in a column, the disc will be added to the corresponding list. This way, occupied will keep track of all discs placed and their positions.

At ❸, we define conn(), which places the disc on the column you click. We declare turn as a global variable, so that its value can be recognized both inside and outside conn(). Then, we convert the x-coordinate of the user's click to the column number on the game board. We then determine the lowest row available in that column, which tells us which row to place the disc in. Note that occupied[col-1] is the list of all discs currently in the column, and we use col-1 instead of col because Python uses zero indexing but our columns are numbered starting at 1.

We then obtain the x- and y-coordinates of the center of the cell in which to place the new disc. The *turtle* module places a dot with a diameter of 80 pixels and the color value stored in turn. We add the disc to the corresponding list within occupied so that next time a disc is placed in the same column, the appropriate cell is marked as invalid. With this, the player's turn is over, and we hand the turn to the other player. Finally, we bind conn() to the mouse-click event.

Run the script, and you should be able to click on the game board and mark the cell with a red or yellow dot. Keep clicking, and the color of the dot will alternate between red and yellow (Figure 11-2).

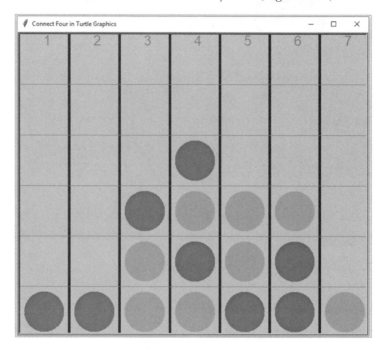

Figure 11-2: Place discs on the Connect Four game board.

Animate the Falling Discs

When you play Connect Four in the real world, you drop the disc at the top, and it falls into the proper position. Next, you'll create the animation effect of the disc falling. This is a good opportunity to learn how to create animation effects using the *turtle* module.

Open *show_disc.py* and add the code in Listing 11-3. Save this as *disc_fall.py* in your chapter folder.

```
import turtle as t
❶ from time import sleep
--snip--
# Keep track of the occupied cells
occupied = [list(),list(),list(),list(),list(),list(),list()]
# Create a second turtle to show disc falling
❷ fall = t.Turtle()
fall.up()
```

```
❸ fall.hideturtle()
# Define a function conn() to place a disc in a cell
def conn(x,y):
    # Make the variable turn a global variable
    global turn
    # Calculate the column number based on x and y values
    if -350<x<350 and -300<y<300:
        col = int((x+450)//100)
    else:
        print('You have clicked outside the game board!')
    # Calculate the lowest available row number in that column
    row = len(occupied[col-1])+1
    # Show the disc fall from the top
❹ if row<6:
        for i in range(6,row,-1):
            fall.goto(xs[col-1],ys[i-1])
            fall.dot(80,turn)
            update()
            sleep(0.05)
            fall.clear()
    # Go to the cell and place a dot of the player's color
    up()
--snip--
```

Listing 11-3: Script to show the animation effect of discs falling

We import sleep() so we can pause the script to let the falling disc stay in a cell for a short while, allowing the user to see its movement ❶. Starting at ❷, we create a second turtle named fall. We lift the drawing pen of the new turtle so that it won't leave a line as it moves. We also use hideturtle() to hide the cursor ❸.

Starting at ❹, we animate the falling disc. We first see if the column is full by checking whether the row number is less than 6. If yes, we'll show the animation effect. If the lower rows in the column are full, the disc can be left in place (there's no need to show the disc falling).

We iterate i through all the empty cells above the lowest available cell. If the lowest available position is row = 2, for example, the command for i in range(6,row,-1) iterates i through values 6, 5, 4, and 3. The -1 tells the range function to count backward. At each iteration, the fall turtle places a dot in the center of the empty cell. The script draws a dot to the screen, pauses for 0.05 seconds, and then erases the dot before going to the next iteration.

The script is now a complete game! However, at the moment, players must use their own judgment to enforce the following rules:

- If a column is already full, you cannot drop a disc in it.
- If a player connects four cells in a straight line, that player wins, and the game should stop.
- If all 42 cells are occupied and nobody has won, the game should stop and a tie be declared.

Let's code that into the game.

Determine Valid Moves, Wins, and Ties

Next, we'll improve the game by blocking invalid moves and declaring wins or ties. Open *disc_fall.py* and add the code in Listing 11-4. Save the new script as *conn_click.py*. The code changes are shown in two sections, so it's easier to refer back to the code when reading the explanations.

```python
import turtle as t
from time import sleep
from tkinter import messagebox

# Set up the screen
--snip--
# Create a second turtle to show disc falling
fall = t.Turtle()
fall.up()
fall.hideturtle()
# Create a list of valid moves
❶ validinputs = [1,2,3,4,5,6,7]
# Define a horizontal4() function to check connecting 4 horizontally
❷ def horizontal4(x, y, turn):
    win = False
    for dif in (-3, -2, -1, 0):
        try:
            if occupied[x+dif][y] == turn\
            and occupied[x+dif+1][y] == turn\
            and occupied[x+dif+2][y] == turn\
            and occupied[x+dif+3][y] == turn\
            and   x+dif >= 0:
                win = True
        except IndexError:
            pass
    return win
# Define a vertical4() function to check connecting 4 vertically
❸ def vertical4(x, y, turn):
    win = False
    try:
        if occupied[x][y] == turn\
        and occupied[x][y-1] == turn\
        and occupied[x][y-2] == turn\
        and occupied[x][y-3] == turn\
        and y-3 >= 0:
          win = True
    except IndexError:
        pass
    return win
```

```
# Define a forward4() function to check connecting 4 diagonally in / shape
def forward4(x, y, turn):
    win = False
    for dif in (-3, -2, -1, 0):
        try:
            if occupied[x+dif][y+dif] == turn\
            and occupied[x+dif+1][y+dif+1] == turn\
            and occupied[x+dif+2][y+dif+2] == turn\
            and occupied[x+dif+3][y+dif+3] == turn\
            and x+dif >= 0 and y+dif >= 0:
                win = True
        except IndexError:
            pass
    return win
# Define a back4() function to check connecting 4 diagonally in \ shape
def back4(x, y, turn):
    win = False
    for dif in (-3, -2, -1, 0):
        try:
            if occupied[x+dif][y-dif] == turn\
            and occupied[x+dif+1][y-dif-1] == turn\
            and occupied[x+dif+2][y-dif-2] == turn\
            and occupied[x+dif+3][y-dif-3] == turn\
            and x+dif >= 0 and y-dif-3 >= 0:
                win = True
        except IndexError:
            pass
    return win
# Define a win_game() function to check if someone wins the game
❹ def win_game(col, row, turn):
    win = False
    # Convert column and row numbers to indexes in the list of lists occupied
    x = col-1
    y = row-1
    # Check all winning possibilities
    if vertical4(x, y, turn) == True:
        win = True
    if horizontal4(x, y, turn) == True:
        win = True
    if forward4(x, y, turn) == True:
        win = True
    if back4(x, y, turn) == True:
        win = True
    # Return the value stored in win
    return win
--snip--
```

Listing 11-4: First half of the script to disallow invalid moves and declare wins and ties

We import the *messagebox* module from the *tkinter* package to allow us to display messages about wins, ties, and invalid moves.

At ❶, we create the list validinputs to keep track of valid moves. All seven columns are valid to start with. If a column contains six discs, it will be removed from the list.

A player can win the game by collecting four discs in a row in one of four orientations: horizontally, vertically, diagonally in a forward-slash fashion (/), or diagonally in a backslash fashion (\). Therefore, we define four functions to check for each way of winning.

At ❷, we define horizontal4(), which checks if a player has won the game by successfully connecting four discs in a row horizontally. In the function, we create the variable win and assign a default value of False. The function then checks whether the player has connected four discs horizontally. If yes, the value of win changes to True. When the function horizontal4() is called, it returns the value stored in the variable win. Let's look at the details of this function.

We'll use x = col-1 and y = row-1 to convert column and row numbers on the game board to indexes in the occupied list. The cell with column number col and row number row corresponds to occupied[x][y] in occupied. For simplicity, we'll call this cell [x][y] for the rest of the chapter.

A player can connect four pieces horizontally in four ways:

- Cells [x-3][y], [x-2][y], and [x-1][y] all have the same color as cell [x][y].
- Cells [x-2][y], [x-1][y], and [x+1][y] all have the same color as cell [x][y].
- Cells [x-1][y], [x+1][y], and [x+2][y] all have the same color as cell [x][y].
- Cells [x+1][y], [x+2][y], and [x+3][y] all have the same color as cell [x][y].

We therefore define a variable dif to iterate through four values (-3, -2, -1, 0). For each value of dif, we check whether all four cells—[x+dif][y], [x+dif+1][y], [x+dif+2][y], and [x+dif+3][y]—have the same color. If yes, we change the value of win to True.

In the process, we need to make exceptions for IndexError because, for example, the value of x+3 may be 8, but the board has only seven columns. If we do not make exceptions for IndexError, the script will crash in the process of checking whether the player has won the game.

Further, we ensure that none of the indexes have negative values, because negative indexing has a very specific meaning in Python. In Python, a negative index wraps around to the beginning of the list instead of falling off at the end. For example, index -1 refers to the last element in a list in Python, -2 to the second to last, and so on. Negative indexing will not raise an IndexOutOfBounds error, but it will also not behave as you expect.

Let's look at a concrete example: for x = 1 and y = 2, when the script checks the cell [x-3][2], it will look at cell [-2][2], which is actually cell [5][2] because -2 refers to the second-to-last value in x, which is 5 (that is, the sixth column, since there is a total of seven columns). Therefore, we put the condition x+dif> = 0 in the function to ensure that we have no negative indexing anywhere.

Finally, we use try and except in every one of the four cases of winning by connecting four discs horizontally. If instead we had used just one set of try and except for all four cases of wins, whenever any IndexError occured, the script would skip all remaining cases and go to the except branch directly. This would cause the script to fail to identify many cases of wins.

Similarly, we define vertical4() to check for a win by connecting four discs in a row vertically ❸. Then forward4() checks for a forward diagonal win, and back4() checks for a backward diagonal win.

At ❹, we define win_game(), which checks for a win in any of the 13 win scenarios (four horizontally, one vertically, four diagonally in a forward-slash fashion, and four diagonally in a backslash fashion). In win_game(), we create the variable win and assign a default value of False. The function first converts column and row numbers, col and row, to indexes in the occupied list, x and y. The function then calls the four functions just defined to see if the player may have won. If any of the four functions returns a value of True, the value of win changes to True, and win_game() will return a value of True when it's called.

Now let's examine the second half of the script (which we are saving as *conn_click.py*), shown in Listing 11-5.

```
--snip--
# Count the number of rounds
❶ rounds=1
# Define a function conn() to place a disc in a cell
def conn(x,y):
    # Declare global variables
  ❷ global turn, rounds, validinputs
    # Calculate the column number based on x and y values
    if -350<x<350 and -300<y<300:
        col = int((x+450)//100)
    else:
        print('You have clicked outside the game board!')
    # Check if it's a valid move
    if col in validinputs:
        # Calculate the lowest available row number in that column
        row = len(occupied[col-1])+1
--snip--
        # Go to the cell and place a dot of the player's color
        t.up()
        t.goto(xs[col-1],ys[row-1])
        t.dot(80,turn)
        t.update()
        # Add the move to the occupied list to keep track
        occupied[col-1].append(turn)
# Check if the player has won
      ❸ if win_game(col, row, turn) == True:
            # If a player wins, invalid all moves, end the game
            validinputs = []
            messagebox.showinfo\
            ("End Game",f"Congrats player {turn}, you won!")
        # If all cells are occupied and no winner, it's a tie
        elif rounds == 42:
            messagebox.showinfo("Tie Game","Game over, it's a tie!")
        # Counting rounds
        rounds += 1

        # Update the list of valid moves
      ❹ if len(occupied[col-1]) == 6:
```

```
            validinputs.remove(col)
        # Give the turn to the other player
        if turn == "red":
            turn = "yellow"
        else:
            turn = "red"
    # If col is not a valid move, show error message
❺ else:
        messagebox.showerror("Error","Sorry, that's an invalid move!")

# Bind the mouse click to the conn() function
t.onscreenclick(conn)
t.listen()
--snip--
```

Listing 11-5: Second half of the script to disallow invalid moves and declare wins and ties

At ❶, we create the variable rounds to keep track of the number of rounds played, corresponding to the number of discs on the game board, so that we can declare a tie when the number reaches 42.

We change conn() ❷ to declare three global variables so that their values can be recognized both inside and outside the function. At ❸, we call win_game() to see whether anyone has won. If yes, we change validinputs to an empty list so no further moves can be made. A message box will pop up that says Congrats player red, you won! or Congrats player yellow, you won!

Figure 11-3 shows the red player winning a game.

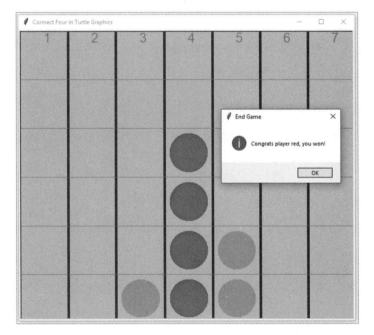

Figure 11-3: Red wins! The darker discs are red, and the lighter are yellow.

If no one has won but rounds reaches 42, the script declares a tie game (Figure 11-4).

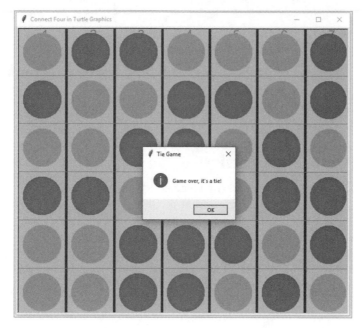

Figure 11-4: A tied game

If no player has won or the game is not tied, we increase the value of rounds by one and assign the turn to the other player. We also update the list of valid moves. If the number of discs in the current column reaches six, we remove the column number from the list validinputs ❹.

During the game, if a player clicks an invalid cell ❺, a message box will say Sorry, that's an invalid move! (Figure 11-5).

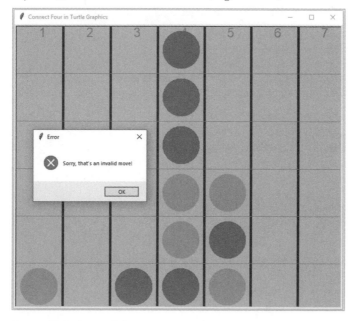

Figure 11-5: An invalid move

The Voice-Controlled Version

Now we're ready to add the voice control functionality!

First, we'll set the computer as your opponent in the game. After you make a move as the red player, the computer will randomly select a yellow move until the game ends. Once you understand how playing against a computer works, a voice-controlled game in which you play against another person is really simple. I'll leave that as an end-of-chapter exercise, and the script is provided at the book's resources website.

NOTE   *We discuss only the one-player version in which you always move first to save space and to focus on creating a voice-controlled Connect Four. In our ultimate VPA in Chapter 17, you'll see a generalized version of the game in which you can choose to play against a computer or a human and whether you move first or second.*

Download *conn_hs.py* from the book's resources and save it in your chapter folder. Listing 11-6 highlights the differences between *conn_hs.py* and *conn_click.py*.

```python
import turtle as t
from time import sleep
from tkinter import messagebox
from random import choice

# Import functions from the local package
from mptpkg import voice_to_text, print_say

# Set up the screen
--snip--
# Create a list of valid moves
validinputs = ['1','2','3','4','5','6','7']
--snip--
# Add a dictionary of words to replace
to_replace = {'number ':'', 'cell ':'',
              'one':'1', 'two':'2', 'three':'3',
              'four':'4', 'for':'4', 'five':'5',
              'six':'6', 'seven':'7'}
# Start an infinite loop to take voice inputs
❶ while True:
    # Ask for your move
```

```
        print_say(f"Player {turn}, what's your move?")
        # Capture your voice input
        inp = voice_to_text().lower()
        print_say(f"You said {inp}.")
        for x in list(to_replace.keys()):
            inp = inp.replace(x, to_replace[x])
        # If it is not a valid move, try again
        if inp not in validinputs:
            print_say("Sorry, that's an invalid move!")
        # If your voice input is a valid move, play the move
❷      else:
            col = int(inp)
            # Calculate the lowest available row number in that column
            row = len(occupied[col-1])+1
            # Show the disc fall from the top
            if row<6:
                for i in range(6,row,-1):
                    fall.goto(xs[col-1],ys[i-1])
                    fall.dot(80,turn)
                    t.update()
                    sleep(0.05)
                    fall.clear()
            # Go to the cell and place a dot of the player's color
            t.up()
            t.goto(xs[col-1],ys[row-1])
            t.dot(80,turn)
            t.update()
            # Add the move to the occupied list to keep track
            occupied[col-1].append(turn)

            # Check if the player has won
            if win_game(col, row, turn) == True:
                # If a player wins, invalid all moves, end the game
                validinputs = []
❸              print_say(f"Congrats player {turn}, you won!")
                messagebox.showinfo/
                ("End Game",f"Congrats player {turn}, you won!")
                break
            # If all cells are occupied and no winner, it's a tie
            elif rounds == 42:
                print_say("Game over, it's a tie!")
                messagebox.showinfo("Tie Game","Game over, it's a tie!")
                break
            # Counting rounds
            rounds += 1
            # Update the list of valid moves
            if len(occupied[col-1]) == 6:
                validinputs.remove(str(col))
            # Give the turn to the other player
            if turn == "red":
                turn = "yellow"
            else:
                turn = "red"
```

```
                # The computer randomly selects a move
        ❹ if len(validinputs)>0:
                col = int(choice(validinputs))
            print_say(f'The computer chooses column {col}.')
            # Calculate the lowest available row number in that column
            row = len(occupied[col-1])+1
            # Show the disc fall from the top
            if row < 6:
                for i in range(6,row,-1):
                    fall.goto(xs[col-1],ys[i-1])
                    fall.dot(80,turn)
                    update()
                    sleep(0.05)
                    fall.clear()
            # Go to the cell and place a dot of the player's color
            t.up()
            t.goto(xs[col-1],ys[row-1])
            t.dot(80,turn)
            t.update()
            # Add the move to the occupied list to keep track
            occupied[col-1].append(turn)

            # Check if the player has won
            if win_game(col, row, turn) == True:
                # If a player wins, invalid all moves, end the game
                validinputs = []
            ❺ print_say(f"Congrats player {turn}, you won!")
                messagebox.showinfo\
                ("End Game",f"Congrats player {turn}, you won!")
                break
            # If all cells are occupied and no winner, it's a tie
            elif rounds == 42:
                print_say("Game over, it's a tie!")
                messagebox.showinfo("Tie Game","Game over, it's a tie!")
                break
            # Counting rounds
            rounds += 1
            # Update the list of valid moves
            if len(occupied[col-1])==6:
                validinputs.remove(str(col))
            # Give the turn to the other player
            if turn == "red":
                turn = "yellow"
            else:
                turn = "red"
t.done()
--snip--
```

Listing 11-6: Script highlights for the voice-controlled Connect Four game

We import a few extra modules. The choice() function from the *random* module lets the computer randomly select a move to play against you. We also import our local print_say() and voice_to_text() functions from the local package *mptpkg* to handle the voice-control functionality.

This time, we'll use string values instead of integers to represent the seven column numbers in the list validinputs, because voice inputs are naturally string variables and, in many cases, attempting to convert voice inputs to integers will crash the script.

At ❶, we start an infinite while loop. At each iteration, the script asks for your move out loud. You speak into the microphone to make your move, and the script captures your voice command and stores it in inp.

Here we did a little tweaking to make voice_to_text() more responsive to your voice commands, as we did in Chapter 10 (see Listing 10-6 as a reminder). Further, the script always interprets *number four* as number for, so we replace for with 4 to get a better response from the script.

If your voice command is not in validinputs, the script reminds you out loud: "Sorry, that's an invalid move!" I've moved up the invalid voice input so that the if and else branches are close together in the script, making it easy for you to understand the logic. If the two branches are far apart, it's easy to get lost in the long lines of code.

If your voice command is a valid move ❷, the script will place the disc as directed, let the disc fall to the lowest available space in the column, add the cell number to your list of occupied cells, remove the cell number from the list of valid inputs, and so on.

The script then checks whether you won the game and, if you have, congratulates you out loud ❸. If not, it will check for a tie and announce accordingly.

When your turn is over, and if you haven't won or tied the game, the computer randomly selects a move from validinputs to play against you ❹, make the move, and check whether the computer has won the game ❺. It will also check for a tie.

WARNING *You need a decent internet connection for the script to work properly. Further, avoid saying a single number as the voice input. Instead, start with "number" so that the script can put your voice command in context.*

Here's the printed message from one interaction with the game:

```
Player red, what's your move?
You said number four.
The computer chooses column 2.
Player red, what's your move?
You said number four.
The computer chooses column 2.
Player red, what's your move?
You said number four.
The computer chooses column 2.
Player red, what's your move?
You said number four.
Congrats player red, you won!
```

Figure 11-6 shows my winning game.

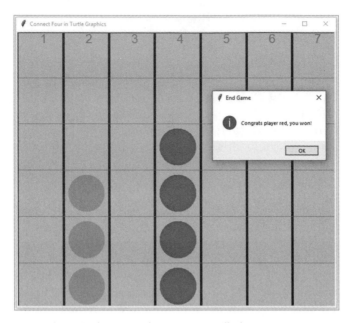

Figure 11-6: Red winning the voice-controlled version

TRY IT OUT

Run *conn_hs.py* and play a complete game with the computer. See if you can make the script understand your every voice command on the first try.

Summary

In this chapter, you created a voice-controlled graphical Connect Four game that talks back to you in a human voice. You set up the game board and mechanisms as you did in Chapter 10, but this time animated the moves.

You learned how to let Python determine whether a player has won the game. In the process, you learned to lay out all cases of winning and use the script to check each one. You also learned how to properly use exception handling and prevent negative indexing from causing mistakes in your script.

You added the voice recognition and text-to-speech features, but also did a bit of refactoring to make sure your code stayed user readable as you added to it. In the next couple of chapters, you'll create more voice-controlled graphical games and make them intelligent.

End-of-Chapter Exercises

1. Modify *conn_board.py* so that six row numbers appear at the right of the screen, with the top row being 6 and the bottom row being 1. Make the x-coordinates of the row numbers 325.

2. Modify *disc_fall.py* so that the discs fall at twice the speed.

3. Modify *conn_click.py* so that a player wins only by connecting four discs of the same color horizontally or diagonally, and not vertically.

4. Currently, when you play Connect Four using the final *conn_hs.py*, you can say either "number four" or "four" if you want to place a disc in column 4. Modify the script so that you can also say "column four" to place a disc in that column.

5. Modify *conn_hs.py* so that you play against a person instead of the computer.

12

GUESS-THE-WORD GAME

In this chapter, you'll build a voice-controlled graphical guess-the-word game. This is an interesting challenge because when playing guess-the-word, players often talk quickly, so we'll need to fine-tune our script's listening abilities.

As usual, we'll go over the game rules and draw a game board; this game board uses six coins to represent your six guesses. You'll learn how to load a picture to a Python script and create multiple images of it onscreen. You'll also learn to make the images disappear one by one.

We'll start the game by using written inputs. Then, when we have it working well, we'll add the speech recognition and text-to-speech features.

All scripts in this chapter are available on the book's resources page at *https://www.nostarch.com/make-python-talk/*. Start by creating the folder */mpt/ch12/* for this chapter.

Game Rules

Our guess-the-word game is loosely based on the hangman game. Our game will present only four-letter words to keep it simple, but you should try adapting it later when you're comfortable with how it all works. Let's go over the rules of the game first.

Similar to hangman, our guess-the-word game involves two players. The first player thinks of a word and draws a number of dashes equal to the number of letters in the word. The first player also draws six coins in the middle of the screen to represent the six incorrect guesses the second player will be allowed.

The second player tries to figure out the word by guessing one letter at a time. If the suggested letter is in the word, the first player fills in the blanks with the letter in the right places. If a suggested letter is not in the word, the first player erases a coin in the middle of the screen. If the second player completes the word before making six incorrect guesses, they win the game. If that player fails to identify the word before using up their six wrong guesses, they lose.

Draw the Game Board

Our game board will preload with four dashes to represent the word. We'll also include the message incorrect guesses onscreen. Open your Spyder editor and enter the code in Listing 12-1, saving it as *guess_word_board.py*.

```
import turtle as t

# Set up the board
t.setup(600,500)
t.hideturtle()
t.tracer(False)
t.bgcolor("lavender")
t.title("Guess the Word Game in Turtle Graphics")
# Define a variable to count how many guesses left
❶ score = 6
# Create a second turtle to show guesses left
left = t.Turtle()
left.up()
left.hideturtle()
left.goto(-290,200)
left.write(f"guesses left:    {score}",font=('Arial',20,'normal'))
```

```
# Put incorrect guesses on top
t.up()
t.goto(-290,150)
t.write("incorrect guesses:",font=('Arial',20,'normal'))
# Put four empty spaces for the four letters at bottom
❷ for x in range(4):
    t.goto(-275+150*x,-200)
    t.down()
    t.goto(-175+150*x,-200)
    t.up()
t.done()
try:
    t.bye()
except t.Terminator:
    print('exit turtle')
```

Listing 12-1: Python script to draw the guess-the-word game board

We import the *turtle* module and set up the screen to be 600 by 500 pixels with a lavender background. The title will read Guess the Word Game in Turtle Graphics. Note that we omitted the last two arguments in setup(), so the game board will appear at the center of your computer screen by default.

At ❶, we create a variable score to keep track of the number of guesses the player has left. It starts with a value of 6. Later in the game, every time the player guesses an incorrect letter, the value will decrease by 1. We also create a new turtle named left, representing the number of guesses remaining. We use the new turtle to write the number of chances the player has left, erasing whatever was there before. By using a new turtle, we limit the number of objects we need to redraw onscreen.

We then add the text incorrect guesses, which will later show the incorrect letters the player guessed. We draw four dashes at the bottom of the board ❸ to hold the four letters in the word. Run the script and you should see a board similar to Figure 12-1.

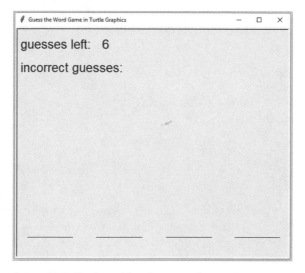

Figure 12-1: The board for the guess-the-word game

The Text Version

In this section, you'll place the six coins on the screen and enable the player to enter letters with the keyboard. You'll then determine whether a player has won or lost the game. This completes the silent version of guess-the-word.

Load the Coins

You'll place six coins at the center of the screen. In the process, you'll learn how to load a picture to the script, resize it to any shape you like, and place as many objects on the turtle screen as you like. As noted, each coin corresponds to one incorrect guess.

Download the picture file *cash.png* from the book's resources and place it in your chapter folder. Open *guess_word_board.py*, add the highlighted code in Listing 12-2, and save the new script as *show_coins.py* in the same chapter folder containing *cash.png*.

```
--snip--
from tkinter import PhotoImage
from time import sleep
--snip--
# Put four empty spaces for the four letters at bottom
for x in range(4):
    t.goto(-275+150*x,-200)
    t.down()
    t.goto(-175+150*x,-200)
    t.up()
# Load a picture of the coin to the script
❶ coin = PhotoImage(file="cash.png").subsample(10,10)
t.addshape("coin", t.Shape("image", coin))
# Create six coins on screen
❷ coins = [0]*6
for i in range(6):
    coins[i] = t.Turtle('coin')
    coins[i].up()
    coins[i].goto(-100+50*i,0)
t.update()
❸ sleep(3)
# Make the coins disappear one at a time
for i in range(6):
    coins[-(i+1)].hideturtle()
    t.update()
    sleep(1)
t.done()
--snip--
```

Listing 12-2: Script to show and remove coins

We import the PhotoImage() class from the *tkinter* module and the sleep() function from the *time* module. We then load *cash.png* by using PhotoImage() ❶. We use subsample() to scale the image to the size we want. In this case, we use scale factors of (10,10), which means that both the width and the height of the picture are one-tenth that of the original picture.

NOTE   *To scale up the size of the image onscreen, you can use the* zoom() *method in the* PhotoImage() *class from* tkinter. *For example,* zoom(2,3) *will double the width and triple the height of the original picture.*

At ❷, we create a list coins with six elements by using [0]*6. If you print out the list, it will look like this:

```
[0, 0, 0, 0, 0, 0]
```

We'll change the elements later; the 0 values are just placeholders.

Next, we create a new turtle in each element in coins. We then make the coin turtles go to the center of the screen and line up horizontally. To demonstrate how to load and then hide the coins, we have them stay onscreen for three seconds ❸ before using hideturtle() from the *turtle* module to make them disappear from the screen one at a time, starting with the last one.

Figure 12-2 shows the screen in the first three seconds, as the coins are lined up.

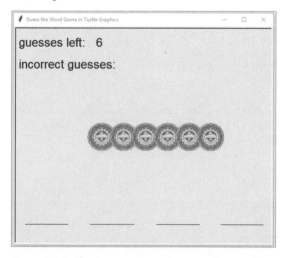

Figure 12-2: Showing coins on the guess-the-word game board

TRY IT OUT

Run *show_coins.py* and see the output screen. Once you confirm it's working, change tracer(False) to tracer(True) in the script and rerun it. You should be able to see the six coins placed onscreen one by one. After that, change tracer(True) back to tracer(False) before continuing to the next subsection.

Guess the Letters

The next version of the game will use 15 four-letter words, picked from a list of the most commonly used four-letter words according to Professor Barry Keating's website at the University of Notre Dame (*https://bit.ly/3g7z7cg*).

Keating has done extensive work in the fields of business forecasting and data mining. He is also the coauthor of the popular textbook *Forecasting and Predictive Analytics* (McGraw Hill, 2018).

After we make the following modifications, the script will randomly choose one word, ask you to guess a letter, and then accept input from the IPython console. If a guess is right, the letter will show up on one of the dashes corresponding to the position of the letter in the word. In the rare case that the letter appears in the word twice, the letter will show up on two of the dashes. If the letter is not in the word, it will show up at the top of the screen in the list of incorrect guesses. We'll skip placing the coins in this script to make testing of the code easier to follow.

Open *guess_word_board.py*, add the highlighted code in Listing 12-3, and save the new script as *guess_letter.py*.

```python
import turtle as t
from random import choice
--snip--
# Put four empty spaces for the four letters at bottom
for x in range(4):
    t.goto(-275+150*x,-200)
    t.down()
    t.goto(-175+150*x,-200)
    t.up()
t.update()
# Put words in a dictionary and randomly pick one
❶ words = ['that', 'with', 'have', 'this', 'will', 'your',
    'from', 'they', 'know', 'want', 'been',
    'good', 'much', 'some', 'time']
word = choice(words)
# Create a missed list
❷ missed = []
# Start the game loop
❸ while True:
    # Take written input
    inp = input("What's your guess?\n").lower()
    # Stop the loop if you key in "done"
    if inp == "done":
        break
    # Check if the letter is in the word
  ❹ elif inp in list(word):
        # If yes, put it in the right position(s)
        for w in range(4):
            if inp == list(word)[w]:
                t.goto(-250+150*w,-190)
                t.write(inp,font=('Arial',60,'normal'))
    # If the letter is not in the word, show it at the top
  ❺ else:
        missed.append(inp)
        t.goto(-290+80*len(missed),60)
        t.write(inp,font=('Arial',60,'normal'))
    # Update everything that happens in the iteration
    t.update()
try:
```

```
    t.bye()
except t.Terminator:
    print('exit turtle')
```

Listing 12-3: Script to put letters on the game board

We first import choice() from the *random* module so the script can randomly pick a word from the list. We put the 15 words in the list words ❶ and allocate the randomly selected word to word. At ❷, we create the list missed to hold all incorrectly guessed letters. We then put the script in an infinite loop ❸ to continuously take your text input. If you want to stop the loop, you can enter done in the Spyder IPython console.

At ❹, we check whether the letter you guess is in one of the letters in word. We use list(), which takes a string variable as input and breaks it into a list of individual letters; for example, the command list("have") produces the list ["h","a","v","e"].

If your guessed letter is in word, the function checks every letter in word to see if your guess matches the letter in that position. If so, the function writes the letter on the corresponding position onscreen.

If your guess is not in word ❺, the letter is added to missed and is written at the top of the screen in the incorrect guesses section.

Note that we also removed the line t.done() in this script. This means that, once you finish guessing and enter done, the script will end and everything will disappear from your screen.

Here's the output from one exchange with the script, when the script randomly selected the word *have* from the list of the 15 words, with my typed input in bold:

```
What's your guess?
a
What's your guess?
b
What's your guess?
v
What's your guess?
v
What's your guess?
b
What's your guess?
h
What's your guess?
e
What's your guess?
f
What's your guess?
g
What's your guess?
h
What's your guess?
u
What's your guess?
done
```

Figure 12-3 shows the resultant screen.

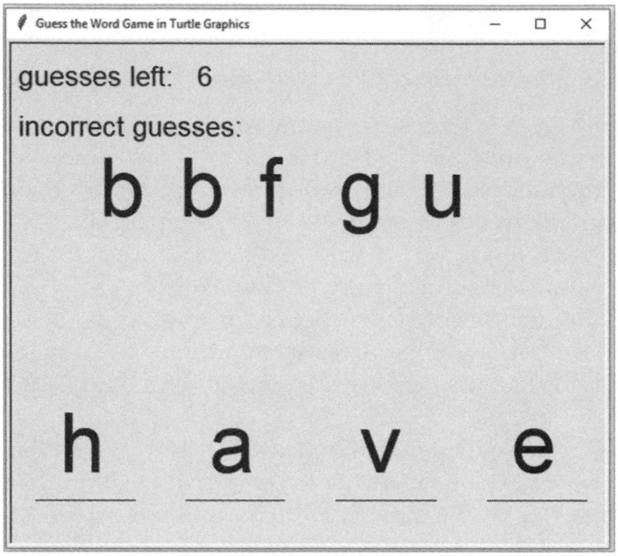

Figure 12-3: A guess-the-word game board with letters on it

It's working, but you may have noticed that some things need improvement. To have a complete version of guess-the-word, we need the script to do the following:

1. Prevent the players from guessing the same letter more than once. In my preceding interaction, I guessed *b*, *v*, and *h* twice, wasting my guesses.
2. Notify the players when a word is complete.
3. Stop taking input after a player completes the word.
4. Put the six coins onscreen and remove one every time a player misses a letter.

Determine Valid Guesses, Wins, and Losses

Next, we'll disallow duplicate-letter guesses, declare a win if you complete the word while missing fewer than six letters, and declare a loss if not.

Open *guess_letter.py* and add the highlighted parts in Listing 12-4. Then save the new script as *guess_word.py*. A block of code in *guess_letter.py* is modified and replaced by the newly added blocks. If you're uncertain what's different, download the script *guess_word.py* from the book's resources page.

```
import turtle as t
from random import choice
from tkinter import messagebox
from tkinter import PhotoImage

--snip--
# Create a missed list
```

```python
missed = []
# Load a picture of the coin to the script
❶ coin = PhotoImage(file = "cash.png").subsample(10,10)
t.addshape("coin", t.Shape("image", coin))
# Create six coins on screen
coins = [0]*6
for i in range(6):
    coins[i] = t.Turtle('coin')
    coins[i].up()
    coins[i].goto(-100+50*i,0)
❷ t.update()
# Prepare the validinputs and gotright lists
❸ validinputs = list('abcdefghijklmnopqrstuvwxyz')
gotright = []
# Start the game loop
while True:
    # Take written input
    inp = input("What's your guess?\n").lower()
    # Stop the loop if you key in "done"
    if inp == "done":
        break
    # If the letter is not a valid input, remind
    elif inp not in validinputs:
        messagebox.showerror("Error","Sorry, that's an invalid input!")
    # Otherwise, go ahead with the game
❹   else:
        # Check if the letter is in the word
        if inp in list(word):
            # If yes, put it in the right position(s)
            for w in range(4):
                if inp == list(word)[w]:
                    t.goto(-250+150*w,-190)
                    t.write(inp,font = ('Arial',60,'normal'))
                    gotright.append(inp)
            # If got four positions right, the player wins
            if len(gotright) == 4:
                messagebox.showinfo\
                ("End Game","Great job, you got the word right!")
                break
        # If the letter is not in the word, show it at the top
❺       else:
            # Reduce guesses left by 1
            score -= 1
            # Remove a coin
            coins[-(6-score)].hideturtle()
            # Update the number of guesses left on board
            left.clear()
            left.write\
            (f"guesses left:   {score}",font = ('Arial',20,'normal'))
            t.update()
            missed.append(inp)
            t.goto(-290+80*len(missed),60)
            t.write(inp,font = ('Arial',60,'normal'))
            if len(missed) == 6:
                # If all six chances are used up, end game
```

```
            messagebox.showinfo\
            ("End Game","Sorry, you used up all your six guesses!")
            break
        # Remove the letter from the validinputs list
        validinputs.remove(inp)
    # Update everything that happens in the iteration
    t.update()
--snip--
```

Listing 12-4: A graphical guess-the-word game that takes written input

We import the *messagebox* module from the *tkinter* Python package again
so we can display messages to the game screen.

Starting at ❶, we display the six coins onscreen. We update the screen
so that everything we put there shows up properly ❷.

At ❸, we create the list validinputs, which has the 26 letters in the alpha-
bet as elements. Later in the script, if the player guesses a letter, we'll remove
the letter from the list so that the same letter can't be guessed more than
once. We also create the empty list gotright. Later we'll use it to keep track of
how many positions the player has guessed right in the word.

We start an infinite while loop that asks for your keyboard input in every
iteration. If you enter done, the loop stops, and the script quits taking input
from you. If you enter invalid input (either a non-letter or a letter you've
already guessed), the script will show a message box indicating Sorry, that's
an invalid input!

If you enter valid input ❹, the script checks whether the letter is in the
word. If yes, the script checks each of the four positions in the word and,
for each match, adds the letter to the list gotright. Note that since the same
letter can appear in a word more than once, a letter may be added to the list
gotright more than once.

The script then checks whether gotright has four elements. If yes, it
means all four letters have been correctly guessed, and a message box will
pop up with Great job, you got the word right!

If the guessed letter is not in the word ❺, the value of score is decreased
by one, meaning the player has one less guess left. The script will remove
a coin from the screen by using hideturtle(). The second turtle will erase
whatever it has drawn on the screen and rewrite the number of guesses left.
If the length of the list missed reaches six, a message box appears: Sorry, you
used up all your six guesses!

Here's one exchange with the script with the user input in bold:

```
What's your guess?
a
What's your guess?
o
What's your guess?
d
What's your guess?
c
What's your guess?
b
```

```
What's your guess?
k
What's your guess?
m
```

My losing game is shown in Figure 12-4.

 NOTE *Since the word is randomly chosen from the 15 words, you won't likely get the same output as mine even if you use the same guesses.*

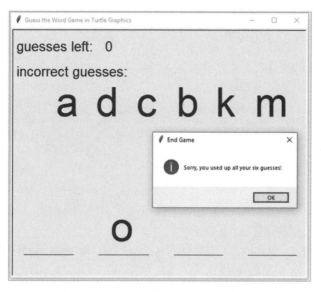

Figure 12-4: A losing game of guess-the-word

TRY IT OUT

Run *guess_word.py* and play a few games, generating the following instances: you make an invalid move, you win the game by completing the word before missing six letters, and you fail to complete the word before missing six letters and hence lose the game.

The Voice-Controlled Version

Now we'll build on the written-input version of the game to add speech functionality. Download *guess_word_hs.py* and save it in your chapter folder. The new code is highlighted in Listing 12-5.

```
--snip--
# Import functions from the local package
from mptpkg import voice_to_text, print_say
```

```
--snip--
# Start the game loop
❶ while True:
    # Ask for your move
    print_say("What's your guess?")
    # Capture your voice input
    inp = voice_to_text().lower()
    print_say(f"you said {inp}")
    inp = inp.replace('letter ','')
# Say "stop listening" or press CTRL-C to stop the game
    if inp == "stop listening":
        break
    # If the letter is not a valid input, remind
    elif inp not in validinputs:
        print_say("Sorry, that's an invalid input!")
    # Otherwise, go ahead with the game
❷ else:
        # Check if the letter is in the word
        if inp in list(word):
            # If yes, put it in the right position(s)
            for w in range(4):
                if inp == list(word)[w]:
                    t.goto(-250+150*w,-190)
                    t.write(inp,font = ('Arial',60,'normal'))
                    gotright.append(inp)
            # If got four positions right, the player wins
            if len(gotright) == 4:
              ❸ print_say("Great job, you got the word right!")
                messagebox.showinfo\
                ("End Game","Great job, you got the word right!")
                break
        # If the letter is not in the word, show it at the top
        else:
            # Reduce guesses left by 1
            score -= 1
            # Remove a coin
            coins[-(6-score)].hideturtle()
            # Update the number of guesses left on board
            left.clear()
            left.write\
            (f"guesses left:   {score}",font = ('Arial',20,'normal'))
            t.update()
            missed.append(inp)
            t.goto(-290+80*len(missed),60)
            t.write(inp,font = ('Arial',60,'normal'))
            if len(missed) == 6:
                # If all six changes are used up, end game
              ❹ print_say("Sorry, you used up all your six guesses!")
                messagebox.showinfo\
                ("End Game","Sorry, you used up all your six guesses!")
--snip--
```

Listing 12-5: A graphical guess-the-word game that takes voice input

We import the usual functions from our local package *mptpkg*: voice_to_text() and print_say(). Because we installed the package (in editable mode), there's no need to tell the system where to find it.

We start an infinite while loop that asks for your choice of letter in each iteration ❶. You speak your guess into the microphone, and the script captures your voice command and stores it in inp. We make allowances so the player can say either "letter a" or just "a." If the former, we replace *letter* with an empty string so that only a is left in the variable inp.

To stop the while loop, you say, "Stop listening." If your guess is not in the list validinputs, the script will answer, "Sorry, that's an invalid input!" out loud. If your guess is in validinputs ❷, the script checks whether the letter is in the word. This time, when you complete the word without missing six times, the game will say, "Great job, you got the word right!" ❸. If you guess wrong six times, the voice will say, "Sorry, you used up your six guesses!" ❹.

Here's an exchange with the script in which the player has successfully guessed the word *good*, missing only two letters:

```
What's your choice?
you said letter a
What's your choice?
you said letter d
What's your choice?
you said letter f
What's your choice?
you said letter o
What's your choice?
you said letter g
Great job, you got the word right!
```

You can see the screen in Figure 12-5.

Figure 12-5: Winning the voice-controlled guess-the-word game

TRY IT OUT

Run *guess_word_hs.py* and try giving voice input in a few different ways to see what the script best understands.

Summary

In this chapter, you created a voice-controlled graphical guess-the-word game that talks back to you in a human voice.

You first learned how to draw the game board. You then learned to upload a picture file to the script and scale it to the size you want. You used the image to create six coins on the screen to represent monetary rewards and made them disappear from the screen one by one. You also learned how to type in your guess and have it show up onscreen. You learned how to disallow guessing the same letter twice and how to determine whether a player has won or lost the game.

You added the speech recognition and text-to-speech features so that the game can be voice controlled. Along the way, you learned how to create an image by manipulating a picture file in *turtle* and how to use multiple turtles to reduce the number of objects you have to redraw on the screen.

End-of-Chapter Exercises

1. Modify *show_coins.py* so that the positions of the six coins are 10 pixels below their current positions vertically. Keep the positions of everything else the same.

2. Modify *show_coins.py* so that the leftmost coin disappears from the screen first and the rightmost one is the last to disappear.

3. Try to figure out what the following line of code will produce. First write down your answer and then run the code in Spyder to verify.

```
list('Hi Python')
```

13

SMART GAMES: ADDING INTELLIGENCE

 In the one-player version of Connect Four we built in Chapter 11, the computer always randomly selects a move. This allowed us to focus on the game's speech recognition and text-to-speech aspects.

However, once you play against the random computer for a few games, you start to wonder if there's a way to make our Connect Four game more challenging. The answer is yes, and in this chapter, you'll learn to make an intelligent Connect Four opponent.

In one approach, we'll ask the script to think three steps ahead, as people do when playing a game: two moves by the computer and one by the player.

In the first step, the computer checks whether a move leads to winning the game right away. If yes, the computer will take it.

Thinking two steps ahead in Connect Four means the computer tries to prevent the opponent from winning in the next turn. This is complicated, because sometimes the computer must block a position and other times it must avoid taking a position. The computer will distinguish these two cases and block some moves and avoid others to prevent the opponent from winning.

By thinking three steps ahead, the computer will follow the path that most likely leads to a victory for the computer after three moves. In many scenarios, thinking three steps ahead can guarantee a win in three steps. In particular, if there is a move that guarantees the computer to win in three moves, the computer will select that as the best next move.

The second method uses an approach that could be classified as a type of *machine learning*. You'll simulate a million games in which both players select random moves. You'll then record the outcome and the intermediate steps. With this data, the computer will learn at each move and select the one most likely to lead to a winning outcome.

We'll assess the effectiveness of the two strategies and choose the one that is more difficult to beat. We'll then add speech recognition and text-to-speech features to the intelligent Connect Four.

Along the way, I'll also challenge you to apply the same methods to the tic-tac-toe game in the "End-of-Chapter Exercises" on page 267. As always, all scripts are available at *https://www.nostarch.com/make-python-talk/*, and you should create the folder */mpt/ch13/* for this chapter.

NEW SKILLS

- Getting your computer games to think one, two, and three steps ahead
- Understanding the difference between deepcopy and assignment statements
- Creating simulated games
- Using basic machine-learning skills to create intelligent games
- Using *pickle* to save and open data files
- Testing the effectiveness of game strategies

The Think-Three-Steps-Ahead Strategy

We'll first use the mouse-click version of Connect Four to speed up the testing of scripts. After we incorporate the strategy of thinking three steps ahead, we'll add the speech features back.

Think One Step Ahead

Thinking one step ahead in Connect Four is easy. The computer checks all possible next moves, and if one of them will lead to a win right away, the computer will take it.

Download *conn_think1.py* from the book's resources and save it in your chapter folder. This is based on the script *conn_click.py* in Chapter 11, but I've altered the code so that you're playing against an automated player that thinks one step ahead rather than another human player.

In Chapter 17, you'll learn how to choose your opponent: a human player, a simple automated player (computer) that chooses random moves, or an automated player that chooses smart moves.

Listing 13-1 highlights the key parts of *conn_think1.py*.

```
--snip--
from random import choice
from copy import deepcopy
--snip--
# Define a horizontal4() function to check connecting 4 horizontally
❶ def horizontal4(x, y, color, board):
    win = False
    for dif in (-3, -2, -1, 0):
        try:
            if board[x+dif][y] == color\
            and board[x+dif+1][y] == color\
            and board[x+dif+2][y] == color\
            and board[x+dif+3][y] == color\
            and  x+dif >= 0:
                win = True
        except IndexError:
            pass
    return win
# Define a vertical4() function to check connecting 4 vertically
def vertical4(x, y, color, board):
--snip--
# Define a win_game() function to check if someone wins the game
❷ def win_game(num, color, board):
    win = False
    # Convert column and row numbers to indexes in the list of lists board
    x = num-1
    y = len(board[x])-1
    # Check all winning possibilities
    if vertical4(x, y, color, board) == True:
        win = True
    if horizontal4(x, y, color, board) == True:
        win = True
    if forward4(x, y, color, board) == True:
        win = True
    if back4(x, y, color, board) == True:
        win = True
    # Return the value stored in win
    return win
    --snip--
# Define the best_move() function
❸ def best_move():
    # Take column 4 in the first move
    if len(occupied[3]) == 0:
        return 4
    # If only one column has free slots, take it
    if len(validinputs) == 1:
```

```
            return validinputs[0]
        # Otherwise, see what will happen in the next move hypothetically
❹   winner = []
        # Go through all possible moves and see if there is a winning move
        for move in validinputs:
            tooccupy = deepcopy(occupied)
            tooccupy[move-1].append('red')
            if win_game(move,'red',tooccupy) == True:
                winner.append(move)
        # If there is a winning move, take it
        if len(winner)>0:
                return winner[0]
❺ def computer_move():
        global turn, rounds, validinputs
        # Choose the best move
        col = best_move()
        if col == None:
            col = choice(validinputs)
        # Calculate the lowest available row number in that column
        row = 1+len(occupied[col-1])
--snip--
        # Check if the player has won the game
    ❻ if win_game(col, turn, occupied) == True:
--snip--
# Computer moves first
computer_move()
# Define a function conn() to place a disc in a cell
def conn(x,y):
        # Declare global variables
        global turn, rounds, validinputs
--snip--
            ❼ if win_game(col, turn, occupied) == True:
--snip--
        # Computer moves next
        if len(validinputs)>0:
            computer_move()
--snip--
```

Listing 13-1: Think one step ahead in the Connect Four game.

We import all needed modules. In particular, we import choice() from the *random* module and deepcopy() from the *copy* module. The *copy* module is in the Python standard library, so no installation is needed.

To search for the best strategy, we'll look one step ahead and see what would happen hypothetically if certain actions were taken. We need deepcopy() to copy a list without altering the original list. We can't simply use assignment statements in this script when copying lists. Assignment statements in Python create a link to the original list object, so if we alter the copy, we alter the original as well. Altering the original list is not what we intend and would cause unexpected behavior.

Assignment statements in Python don't copy objects. Instead, they create bindings between a target and an object. If we use an assignment statement to create a copy of the list occupied *in* conn_think1.py *and make changes to the copy, the original will be altered as well.*

At **❶**, we make horizontal4(x,y,color,board)more general so that it can be applied to any four arguments. Later in the script, we'll use it to check whether certain moves win the game by collecting four discs horizontally in a hypothetical situation. We define the functions vertical4(), forward4(), and back4() in a similar way.

At **❷**, we define win_game(num,color,board), which checks whether the player has won in any of the preceding four scenarios. We've also omitted the row number as an argument because it will be inferred from the argument board.

The main action is in best_move(), starting at **❸**. This function searches for the best move for the computer (the red player). If column 4 is empty, the computer takes the center column. Since the red player moves first, this line of code ensures that the very first move of the game is always the center column 4, giving whoever makes the first move an advantage.

Since our goal in this chapter is to make Connect Four more challenging, we let the computer move first. However, letting the human play first is straightforward, and we'll leave that as an exercise at the end of the chapter. In Chapter 17, you'll see how to choose who plays first.

If only one move is left (that is, six columns are full and only one column has empty cells), there's no point searching for a best move, so the computer takes the only remaining move.

If more than one move remains, the function checks every possible move to see if any will lead to a win for the computer right away. The script creates the list winner to contain the potentially winning moves **❹**. We go through all possible next moves. We use win_game() to check whether a move will win the game hypothetically. If yes, the move is added to winner. The function then checks whether winner is empty, and if it isn't, the computer takes the first available move in the list.

We then define computer_move() **❺**. When called, this function tells the computer to make the move produced by best_move(). The computer then places a disc in the corresponding column. Once the computer places the disc, the script uses win_game() to check if the move wins the game **❻**.

The computer makes the first move of the game. After that, we define conn(), which allows you to click the screen to play your move. The script checks whether your move wins the game **❼**. The computer will move after you if the game isn't over.

Run the script several times and play against the computer. You'll notice that the computer will always take the winning move if there is one. For example, at the left of Figure 13-1, an opportunity emerges for the red player to take column 7 and win the game. The computer thinks one step ahead and takes the winning move.

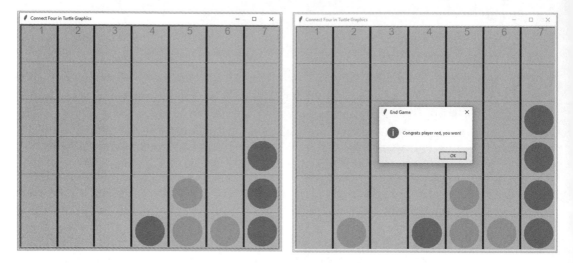

Figure 13-1: A Connect Four game that thinks one step ahead

TRY IT OUT

Run *conn_think1.py* and create opportunities for the computer to win. See if the computer takes the winning move right away.

Think Two Steps Ahead

Thinking two steps ahead in Connect Four is a little complicated. The computer's next move can either block the opponent (which is you) or help the opponent's chance of winning the game on the next turn.

We'll separate these two cases: if the computer's move blocks the opponent's chance of winning, the script will take it; if the computer's move helps the opponent's chance of winning, the script will avoid it. Let's use examples to demonstrate the two cases.

Moves to Avoid

In this example, the computer should avoid a certain move so that the opponent won't win on the next turn.

At the left of Figure 13-2, it's the red player's turn. If the red player chooses column 6 as the next move, the opponent can win on the following turn, as shown on the right in the figure. Therefore, the red player should avoid this move.

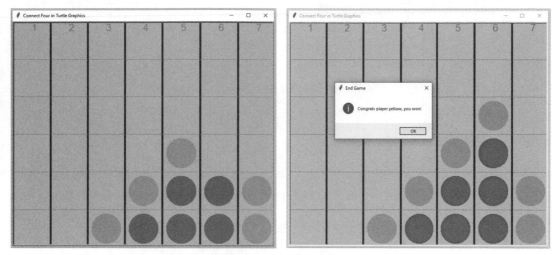

Figure 13-2: The red player should avoid column 6 in this example.

Here, the red player has made a move that allows yellow to win. We can avoid that win with this rule: if you make a next move *x*, and your opponent places a disc in the same column *x* two steps ahead and wins the game, you should avoid the move *x* in the next step.

Moves to Block

In the next case, the computer should block a certain move so the opponent won't win in two steps.

At the left in Figure 13-3, it's the red player's turn. If the red player doesn't choose column 3 in the next move, the opponent can choose column 3 and win on the following turn. Therefore, the red player should block this move.

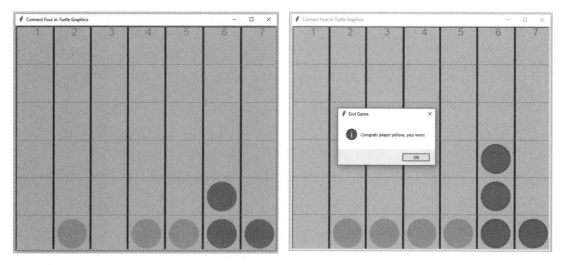

Figure 13-3: The red player should block column 3.

Here, the red player makes a different move—column 6—and loses the game. So the rule is as follows: if red makes the next move, *x*, and the yellow opponent can make a different move *y* within two steps and win, red should block yellow's move *y* in the next step.

Implement the Think-Two-Steps-Ahead Strategy

Let's allow the computer to think up to two steps ahead by using the three techniques just discussed (one for thinking one step ahead, two for thinking two steps ahead).

Open *conn_think1.py*, replace its best_move() with the new best_move() function defined in Listing 13-2, and save the new script as *conn_think2.py* in your chapter folder (or you can download it from the book's resources).

```
--snip--
# Define the best_move() function
def best_move():
    # Take column 4 in the first move
    if len(occupied[3]) == 0:
        return 4
    # If only one column has free slots, take it
    if len(validinputs) == 1:
        return validinputs[0]
    # Otherwise, see what will happen in the next move hypothetically
    winner = []
    # Go through all possible moves and see if there is a winning move
❶   for move in validinputs:
        tooccupy = deepcopy(occupied)
        tooccupy[move-1].append('red')
        if win_game(move,'red',tooccupy) == True:
            winner.append(move)
    # If there is a winning move, take it
    if len(winner)>0:
        return winner[0]
    # If no winning move, look two steps ahead
❷   if len(winner) == 0 and len(validinputs)>=2:
        loser = []
        # Check if your opponent has a winning move
        for m1 in validinputs:
            for m2 in validinputs:
                if m2 != m1:
                    tooccupy = deepcopy(occupied)
                    tooccupy[m1-1].append('red')
                    tooccupy[m2-1].append('yellow')
                    if win_game(m2, 'yellow',tooccupy) == True:
                        winner.append(m2)
                if m2 == m1 and len(occupied[m1-1]) <= 4:
                    tooccupy2 = deepcopy(occupied)
                    tooccupy2[m1-1].append('red')
                    tooccupy2[m2-1].append('yellow')
                    if win_game(m2,'yellow',tooccupy2) == True:
                        loser.append(m2)
        # If your opponent has a winning move, block it
        if len(winner)>0:
            return winner[0]
```

```
        # If you can make a move to help your opponent to win, avoid it
❸   if len(loser)>0:
        myvalids = deepcopy(validinputs)
        for i in range(len(loser)):
            myvalids.remove(loser[i])
        if len(myvalids)>0:
            return choice(myvalids)
--snip--
```

Listing 13-2: Allow the computer to think up to two steps ahead.

In the newly defined function best_move(), the script searches for the best move based on discs currently on the board. If this is the very first move of the game, the function takes the column in the middle. If only one move is left, the function defines the best move to be the only move left.

If more than one move remains, the function checks every possible move to see if any will lead to a win for the red player (the computer) right away ❶. If yes, the function returns the move as the best move and stores it in winner. If not, the function will look two steps ahead to see if the opponent can win within two steps ❷.

The function checks two separate cases: if the red player's move m1 (the first move) and the yellow player's move m2 (the second move) lead to a win for the yellow player in two steps, we add the move m2 to the list winner. If the red player's move m1 and the yellow player's move m2=m1 lead to a win for the yellow player in two steps, we add the move m2 to the list loser.

The script checks whether winner is empty. If it isn't, the computer will select the opponent's winning move to block the opponent from winning. Otherwise, the computer will check whether the list loser is empty. If not, the computer will avoid all elements in loser so as not to help the opponent win ❸.

Run *conn_think2.py* and play a few times against the computer. You'll notice an improvement in the game in the sense that the computer can now think two steps ahead and try to prevent you from winning on your next turn.

TRY IT OUT

Run *conn_think2.py* and try to win the game yourself. Pay attention to whether the computer prevents you from winning if such opportunities arise.

Think Three Steps Ahead

This next section will allow the computer to think up to three steps ahead before taking its turn. If the computer has no winning move in the next step and the opponent has no winning moves two steps ahead, the computer will look three steps ahead.

The computer will take the next move that most likely leads to a win in three steps. In particular, if there's a next move that guarantees the computer to win in three steps, the computer will select that next move as the best one. Let's use an example to demonstrate.

An Example of a Win in Three Steps

The script *conn_think2.py* is harder to beat than *conn_think1.py*, but not impossible. A sophisticated player will notice that the computer misses some moves that could have led to a win in three steps.

Here's an example. At the left of Figure 13-4, it's the computer's (the red player's) turn to move. If the computer drops a disc in column 3, the computer is guaranteed to win on its next turn, because the opponent (the yellow player) can block only either column 1 or column 5. The computer can then occupy the other column (either column 5 or column 1) in this third step and win the game.

But instead, the computer chooses column 6, as shown at the right of Figure 13-4, missing a chance to guarantee a win.

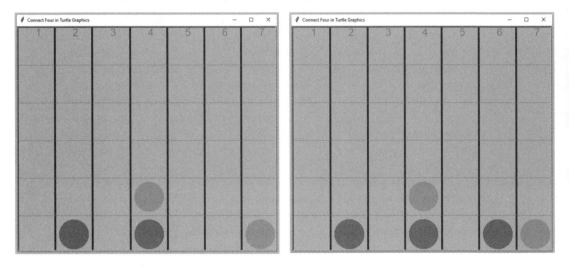

Figure 13-4: The computer (the red player) fails to make a move that guarantees a win.

We should, therefore, make further improvements on the game. You'll build a game that thinks three steps ahead.

Implement the Think-Three-Steps-Ahead Strategy

Let's allow the computer to think up to three steps ahead.

Open *conn_think2.py*, add the newly defined validmoves() function and the highlighted part in Listing 13-3 to the best_move() function, and save the new script as *conn_think.py* in your chapter folder. Alternatively, you can download it from the book's resources. This is the complete script for our think-ahead strategy.

```
--snip--
# Define the validmoves() function to ensure three future moves
# will not cause any column to have more than six discs in it
def validmoves(m1,m2,m3,occupied):
    validmove = False
    if m1 == m2 == m3 and len(occupied[m1-1]) <= 3:
```

```
                 validmove = True
        if m1 == m2 and m2 != m3 and len(occupied[m1-1]) <= 4:
            validmove = True
        if m1 == m3 and m2 != m3 and len(occupied[m1-1]) <= 4:
            validmove = True
        if m3 == m2 and m2 != m1 and len(occupied[m3-1]) <= 4:
            validmove = True
    return validmove
# Define the best_move() function
def best_move():
    # Take column 4 in the first move
--snip--
# Otherwise, look 3 moves ahead
❶ if len(winner) == 0 and len(loser) == 0:
        # Look at all possible combinations of 3 moves ahead
        for m1 in validinputs:
            for m2 in validinputs:
                for m3 in validinputs:
                    if validmoves(m1,m2,m3,occupied) == True:
                        tooccupy3 = deepcopy(occupied)
                        tooccupy3[m1-1].append('red')
                        tooccupy3[m2-1].append('yellow')
                        tooccupy3[m3-1].append('red')
                        if win_game(m3, 'red', tooccupy3) == True:
                            winner.append(m1)
        # See if there is a move now that can lead to winning in 3 moves
        if len(winner)>0:
❷          cnt = {winner.count(x):x for x in winner}
           maxcnt = sorted(cnt.keys())[-1]
           return cnt[maxcnt]
--snip--
```

Listing 13-3: Allow the computer to think up to three steps ahead.

We first define validmoves(m1,m2,m3,occupied) to ensure that none of the three future hypothetical moves m1, m2, and m3 on the game board (represented by the list of lists occupied) will cause any columns to have more than six discs. If the three moves cause any of the seven columns to contain more than six discs, the function returns False; otherwise, it returns True.

As in *conn_think2.py*, the computer first checks whether a winning move could be made right away. If yes, it will take it. If not, it checks whether a winning move could be made two steps ahead for the opponent. If yes, the computer tries to prevent it.

If no winning moves are available for the opponent two steps ahead, the computer looks three steps ahead ❶. It checks all combinations of three moves: the computer's next move, m1; the opponent's move two steps ahead, m2; and the computer's move at the third step, m3. If a combination leads to a win for the player, the next move m1 is added to the list winner.

However, just because a move *x* is in winner doesn't mean this move will guarantee a computer win in three steps, because it can't guarantee that the opponent will choose m2 in the second step. Further, winner could contain multiple values. The function best_move() therefore looks for the most frequent value in winner, since that's the move most likely to lead to a win for the computer in three steps.

As with most things in Python, there are many ways to find the most frequent value in a list. We utilize a trick known as a *list comprehension* to create an inline dictionary cnt. In this dictionary, the key is the number of times a move appears in winner, and the value is the move ❷. For example, if winner has six elements [7, 6, 6, 5, 5, 5], the dictionary cnt would be {1:7, 2:6, 3:5}. We then sort the keys in cnt to find the highest frequency and call it maxcnt. Here, maxcnt has a value of 3 because the highest number of times a value appears is three. Finally, we use maxcnt to retrieve the dictionary element with the highest frequency. Here, the move 5 appears most frequently in winner.

If you run *conn_think.py* and play the game, you'll find the computer almost impossible to beat. If you do everything right, you can tie the game. The moment you make a wrong move, the computer will seize the opportunity and win the game.

TRY IT OUT

Run *conn_think.py* five times and try your best to win each game. See how many games you can manage to win.

The Machine-Learning Strategy

Another way to make Connect Four smart is to let the computer learn from actual game outcomes. You'll generate a million games in which both players use random moves. You'll record the intermediate steps and the outcome of each game. The computer will use the game outcome data to design the best strategy.

At each move, the computer looks at all games with the same game history as the current game board. It calculates the average outcome for each possible next move and chooses the one that most likely leads to a favorable outcome.

Create a Dataset of Simulated Games

The first step in the machine-learning strategy is to generate data to learn from. We'll simulate two players choosing random moves and record both the outcome and the steps taken to reach that outcome. Even though the moves by both players are random, we repeat the game many times. The randomness in all these games is washed out by the law of large numbers. As a result, the outcome data will be useful to the computer to predict the outcome of a move.

In statistics, the law of large numbers *says that if you perform the same experiment many times, the average outcome should be close to the expected value. See an example at* https://en.wikipedia.org/wiki/Law_of_large_numbers. *In our setting, if the average outcome from playing move A is better than the average outcome from playing move B over a large number of trials, move A should be chosen over move B.*

Download *conn_simulation.py* from the book's resources. I explain the script in Listing 13-4.

```
from random import choice
import pickle

# Define a simulate() function to generate a complete game
def simulate():
    occupied=[list(),list(),list(),list(),list(),list(),list()]
    validinputs=[1,2,3,4,5,6,7]
# Define a horizontal4() function to check connecting 4 horizontally
def horizontal4(x, y, turn):
    win=False
    for dif in (-3, -2, -1, 0):
--snip--
❶ def win_game(col, row, turn):
      win=False
--snip--
      # Return the value stored in win
      return win
    # The red player takes the first move
❷ turn="red"
    # Keep track of all intermediate moves
    moves=[]
    # Use winlose to record game outcome, default value is 0 (a tie)
    winlose=[0]
    # Play a maximum of 42 steps
❸ for i in range(42):
      # The player randomly selects a move
      col=choice(validinputs)
      row=len(occupied[col-1])+1
      moves.append(col)
      # Check if the player has won
      if win_game(col, row, turn)==True:
          if turn=='red':
              winlose[0]=1
          if turn=='yellow':
              winlose[0]=-1
          break
      # Add the move to the occupied list to keep track
      occupied[col-1].append(turn)
      # Update the list of valid moves
      if len(occupied[col-1])==6 and col in validinputs:
          validinputs.remove(col)
      # Give the turn to the other player
      if turn=="red":
          turn="yellow"
      else:
```

```
            turn="red"
        # Record both game outcome and intermediate steps
        return winlose+moves
    # Simulate the game 1 million times and record all games
    results=[]
❹ for x in range(1000000):
        result=simulate()
        results.append(result)
    # Save the simulation data on your computer
❺ with open('conn_simulates.pickle', 'wb') as fp:
        pickle.dump(results,fp)
    # Read the data and print out the first 10 games
    with open('conn_simulates.pickle', 'rb') as fp:
        mylist=pickle.load(fp)
print(mylist[0:10])
```

Listing 13-4: Simulating a million Connect Four games

We first define simulate(). When called, it simulates a complete Connect Four game and records each move and the game outcome. We omit the graphics part of the game to save time.

We define win_game() to check if a player has won the game ❶. In each game, the red player moves first ❷. We create the two lists moves and winlose to record the intermediate moves and the game outcome, respectively.

We create a game loop to iterate a maximum of 42 times because each Connect Four game has a maximum of 42 moves ❸. In each iteration, a player randomly selects a move. The move is added to moves to keep track of the history of the game. At each step, we check whether a player wins. If yes, we'll record an outcome of 1 if the winner is the red player and -1 if the winner is the yellow player. The default outcome is a tie, in which case we'll record a value of 0.

We then call simulate() a million times ❹. The result of each game is saved in a list result, with its first element being the outcome of the game (-1, 1, or 0), followed by the intermediate steps of the game.

The outcomes and intermediate steps of the million games are saved in *conn_simulates.pickle* for later use ❺. We print out the results of the first 10 games, shown in Listing 13-5.

```
[[1, 1, 7, 1, 5, 7, 6, 5, 1, 5, 7, 5, 2, 5],
 [1, 5, 4, 2, 7, 5, 2, 5, 6, 2, 7, 5],
 [1, 7, 3, 5, 5, 3, 7, 3, 7, 4, 2, 7, 7, 6],
 [-1, 6, 7, 6, 6, 5, 1, 5, 3, 5, 7, 6, 5, 4, 2, 5, 7, 3, 4,
 7, 1, 1, 6, 4, 5, 6, 1, 1, 4, 1, 7, 3, 3, 7, 2, 3, 2, 3, 4],
 [-1, 1, 3, 5, 1, 4, 5, 4, 6, 2, 7, 3, 2, 3, 4, 2, 3],
 [1, 6, 5, 7, 1, 3, 3, 1, 5, 5, 5, 2, 3, 6, 7, 2, 6, 3, 2, 7,
 5, 4, 3, 7, 6, 7, 6, 6, 1, 2, 2, 4, 5, 4, 7, 3, 2, 1, 1, 4],
 [1, 2, 5, 3, 5, 3, 4, 7, 7, 5, 3, 4, 2, 2, 2, 5, 4, 4, 4, 4, 6, 6],
 [1, 2, 5, 6, 4, 6, 7, 5, 5, 7, 4, 1, 3, 6, 3, 2, 1, 7, 1, 6],
 [1, 7, 4, 4, 6, 3, 1, 2, 2, 3, 3, 4, 6, 3, 6, 1, 3, 4, 1, 3, 7, 7, 5, 4],
 [-1, 1, 4, 1, 4, 1, 2, 4, 5, 6, 6, 6, 3]]
```

Listing 13-5: The first 10 simulated Connect Four games

For example, the output for the first game is [1, 1, 7, 1, 5, 7, 6, 5, 1, 5, 7, 5, 2, 5]. The first element, 1, means that the red player has won the game. The remaining elements, 1, 7, 1 ... , indicate the columns the players dropped their discs into, alternating between red and yellow. The red player eventually wins this game by connecting four red discs vertically in column 5.

TRY IT OUT

Run *conn_simulation.py* and print out the first 10 games in the generated dataset. Interpret the numbers in each game and confirm that the intermediate steps are consistent with the game's outcome.

Apply the Data

The next step is to use the outcome data to design intelligent moves for the computer. At each move, the computer will turn to the simulated data to retrieve all games with the same history. It searches through all possible next moves, finds the one that leads to the most favorable outcome, and uses that as the next move.

Download *conn_ml.py* and save it in your chapter folder. The script is based on *conn_think.py*. Listing 13-6 highlights the main differences.

```
--snip--
# A history of moves made
moves_made=[]
# Obtain game data
with open('conn_simulates.pickle', 'rb') as fp:
    gamedata=pickle.load(fp)
# Define the best_move() function
❶ def best_move():
    # Take column 4 in the first move
    if len(occupied[3])==0:
        return 4
    # If there is only one column has free slots, use the column
    if len(validinputs)==1:
        return validinputs[0]
    simu=[]
    for y in gamedata:
        if y[1:len(moves_made)+1]==moves_made:
            simu.append(y)
    # Now we look at the next move;
    outcomes={x:[] for x in validinputs}
    # We collect all the outcomes for each next move
    for y in simu:
        outcomes[y[len(moves_made)+1]].append(y[0])
    # Set the initial value of bestoutcome
    bestoutcome=-2;
    # Randomly select a move to be best_move
```

```
        best_move=validinputs[0]
        # iterate through all possible next moves
        for move in validinputs:
            if len(outcomes[move])>0:
                outcome=sum(outcomes[move])/len(outcomes[move])
                # If the average outcome beats the current best
                if outcome>bestoutcome:
                    # Update the bestoutcome
                    bestoutcome=outcome
                    # Update the best move
                    best_move=move
        return best_move
    # Define a function computer_move()
❷ def computer_move():
        # Declare global variables
        global turn, rounds, validinputs
        # Get the best move
        col=best_move()
        if col==None:
            col=choice(validinputs)
    --snip--
        moves_made.append(col)
    --snip--
    # Computer moves first
❸ computer_move()
    # Define a function conn() to place a disc in a cell
❹ def conn(x,y):
        # Declare global variables
        global turn, rounds, validinputs
    --snip--
        moves_made.append(col)
    --snip--
        # Computer moves next
        if len(validinputs)>0:
            computer_move()
    --snip--
```

Listing 13-6: A Connect Four game player with the machine-learning strategy

We create the new list moves_made to keep track of all moves in the game so far; we'll use it later in best_move(). We open the simulated Connect Four game data and save it in a list gamedata.

In best_move(), we make sure the first move is always to place a disc in column 4, as that gives the computer a starting advantage ❶. We check if only one move is left and, if so, just take it as the next best move. Otherwise, we check all simulated games with the same history as the current game and see which next move will be most favorable to the red player. We assign that move as the best move. I'll explain how we do that in detail in *ml_move.py*, using a concrete example.

At ❷, we define computer_move(). When it's the computer's turn to play, it calls best_move() to generate a move. The computer makes the move, and we add that move to the list moves_made to track the game history.

We set the computer to make the first move ❸. After that, the player clicks to make their move ❹. The human player's move is also added to moves_made. The computer will move after you if the game isn't over.

Run *conn_ml.py* and play the game a few times. You might be surprised to find that it's relatively easy to win. The machine-learning strategy is not nearly as effective as our three-steps method. We'll look into why later in the chapter.

TRY IT OUT

Run *conn_ml.py* and play five games against the computer. See how many games you can win.

Test the Effectiveness of the Two Strategies

Next, we want to measure how intelligent the two strategies are. We'll simulate 1,000 games and record the outcomes. In each game, the intelligent computer version will play against a simple computer player that selects random moves. We'll see how many times the intelligent player wins or ties the game.

The Think-Three-Steps-Ahead Strategy

We'll start with the three-steps version. The script *outcome_conn_think.py*, shown in Listing 13-7, has our two computer players play 1,000 times, then prints out the number of winning, tying, and losing games.

```
import pickle
from random import choice
from copy import deepcopy

# Define the simulate() function to play a complete game
❶ def simulate():
    occupied=[list(),list(),list(),list(),list(),list(),list()]
    validinputs=[1,2,3,4,5,6,7]
--snip--
    def win_game(num, color, lst):
        win=False
--snip--
    def best_move():
        # Take column 4 in the first move
        if len(occupied[3])==0:
            return 4
--snip--
    # The red player takes the first move
    turn="red"
    # Keep track of all intermediate moves
    moves_made=[]
```

```
❷ winlose=[0]
   # Play a maximum of 42 steps (21 rounds)
   for i in range(21):
       # The player selects the best move
     ❸ col=best_move()
       if col==None:
           col=choice(validinputs)
       moves_made.append(col)
--snip--
       # The other player randomly selects a move
       col=choice(validinputs)
       moves_made.append(col)
--snip--
   # Record both game outcome and intermediate steps
 ❹ return winlose+moves_made
# Repeat the game 1000 times and record all game outcomes
results=[]
❺ for x in range(1000):
   result=simulate()
   results.append(result)
with open('outcome_conn_think.pickle', 'wb') as fp:
   pickle.dump(results,fp)
with open('outcome_conn_think.pickle', 'rb') as fp:
   mylist=pickle.load(fp)
winlose=[x[0] for x in mylist]
# Print out the number of winning games
print("the number of winning games is", winlose.count(1))
# Print out the number of tying games
print("the number of tying games is", winlose.count(0))
# Print out the number of losing games
print("the number of losing games is", winlose.count(-1))
```

Listing 13-7: Test the effectiveness of the think-three-steps-ahead strategy.

At ❶, we define simulate(), which pits the intelligent computer (the red player) using the think-three-steps-ahead strategy against a computer player that selects random moves.

The win_game() and best_move() functions are the same as those defined in *conn_think.py*. We use the list winlose to record the game outcomes ❷: 1 if the red player wins, -1 if the yellow player wins, and 0 if it's a tie.

Once the game starts, the red player calls best_move() to obtain a move ❸, while the yellow player randomly selects a move ❹.

At ❺, we call simulate() 1,000 times and record the outcome of all games. We then print out the number of winning, tying, and losing games, summing the count of 1, -1, and 0 to make it easier to read. Here's an example of the output:

```
the number of winning games is 995
the number of tying games is 0
the number of losing games is 5
```

Out of all the games, the intelligent player with the think-three-steps-ahead strategy has won 995 times, never tied, and lost 5 times.

TRY IT OUT

Rerun *outcome_conn_think.py* a few times to see how many times the "intelligent" computer wins.

The Machine-Learning Strategy

Now we'll test the machine-learning strategy in the same way. Download *outcome_conn_ml.py* and save it in your chapter folder. This is similar to *outcome _conn_think.py*, so I'll just highlight the differences here:

```
--snip--
    # Obtain gamedata
    with open('conn_simulates.pickle', 'rb') as fp:
        gamedata=pickle.load(fp)
# Define the best_move() function based on the machine-learning strategy
    def best_move():
        # Take column 4 in the first move
        if len(occupied[3])==0:
            return 4
--snip--
with open('outcome_conn_ml.pickle', 'wb') as fp:
    pickle.dump(results,fp)
with open('outcome_conn_ml.pickle', 'rb') as fp:
    mylist=pickle.load(fp)
--snip--
```

First, we obtain the simulated game outcome data that we've generated from *conn_simulation.py*. Second, we base the definition of best_move() on the machine-learning strategy instead of the three-steps strategy.

WARNING *The script* outcome_conn_ml.py *may take a long time (up to a couple of hours) to run, depending on the speed of your computer. If you aren't sure about your computer's speed, change the number of games from 1,000 to 100 and run the script first.*

We call simulate() 1,000 times and record the outcomes, printing them as before. Here's an example output:

```
the number of winning games is 882
the number of tying games is 0
the number of losing games is 118
```

Out of all the games, the computer has won 882 times, never tied, and lost 118 times—it did significantly worse than with the three-steps strategy. Let's look at why.

Why Doesn't the Machine-Learning Strategy Work Well in Connect Four?

The machine-learning strategy is less effective in our game mainly because so many moves are available in a Connect Four game: a maximum of 42. That means, exponentially, that a very large number of possible game outcomes exist. We simulated a million games, which sounds like a lot, but when the data is spread among many game outcomes, it's inevitable that some game outcomes will not be in the simulated data. As a result, it's impossible to find a best strategy for many of the game histories.

As an example, we'll test the machine-learning strategy with one particular game history. Assume that the red and yellow players have both made three moves and next it's the red player's turn. The game board at this stage is as shown in Figure 13-5.

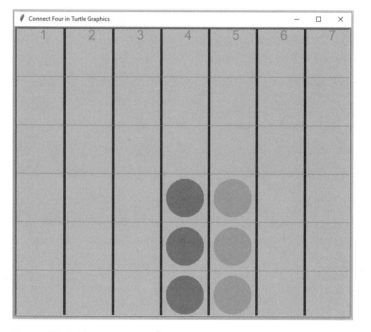

Figure 13-5: One game simulation

We'll simulate this game setup in code to see how our machine-learning strategy decides which move to make next. Enter *ml_move.py*, shown in Listing 13-8.

```
import pickle
validinputs=[1,2,3,4,5,6,7]
# A game history
moves_made=[4,5,4,5,4,5]
# The game board
occupied=[list(),list(),list(),
          ['red','red','red'],
          ['yellow','yellow','yellow'],
          list(),list()]
```

```
# Obtain gamedata
with open('conn_simulates.pickle', 'rb') as fp:
    gamedata=pickle.load(fp)
❶ simu=[]
for y in gamedata:
    if y[1:len(moves_made)+1]==moves_made:
        simu.append(y)
# Now we look at the next move
outcomes={x:[] for x in validinputs}
# We collect all the outcomes for each next move
for y in simu:
    outcomes[y[len(moves_made)+1]].append(y[0])
❷ print(outcomes)
# Set the initial value of bestoutcome
bestoutcome=-2;
# Randomly select a move to be best_move
best_move=validinputs[0]
# Iterate through all possible next moves
❸ for move in validinputs:
    if len(outcomes[move])>0:
        outcome=sum(outcomes[move])/len(outcomes[move])
        print\
        (f'when the next move is {move}, the average outcome is {outcome}')
        # If the average outcome from that move beats the current best move
        if outcome>bestoutcome:
            # Update the best outcome
            bestoutcome=outcome
            # Update the best move
            best_move=move
❹ print(f'the best next move is {best_move}')
```

Listing 13-8: Search for the best machine learning strategy move.

We import *pickle*, which enables us to work with datasets saved in the *pickle* format. We open the simulation data file, *conn_simulates.pickle*, which was created earlier in *conn_simulation.py*. The data is saved in the gamedata list.

At this point, the red player is able to place a disc in any of the seven columns in the next move, so we have all seven values in validinputs. We save the six moves already made in Figure 13-4, [4, 5, 4, 5, 4, 5], in the list moves_made. The list of lists occupied keeps track of the disc positions currently on the game board.

We check the million simulated games data to see if any of those games match the game history of the current game. If yes, we put all the historical games that match in the list simu ❶. We then focus on the seventh move in all those games. We look at the outcomes (win, lose, or tie) of all games associated with each of the seven possible moves, 1 through 7, and put them in a dictionary outcomes.

We then print out the content of outcomes ❷:

```
{1: [], 2: [-1, 1], 3: [1], 4: [1], 5: [-1], 6: [-1, -1, 1], 7: [-1]}
```

WARNING *The outcome will be different when you run* ml_move.py *because the simulated data is generated randomly.*

As you can see, nine games have the same game history: none of which placed the next disc in column 1, two that used column 2 for the next move, one that used column 3, and so on. The values -1, 0, and 1 inside the square brackets indicate that the red player loses, ties, and wins the game, respectively.

To help us compare which of the seven moves leads to the best outcome for the red player, we calculate the average outcome for each move ❸. If a move leads to wins 100 percent of the time, the average outcome is 1; if a move leads to 50 percent wins and 50 percent losses, the average outcome is 0; if a move leads to a loss 100 percent of the time, the average is -1.

We print the average outcomes (we don't have results for move 1 because no simulated game in simu used this move):

```
when the next move is 2, the average outcome is 0.0
when the next move is 3, the average outcome is 1.0
when the next move is 4, the average outcome is 1.0
when the next move is 5, the average outcome is -1.0
when the next move is 6, the average outcome is -0.3333333333333333
when the next move is 7, the average outcome is -1.0
```

Both moves 3 and 4 lead to an average outcome of 1. The script prints out the first best move, which is 3 in this case ❹:

```
the best next move is 3
```

However, when we look at this move in the game (Figure 13-6), we can see it clearly isn't the best move we could have made.

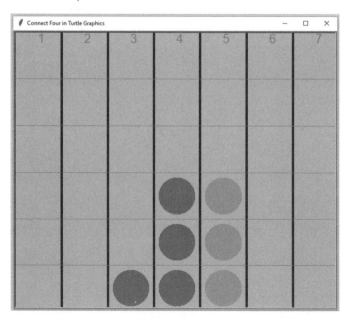

Figure 13-6: The machine-learning computer makes a mistake.

As you can see, the problem with the machine-learning strategy is that we don't have enough simulated games that match our game history.

You may wonder whether we can just increase the number of simulated games to solve the problem. The answer is yes and no. Increasing the number of simulated games will make the strategy more intelligent, but it will also increase the data size enough to slow the response of the machine-learning script. Thus, the player will have to wait a long time for the computer to make a move. This is the trade-off when using machine learning.

Let's test this by increasing the size of the simulated games to 10 million. Generating this data takes several hours. We rerun *ml_move.py* with the larger dataset and get the following output:

```
{1: [-1, 1, -1, 1, -1, -1, 1, 1, -1, -1, -1, 1, 1, -1, 1],
2: [1, 1, -1, 1, 1, 1, 1, -1, -1, 1, 1, -1, 1, 1],
3: [-1, -1, -1, -1, -1, 1, -1, -1, -1, -1, -1],
4: [1, 1, 1, 1, 1, 1, 1, 1, 1],
5: [1, 1, 1, 1, 1, 1, -1],
6: [-1, -1, 1, -1, -1, 1, 1, -1, 1, 1, -1, 1, -1],
7: [1, -1, 1, -1, -1, -1, 1, -1, -1, 1]}
when the next move is 1, the average outcome is -0.06666666666666667
when the next move is 2, the average outcome is 0.42857142857142855
when the next move is 3, the average outcome is -0.8181818181818182
when the next move is 4, the average outcome is 1.0
when the next move is 5, the average outcome is 0.7142857142857143
when the next move is 6, the average outcome is -0.07692307692307693
when the next move is 7, the average outcome is -0.2
the best next move is 4
```

Now that we have much more data to base our decision on, the machine-learning strategy correctly recommends column 4, resulting in Figure 13-7.

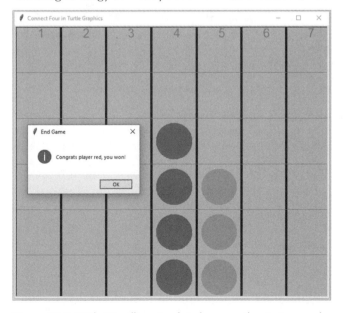

Figure 13-7: With 10 million simulated games, the strategy makes the correct move.

Voice-Controlled Intelligent Connect Four Games

Let's wrap up this chapter by adding speech recognition and text-to-speech features to the intelligent Connect Four games.

A Voice-Controlled Game That Thinks Ahead

We'll mesh together two scripts, *conn_think.py* and *conn_hs.py*, into *conn_think_hs.py*. Download this file from the book's resources and save it in your chapter folder. The main differences are shown in Listing 13-9.

```
--snip--
❶ def best_move():
       # Take column 4 in the first move
       if len(occupied[3])==0:
           return 4
--snip--
   # Define the computer_move() function
❷ def computer_move():
       global turn, rounds, validinputs
       # Choose the best move
       col=best_move()
       if col==None:
           col=choice(validinputs)
       print_say(f"The computer chooses column {col}.")
--snip--
       # Check if the player has won
       if win_game(col, turn, occupied)==True:
           # If a player wins, invalid all moves, end the game
           validinputs=[]
         ❸ print_say(f"Congrats player {turn}, you won!")
           messagebox.showinfo("End Game",f"Congrats player {turn}, you won!")
       # If all cells are occupied and no winner, it's a tie
       if rounds==42:
           print_say("Game over, it's a tie!")
           messagebox.showinfo("Tie Game","Game over, it's a tie!")
--snip--
   # Computer moves first
❹ computer_move()
   # Add a dictionary of words to replace
```

```
    to_replace = {'number ':'', 'cell ':'', 'column ':'',
                  'one':'1', 'two':'2', 'three':'3',
                  'four':'4', 'for':'4', 'five':'5',
                  'six':'6', 'seven':'7'}
    # Start a while loop to take voice inputs
❺ while len(validinputs)>0:
        # Ask for your move
        print_say(f"Player {turn}, what's your move?")
        # Capture your voice input
        inp= voice_to_text().lower()
        print_say(f"You said {inp}.")
        for x in list(to_replace.keys()):
            inp = inp.replace(x, to_replace[x])
        try:
            col=int(inp)
        except:
            print_say("Sorry, that's an invalid input!")
            continue
        # If col is not a valid move, try again
    ❻ if col not in validinputs:
            print_say("Sorry, that's an invalid move!")
            continue
        # If your voice input is a valid column number, play the move
        else:
            # Calculate the lowest available row number in that column
            row=len(occupied[col-1])+1
--snip--
            print_say(f"Congrats player {turn}, you won!")
--snip--
            print_say("Game over, it's a tie!")
--snip--
        if len(validinputs)>0:
            computer_move()
--snip--
```

Listing 13-9: A voice-controlled Connect Four game with the three-steps strategy

The function best_move() is the same as in the script *conn_think.py* ❶. We define computer_move() ❷, which uses best_move() to choose a move and speaks aloud the selected column. If the computer's move wins or ties the game, the script also announces it ❸.

The computer then makes the first move of the game ❹, and it starts a while loop that keeps running as long as the list validinputs isn't empty ❺. At each iteration, the script captures your voice input, which should be the number of the column you want to drop a disc in. You can say "number five," "column five," or "5." It then converts the voice command to an integer number to match the format in validinputs so it can compare your input to the list. If you said something that isn't convertible to an integer, the script will say, "Sorry, that's an invalid input."

If you've given an invalid move ❻, the script will say, "Sorry, that's an invalid move." If your move is valid, the script places the disc on the game board. In the process, it will check whether you've won or tied the game and, if so, will announce the result aloud. If the game is not yet over, the computer makes a move.

Run the script and play the voice-controlled game with the computer. You'll notice that the game is more challenging and more interesting to play.

A Voice-Controlled Game Using Machine Learning

We'll mesh together two scripts we created before, *conn_ml.py* and *conn _hs.py*, into *conn_ml_hs.py*. Download the file from the book's resources and save it in your chapter folder. Listing 13-10 shows the main differences.

```
--snip--
import pickle
--snip--
# A history of moves made
moves_made=[]
# Obtain gamedata
with open('conn_simulates.pickle', 'rb') as fp:
    gamedata=pickle.load(fp)
# Define the best_move() function based on machine learning
def best_move():
    # Take column 4 in the first move
    if len(occupied[3])==0:
        return 4
--snip--
# Define the computer_move() function
def computer_move():
    global turn, rounds, validinputs
    # Choose the best move
    move=best_move()
    if move==None:
        move=choice(validinputs)
    print_say(f"The computer decides to occupy cell {move}.")
--snip--
    moves_made.append(move)
--snip--
# Computer moves first
computer_move()
# Start an infinite loop to take voice inputs
while len(validinputs)>0:
    # Ask for your move
    print_say(f"Player {turn}, what's your move?")
    # Capture your voice input
    inp= voice_to_text().lower()
--snip--
    moves_made.append(inp)
--snip--
    # Computer moves
    if len(validinputs)>0:
        computer_move()
--snip--
```

Listing 13-10: A voice-controlled Connect Four game using the machine-learning strategy

This works in the same way as the voice-controlled three-steps version. Run the script and play a game. You should find the game interesting but easier to beat than the three-steps strategy.

Summary

In this chapter, you created intelligent, voice-controlled graphical Connect Four games by using two methods: the think-three-steps-ahead strategy and the machine-learning strategy. This taught some important reasoning skills—how do we make a script intelligent?—as well as some basic machine-learning skills.

You learned to generalize these two strategies and apply them to specific games. You can apply these skills to create your own intelligent voice-controlled games.

End-of-Chapter Exercises

1. Modify *conn_think1.py* so that the human player moves first and the computer moves second.

2. Mesh together *ttt_click.py* from Chapter 10 and *conn_think1.py* to create a mouse-click version of the tic-tac-toe game in which the computer thinks one step ahead.

3. Create a mouse-click version of the tic-tac-toe game in which the computer thinks two steps ahead, based on *ttt_click.py* and *conn_think2.py*.

4. In best_move(), defined in *conn_think.py*, if the list winner has eight elements [7, 7, 4, 5, 6, 6, 6, 6], what's the value of cnt, maxcnt, and cnt[maxcnt], respectively?

5. Design a mouse-click version of the tic-tac-toe game in which the computer thinks three steps ahead, based on *ttt_click.py* and *conn_think.py*.

6. Simulate a million tic-tac-toe games and save the game outcome and intermediate steps as *ttt_simulates.pickle*. Then create a mouse-click version of tic-tac-toe in which the computer uses the machine-learning strategy, similar to what we've done in *conn_simulation.py* and *conn_ml.py*.

7. Modify *outcome_conn_think.py* and *outcome_conn_ml.py* to test the effectiveness of the three-steps strategy and the machine-learning strategy in the tic-tac-toe games you just created.

8. After running *conn_simulation.py*, we printed out 10 observations from the dataset *conn_simulates.pickle*, as shown in Listing 13-5. The 10th observation is [-1, 1, 4, 1, 4, 1, 2, 4, 5, 6, 6, 6, 3]. Who has won the 10th game? Are the four discs connected vertically, horizontally, or diagonally?

PART IV

GOING FURTHER

14

FINANCIAL APPLICATIONS

The speech recognition and text-to-speech techniques can be applied to many aspects of life. In this chapter, we'll focus on tracking the financial markets, but the techniques you learn here can be easily generalized and applied to your own area of interest, whatever that may be.

You'll build three projects in this chapter: an app that reports the up-to-date stock price of any publicly traded company; a script that builds visualizations of stock prices; and an app that uses recent daily stock prices to calculate returns, run regressions, and perform detailed analyses.

As always, all scripts are available through the book's resources page at *https://www.nostarch.com/make-python-talk/*. Start by creating the folder */mpt/ch14/* for this chapter.

Python, What's the Facebook Stock Price?

In this project, you'll use the *yahoo_fin* package to obtain real-time price information based on the ticker symbol of a stock. A *ticker symbol* is a sequence of characters, or code, used to uniquely identify a stock. Most people will not know a company's associated ticker symbol.

This provides the opportunity to work backward. You'll learn to scrape the web to get a stock's ticker symbol from the company name. When you enter the name of a firm into the script, Python will tell you the ticker symbol of the firm's stock. Finally, you'll add the text-to-speech and speech recognition features.

Obtain the Latest Stock Price

The *yahoo_fin* package lets you obtain the latest stock price information from Yahoo! Finance. This package isn't in the Python standard library, so you need to pip install it first.

Open your Anaconda prompt (in Windows) or a terminal (in Mac or Linux), activate the virtual environment *chatting*, and run the following command (note the underscore in the middle of the package name):

```
pip install yahoo_fin
```

Next, open your Spyder editor and save Listing 14-1 as *live_price.py* in your chapter folder. To use this script, you need to find the ticker symbol for the stock you're interested in beforehand.

```
from yahoo_fin import stock_info as si

# Start an infinite loop
❶ while True:
    # Obtain ticker symbol from you
```

```
  ticker = input("Which stock (ticker symbol) are you looking for?\n")
  # If you want to stop, type in "done"
❷ if ticker == "done":
      break
  # Otherwise, type in a stock ticker symbol
  else:
      # Obtain stock price from Yahoo!
    ❸ price = si.get_live_price(ticker)
      # Print out the stock price
      print(f"The stock price for {ticker} is {price}.")
```

Listing 14-1: Retrieving real-time stock prices

We import the *stock_info* module from the *yahoo_fin* package under the alias si. We then put the script in an infinite loop ❶ to continuously take your written input requesting stock ticker symbols. Whenever you want to stop the script, you can enter done ❷. Otherwise, the script automatically continues to obtain the latest stock price information for your requested company from Yahoo! Finance ❸. Finally, the script prints out the stock price information.

Here's the output from an exchange with the script, with user input in bold:

```
Which stock (ticker symbol) are you looking for?
MSFT
The stock price for MSFT is 183.25.

Which stock (ticker symbol) are you looking for?
AAPL
The stock price for AAPL is 317.94000244140625.

Which stock (ticker symbol) are you looking for?
done
```

As you can see, I entered ticker symbols for Microsoft and Apple (MSFT and AAPL, respectively), and the script returned their latest prices.

Notice that the price of the Apple stock has many digits after the decimal. We'll adjust the code a little later to show only two digits after the decimal for all stock prices.

TRY IT OUT

Run *live_price.py* and find the stock prices for Amazon (AMZN) and Tesla (TSLA). Then go to the website *https://finance.yahoo.com/* to check if the prices are close to your output.

For the script to work, you need the company's stock ticker symbol, such as MSFT or AAPL. You may wonder, what if I don't know the ticker symbols of the stocks that I'm interested in? Can Python find it if I know only the company name, such as Microsoft or Apple? The answer is yes, and this is when the web-scraping skills you learned in Chapter 6 become handy.

Find Ticker Symbols

Many times, you'll know the name of the company you're interested in but not its ticker symbol. This script will find the ticker symbol when you enter the name of the company. This is important because our end goal is to create voice-controlled applications in the financial market. It's relatively difficult for the Python script to pick up the ticker symbol via voice commands, but picking up the company name is much easier.

We need to first find a website that can reliably provide a company's ticker symbol. We'll use Yahoo! Finance and query the site using the URL *https://query1.finance.yahoo.com/v1/finance/search?q=* followed by the name of the company you want to query. For example, if you put *Bank of America* at the end, you'll get a set of Python-friendly data results, as shown in Figure 14-1.

{"explains":[],"count":18,"quotes":[{"exchange":"NYQ","shortname":"Bank of America Corporation","quoteType":"EQUITY","symbol":"BAC","index":"quotes","score":208707.0,"typeDisp":"Equity","longname":"Bank of America Corporation","isYahooFinance":true},{"exchange":"NYQ","shortname":"Bank of America Corporation Non","quoteType":"EQUITY","symbol":"BAC-PL","index":"quotes","score":20322.0,"typeDisp":"Equity","longname":"Bank of America Corporation","isYahooFinance":true},{"exchange":"NYQ","shortname":"Bank of America Corporation Dep","quoteType":"EQUITY","symbol":"BAC-PC","index":"quotes","score":20183.0,"typeDisp":"Equity","longname":"Bank of America Corporation","isYahooFinance":true},{"exchange":"NYQ","shortname":"Bank of America Corporation Dep","quoteType":"EQUITY","symbol":"BAC-PB","index":"quotes","score":20141.0,"typeDisp":"Equity","longname":"Bank of America Corporation","isYahooFinance":true},{"exchange":"NYQ","shortname":"Bank of America Corporation Inc","quoteType":"EQUITY","symbol":"MER-PK","index":"quotes","score":20095.0,"typeDisp":"Equity","longname":"Merrill Lynch Capital Trust I GTD CAP 6.45%","isYahooFinance":true},{"exchange":"NYQ","shortname":"Bank of America Corporation Dep","quoteType":"EQUITY","symbol":"BAC-PE","index":"quotes","score":20094.0,"typeDisp":"Equity","longname":"Bank of America Corporation","isYahooFinance":true},{"exchange":"NYQ","shortname":"Bank of America Corporation Ban","quoteType":"EQUITY","symbol":"BML-PL","index":"quotes","score":20081.0,"typeDisp":"Equity","longname":"Bank of America Corporation","isYahooFinance":true}],"news":[{"uuid":"018f2e3d-cd78-39a5-b97f-4e9508f6e4c3","title":"Get ready for a good earnings season for big U.S.

Figure 14-1: Results when you search for the ticker symbol for Bank of America

This data is formatted in *JSON*, short for *JavaScript Object Notation*. This file format is used for browser-server communication that uses human-readable text to store and transmit data objects. JSON was derived from JavaScript, but it's now a language-independent data format that's used by many programming languages, include Python.

To make the JSON data easier to read, we'll use the online JSON data formatter at *https://jsonformatter.curiousconcept.com/*. Open the URL and you'll see a screen similar to Figure 14-2.

Figure 14-2: A website to format JSON data

Paste the data from Figure 14-1 into the designated space and click **Process**. The formatter will convert the data into a much more readable format, shown in Listing 14-2.

```
{
    "explains":[

    ],
    "count":18,
    "quotes":[
        {
            "exchange":"NYQ",
            "shortname":"Bank of America Corporation",
            "quoteType":"EQUITY",
          ❶ "symbol":"BAC",
            "index":"quotes",
            "score":208707.0,
            "typeDisp":"Equity",
            "longname":"Bank of America Corporation",
            "isYahooFinance":true
        },
        {
            "exchange":"NYQ",
            "shortname":"Bank of America Corporation Non",
            "quoteType":"EQUITY",
            "symbol":"BAC-PL",
            "index":"quotes",
            "score":20322.0,
            "typeDisp":"Equity",
            "longname":"Bank of America Corporation",
            "isYahooFinance":true
        },
        {
            "exchange":"NYQ",
            "shortname":"Bank of America Corporation Dep",
```

```
        "quoteType":"EQUITY",
        "symbol":"BAC-PC",
        "index":"quotes",
        "score":20183.0,
        "typeDisp":"Equity",
        "longname":"Bank of America Corporation",
        "isYahooFinance":true
    },


--snip--
}
```

Listing 14-2: The formatted JSON data for the ticker symbol search

The dataset is a large dictionary of several elements with the key values explains, count, quotes, and so on. The value for the quotes key is a list of several dictionaries. The first dictionary contains the keys exchange, shortname, quoteType—and importantly, symbol, which contains the value BAC, the ticker symbol we need ❶.

Next, we use a Python script to extract the ticker symbol based on the preceding pattern. The script *get_ticker_symbol.py*, shown in Listing 14-3, accomplishes that.

```
import requests

# Start an infinite loop
❶ while True:
    # Obtain company name from you
    firm = input("Which company's ticker symbol are you looking for?\n")
    # If you want to stop, type in "done"
    if firm == "done":
        break
    # Otherwise, type in a company name
  ❷ else:
      ❸ try:
            # Extract the source code from the website
            url = 'https://query1.finance.yahoo.com/v1/finance/search?q='+firm
            response = requests.get(url)
            # Read the JSON data
            response_json = response.json()
            # Obtain the value corresponding to "quotes"
          ❹ quotes = response_json['quotes']
            # Get the ticker symbol
            ticker = quotes[0]['symbol']
            # Print out the ticker
            print(f"The ticker symbol for {firm} is {ticker}.")
        except:
            print("Sorry, not a valid entry!")
        continue
```

Listing 14-3: Finding a stock's ticker symbol based on the company name

We import the *requests* module, which allows Python to send HyperText Transfer Protocol (HTTP) requests. At ❶, we start an infinite loop that asks for your written input in each iteration. To exit the loop, enter done. Otherwise, you enter in the company name ❷. We use exception handling to prevent a crash ❸.

We go into the JSON data and extract the list corresponding to the key quotes ❹. We then go to the first element and look for the value corresponding to the key symbol. The script prints out the ticker symbol at the IPython console. If there are no results, the script will print Sorry, not a valid entry!.

Run the script a few times and search for several companies to check that it works. The following output is one interaction with the script:

```
Which company's ticker symbol are you looking for?
ford motor
The ticker symbol for ford motor is F.

Which company's ticker symbol are you looking for?
walt disney company
The ticker symbol for walt disney company is DIS.

Which company's ticker symbol are you looking for?
apple
The ticker symbol for apple is AAPL.

Which company's ticker symbol are you looking for?
done
```

As you can see, the script works for companies with one-word names, like Apple, as well as longer names, such as Walt Disney Company.

TRY IT OUT

Use *get_ticker_symbol.py* to find the ticker symbols for General Motors and Procter & Gamble.

Retrieve Stock Prices via Voice

Now we'll mesh together the scripts *live_price.py* and *get_ticker_symbol.py* and add in the speech recognition and text-to-speech features. Enter Listing 14-4 in a Spyder editor and save it as *live_price_hs.py* in your chapter folder, or download the script from the book's resources.

```
import requests
from yahoo_fin import stock_info as si

from mptpkg import voice_to_text, print_say
```

```
      # Start an infinite loop
❶ while True:
      # Obtain company name from you
      print_say("Which company's stock price do you want to know?")
      firm = voice_to_text()
      print_say(f"You just said {firm}.")
      # If you want to stop, type in "stop listening"
      if firm == "stop listening":
          print_say("OK, goodbye then!")
          break
      # Otherwise, say a company name
  ❷ else:
      try:
              # Extract the source code from the website
              url = 'https://query1.finance.yahoo.com/v1/finance/search?q='+firm
              response = requests.get(url)
              # Read the JSON data
              response_json = response.json()
              # Obtain the value corresponding to "quotes"
              quotes = response_json['quotes']
              # Get the ticker symbol
              ticker = quotes[0]['symbol']

              # Obtain live stock price from Yahoo!
          ❸ price = round(float(si.get_live_price(ticker)),2)
              # Speak the stock price
              print_say(f"The stock price for {firm} is {price}.")
      # In case the price cannot be found, the script will tell you
      except:
              print_say("Sorry, I cannot find what you are looking for!")
      continue
```

Listing 14-4: Use voice to retrieve real-time stock price

We now import print_say() and voice_to_text() from the local *mptpkg* package to add the text-to-speech and speech recognition features.

At ❶, we start an infinite loop that asks for your voice input. To exit the loop, you say, "Stop listening." Otherwise, you say a company name ❷, and the script searches for the ticker symbol. We use try and except here to prevent the script from crashing because of a lack of results from Yahoo! Finance.

We save the stock price from Yahoo! Finance in price ❸. Note that we use round() to round the stock price to two digits after the decimal. The script will speak the company's stock price or, if there are no results, will say, "Sorry, I cannot find what you are looking for!"

NOTE *While the result from the ticker symbol search in this script is relatively accurate, mistakes do happen. Be sure to say the company name in a clear enough way that the script returns the correct ticker symbol. For example, use "Ford Motor" instead of "Ford."*

Here's a sample interaction:

```
Which company's stock price do you want to know?
You just said JPMorgan Chase.
The stock price for JPMorgan Chase is 97.31.

Which company's stock price do you want to know?
You just said Goldman Sachs.
The stock price for Goldman Sachs is 196.49.

Which company's stock price do you want to know?
You just said stop listening.
OK, goodbye then!
```

TRY IT OUT

Use *live_price_hs.py* to find out the latest stock price for Johnson & Johnson and McDonald's.

Voice-Controlled Data Visualization

One efficient way to analyze data—for example, to find patterns in stock movements—is through data visualization. *Data visualization* puts data into visual contexts such as plots and charts to make it easy for human brains to understand.

The price you obtained in the first project of this chapter is the latest price for the stock. That is, you have one data point for each stock you query. However, in order to learn more about a stock, it's better to obtain a number of recent prices for the stock so that you can get a sense of velocity and direction. Is the stock staying at about the same value, rising, or falling? If the price is changing, how rapid is this change?

In this project, you'll obtain recent daily stock price information from Yahoo! Finance. You'll then plot a graph to see the price movements over time. You'll also learn to create candlestick charts so that you can see intraday stock movement patterns. With that set up, we'll add the speech recognition and text-to-speech features.

Create Stock Price Plots

We'll use the *pandas_datareader* module with *matplotlib* to create plots for stock prices over the last six months. First you'll learn how to extract data, and then you'll learn how to create plots.

Before we begin, you need to install a few third-party modules. Go to your Anaconda prompt (in Windows) or a terminal (in Mac or Linux) and activate the virtual *chatting* environment. Then run the following lines of code one by one:

```
conda install pandas
conda install matplotlib
pip install pandas_datareader
```

Follow the instructions to finish the installations. The *pandas_datareader* module extracts online data from various sources into a *pandas* DataFrame. Then enter Listing 14-5 in your Spyder editor and save the script as *price_plot.py* in your chapter folder.

```
import matplotlib.pyplot as plt
from pandas_datareader import data as pdr
import matplotlib.dates as mdates

# Set the start and end dates
❶ start_date = "2020-09-01"
end_date = "2021-02-28"

# Choose stock ticker symbol
❷ ticker = "TSLA"
# Get stock price
❸ stock = pdr.get_data_yahoo(ticker, start=start_date, end=end_date)
print(stock)
# Obtain dates
❹ stock['Date']=stock.index.map(mdates.date2num)
# Choose figure size
❺ fig = plt.figure(dpi=128, figsize=(10, 6))
# Format date to place on the x-axis
❻ formatter = mdates.DateFormatter('%m/%d/%Y')
plt.gca().xaxis.set_major_formatter(formatter)
# Plot data
❼ plt.plot(stock['Date'], stock['Adj Close'], c='blue')
# Format plot
❽ plt.title("The Stock Price of Tesla", fontsize=16)
plt.xlabel('Date', fontsize=10)
fig.autofmt_xdate()
plt.ylabel("Price", fontsize=10)
❾ plt.show()
```

Listing 14-5: The script to create a stock price plot

We import the modules, then specify the start and end dates of the data we want to extract ❶. These will be hardcoded for now; we'll make the dates dynamic later. The dates should be in the format *YYYY-MM-DD*. In this case, we'll use the six-month period from September 1, 2020, to February 28, 2021. We also provide the ticker symbol of the stock—in this case, Tesla with the ticker symbol TSLA ❷.

We use get_data_yahoo() in the *pandas_datareader* module to extract daily stock price information and save the data as a *pandas* DataFrame named stock ❸. The dataset looks like this:

	High	Low	...	Volume	Adj Close
Date			...		
2020-09-01	502.489990	470.510010	...	90119400	475.049988
2020-09-02	479.040009	405.119995	...	96176100	447.369995
2020-09-03	431.799988	402.000000	...	87596100	407.000000
2020-09-04	428.000000	372.019989	...	110321900	418.320007
2020-09-08	368.739990	329.880005	...	115465700	330.209991
...	...	... ...		...	...
2021-02-22	768.500000	710.200012	...	37269700	714.500000
2021-02-23	713.609985	619.000000	...	66606900	698.840027
2021-02-24	745.000000	694.169983	...	36767000	742.020020
2021-02-25	737.210022	670.580017	...	39023900	682.219971
2021-02-26	706.700012	659.510010	...	41011300	675.500000

```
[123 rows x 6 columns]
```

The dataset uses dates as indexes. The 123 rows represent the 123 trading days during the six-month period. The six columns represent the following information in each trading day: high price, low price, open price, closing price, trading volume, and adjusted closing price.

We then read the timestamp index of the dataset as a number and save it as an additional (seventh) column ❹. This step is necessary because the dataset doesn't recognize the index as a separate variable, but we need the date information to use as our x-axis in the charts. We then use the figure() function in *matplotlib.pyplot* to specify the size and resolution of the plot and name the generated figure fig ❺. The dpi=128 argument makes the output 128 pixels per inch. The figsize=(10,6) argument sets the plot 10 inches wide and 6 inches tall.

NOTE *DPI stands for (printer) dots per inch from predigital days. Nowadays, it actually stands for pixels per inch, so DPI is a bit of a misnomer.*

We use the DateFormatter() method from *matplotlib.dates* to specify the format of the dates we want to show ❻. We do the actual plotting by using plot() ❼. The first two arguments are the variables to use on the x- and y-axis, respectively. We also use a third argument to specify the color. In this case, we plot the adjusted closing price against the date and use blue as the color.

NOTE *The adjusted closing price is the closing price adjusted for stock splits and cash dividends. In many cases, it's identical to the unadjusted closing price. When it differs, it is a more accurate measure of total returns to investors since it takes into account both dividend yields and capital gains.*

Starting at ❽, we put a title on the graph and label the x- and y-axis. We also use autofxt_xdate() to show the dates on the x-axis diagonally to prevent overlapping text.

Finally, show() is called to display the plot ❾. Figure 14-3 shows the output.

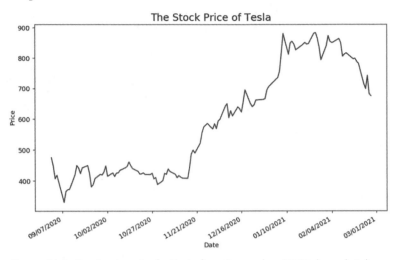

Figure 14-3: Stock price plot for Tesla from September 2020 through February 2021

We can see the price movement patterns of Tesla over the six-month period. The stock was at less than $500 per share in early September 2020 but shot up to over $800 per share in late December, before dropping slightly in mid-February. This visualization is much more reader-friendly (and informative) than the stock DataFrame output earlier!

NOTE *In case you can't locate the generated plot, the plots and charts appear in the Plots pane in the Spyder IDE. You may need to click the Plots tab to see them.*

TRY IT OUT

Run *price_plot.py* and generate a stock price plot for Facebook (ticker symbol FB) from September 1, 2020 to February 28, 2021.

Create Candlestick Charts

Price plots are great for summarizing patterns using one observation per day. Sometimes you're interested in several intraday price movements, such as the range of the price fluctuation in a given day, whether the closing price is higher or lower than the opening price, and so on. With *candlestick charts*, you can visualize four pieces of information each day for a stock: daily high, daily low, opening price, and closing price.

The following script generates the candlestick chart for Amazon stock in the month of February 2021. I don't recommend plotting stock prices from more than one month because the chart may become too crowded, making it hard to detect patterns.

First, you need to install the third-party *mplfinance* module. Open your Anaconda prompt (in Windows) or a terminal (in Mac or Linux), activate the virtual environment *chatting*, and run the following command:

```
pip install mplfinance
```

Then open your Spyder editor and save Listing 14-6 as *candle_stick.py* in your chapter folder.

```
import matplotlib.pyplot as plt
from pandas_datareader import data as pdr
import matplotlib.dates as mdates
from mplfinance.original_flavor import candlestick_ohlc

# Set the start and end date
start_date = "2021-02-01"
end_date = "2021-02-28"
# Choose stock ticker symbol
ticker = "AMZN"
# Get stock price
stock = pdr.get_data_yahoo(ticker, start=start_date, end=end_date)
# Obtain dates
stock['Date'] = stock.index.map(mdates.date2num)
# Choose the four daily prices: open, high, low, and close
❶ df_ohlc = stock[['Date','Open', 'High', 'Low', 'Close']]
# Choose figure size
figure, fig = plt.subplots(dpi=128, figsize = (8,4))
# Format dates
formatter = mdates.DateFormatter('%m/%d/%Y')
# Choose x-axis
fig.xaxis.set_major_formatter(formatter)
fig.xaxis_date()
❷ plt.setp(fig.get_xticklabels(), rotation = 10)
# Create the candlestick chart
❸ candlestick_ohlc(fig,
                   df_ohlc.values,
                   width=0.8,
                   colorup='black',
                   colordown='gray')
# Put text in the chart that black color means close > open
❹ plt.figtext(0.3,0.2,'Black: Close > Open')
# Put text in the chart that gray color means close < open
plt.figtext(0.3,0.15,'Gray: Close < Open')
# Put chart title and axis labels
❺ plt.title(f'Candlesticks Chart for {ticker}')
plt.ylabel('Price')
plt.xlabel('Date')
plt.show()
```

Listing 14-6: The script to create a candlestick chart

We import all needed modules and functions, including the `candlestick_ohlc()` function from the *mplfinance* module that we'll use to create the candlestick chart.

At ❶, we select the four daily prices that we want to extract and visualize in the chart: opening price, daily high, daily low, and closing price.

The `setp()` function from *matplotlib* sets object properties, and we invoke it to rotate the dates on the x-axis ❷. We pass two arguments (the first to obtain the x-axis label and the second to set the property) to rotate the x-axis label 10 degrees, so text doesn't overlap. At ❸, we use `candlestick_ohlc()` to generate the candlestick chart. The first argument specifies where to place the chart, and the second specifies the data to use. The third argument is the width of the candle body relative to the distance between two observations (the distance on the x-axis between two trading days).

The candlestick chart uses colors to convey additional data. We use black to indicate that the closing price is higher than the opening price; otherwise, the value is gray. The information is also conveyed in the legend ❹. Finally, we give the chart a title and label the two axes ❺.

The candlestick chart for Amazon stock prices in February 2021 is shown in Figure 14-4. The blank spaces in the chart are non-trading days (weekends and holidays).

The daily high and daily low are at the ends of the thin lines (which look like candle wicks), while the opening and closing prices are at the ends of the wide lines (which look like candle bodies). Hence the name!

From this, we can quickly see that, on February 1, the price jumped up: the body of the candle spans nearly $100 and is colored black. Compare this to the following day, where, although the thin line is relatively long, the candle body is short, showing that despite fluctuations, it closed at nearly the same price that it opened at.

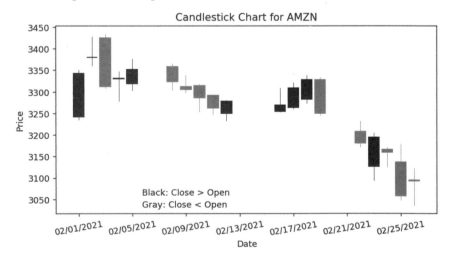

Figure 14-4: A candlestick chart for Amazon daily stock prices in February 2021

Add Voice Control

Let's add the speech functionality. When you say the company name, the script will search for the ticker symbol of the firm's stock, retrieve daily price information, and display the plot or chart. We first need to create two local modules: one to display stock price plots and one to show candlestick charts.

The Price Plot Module

We'll create a stock price plot module based on *price_plot.py*. Enter Listing 14-7 in your Spyder editor and save it as *myplot.py*.

```python
--snip--
from datetime import date, timedelta

from mptpkg import print_say

❶ def price_plot(firm):
    try:
        # Extract the source code from the website
      ❷ url = 'https://query1.finance.yahoo.com/v1/finance/search?q='+firm
        response = requests.get(url)
        # Read the JSON data
        response_json = response.json()
        # Obtain the value corresponding to "quotes"
        quotes = response_json['quotes']
        # Get the ticker symbol
        ticker = quotes[0]['symbol']
        # Set the start and end date
      ❸ end_date = date.today().strftime("%Y-%m-%d")
        start_date = (date.today() - timedelta(days=180)).strftime("%Y-%m-%d")
        # Get stock price
        stock = pdr.get_data_yahoo(ticker, start=start_date, end=end_date)
        # Obtain dates
        stock['Date']=stock.index.map(mdates.date2num)
        # Choose figure size
      ❹ fig = plt.figure(dpi=128, figsize=(10, 6))
        # Format date to place on the x-axis
        formatter = mdates.DateFormatter('%m/%d/%Y')
        plt.gca().xaxis.set_major_formatter(formatter)
        # Plot data
        plt.plot(stock['Date'], stock['Adj Close'], c='blue')
        # Format plot
        plt.title\
        (f"The Stock Price of {firm} in the Last Six Months", fontsize=16)
```

```
        plt.xlabel('Date', fontsize=10)
        fig.autofmt_xdate()
        plt.ylabel("Price", fontsize=10)
        plt.show()
        # Let you know that the plot is ready via voice and print
    ❺ print_say(f"OK, here is the stock price plot for {firm}.")
    except:
        print_say("Sorry, not a valid entry!")
```

Listing 14-7: The script for the stock plot module

We import the modules, including those we used to plot stock prices and to parse the HTML source file to find the firm's ticker symbol. We also import the print_say() function from the local *mptpkg* package.

At ❶, we start stock_plot(), which takes the company name as the argument. We again use try and except to prevent crashes. We first find the ticker symbol of the firm ❷.

Here we make the price information dynamic ❸. The end date is today's date, while the start date is six months ago. The script will generate a plot ❹ and then tell you the plot is ready ❺. If the ticker symbol or the price information can't be found, the script will print and say, "Sorry, not a valid entry!"

The Candlestick Chart Module

Next we'll create the candlestick chart module. Open *mychart.py* from the book's resources, as shown in Listing 14-8.

```
from mplfinance.original_flavor import candlestick_ohlc
from mptpkg import print_say
from datetime import date, timedelta
--snip--
❶ def candle_stick(firm):

--snip--
        # Set the start and end date
        start_date = (date.today() - timedelta(days=14)).strftime("%Y-%m-%d")
        end_date = date.today().strftime("%Y-%m-%d")
--snip--
        # Choose the four daily prices: open, high, low, and close
    ❷ df_ohlc = stock[['Date','Open', 'High', 'Low', 'Close']]
        # Choose figure size
        figure, fig = plt.subplots(dpi=128, figsize = (8,4))
--snip--
        plt.show()
    ❸ print_say(f"Here is the candlestick chart for {firm}.")
--snip--
    except:
        print_say("Sorry, not a valid entry!")
```

Listing 14-8: The script to create the candlestick chart module

We import the modules, including the candlestick_ohlc() function from the *mplfinance* module.

We define `candle_stick()` at ❶. Here we make the price information dynamic. The end date is today's date, while the start date is two weeks ago. We then perform the same actions as in *myplot.py* to search for the ticker symbol. With the ticker symbol, we retrieve the daily stock price information in the past 14 days from Yahoo! Finance. I've snipped this part of the script to save space.

The data used for the candlestick chart will be the date plus the opening price, daily high and low prices, and closing price ❷. The script builds the candlestick chart and lets you know when it's done ❸.

The Main Script

Next, we'll import the two modules to the main script so that we can voice-activate a stock price plot or a candlestick chart. Enter Listing 14-9 in your Spyder editor and save it as *plot_chart_hs.py* in your chapter folder.

```
from myplot import price_plot
from mychart import candle_stick
from mptpkg import voice_to_text, print_say

# Start an infinite loop
❶ while True:
    # Obtain voice input from you
    print_say("How may I help you?")
    inp = voice_to_text()
    print_say(f"You said {inp}.")
    # If you want to stop, say "stop listening"
❷   if "stop listening" in inp:
        print_say("Nice talking to you, goodbye!")
        break
    # If "price pattern for" in voice, activate plot functionality
❸   elif "price pattern for" in inp:
        pos = inp.find('price pattern for ')
        firm = inp[pos+len('price pattern for '):]
        price_plot(firm)
        continue
    # If "candlestick chart for" in voice, activate chart functionality
❹   elif "chart for" in inp:
        pos = inp.find('chart for ')
        firm = inp[pos+len('chart for '):]
        candle_stick(firm)
        continue
    # Otherwise, go to the next iteration
    else:
        continue
```

Listing 14-9: The script to voice-control plot and chart creation

We import the modules and add the `print_say()` and `voice_to_text()` functions. We also import `price_plot()` from the local *myplot* module and `candle_stick()` from the local *mychart* module that we just created.

At ❶, we start an infinite loop that asks for your voice input. To exit the script, you say, "Stop listening" ❷. To see the stock plot of a firm (say, Goldman Sachs), you say, "Stock pattern for Goldman Sachs." The "stock pattern for" will trigger the stock plot functionality ❸. We use "stock pattern" instead of "stock plot" because it's easier for the microphone to pick up. The script then extracts the company name, which is Goldman Sachs in this case, and uses it as the argument in the price_plot() function.

To see the candlestick chart of a firm (say, General Motors), you say, "Chart for General Motors." The "chart for" part of the voice command will trigger the candlestick chart functionality ❹. The script then extracts the company name and uses it as the argument in the candle_stick() function.

NOTE *Depending on your operating system, you may want to change the trigger words in the script. For example, if the microphone can't pick up "Stop listening," you can change it to* stop *or* stop running.

Here's my sample output:

```
How may I help you?
You said price pattern for Oracle.
OK, here is the stock price plot for Oracle.

How may I help you?
You said chart for Intel.
Here is the candlestick chart for Intel.

How may I help you?
You said stop listening.
Nice talking to you, goodbye!
```

The "price pattern for Oracle" phrase triggered the price plot functionality, and the script generated the price plot for Oracle, shown in Figure 14-5.

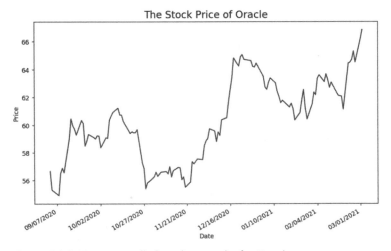

Figure 14-5: Voice-controlled stock price plot for Oracle

The "chart for Intel" phrase prompted the script to create a candlestick chart for Intel, shown in Figure 14-6.

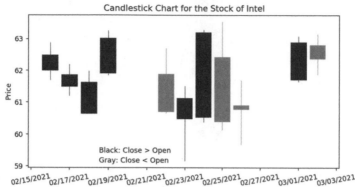

Figure 14-6: Voice-controlled candlestick chart for Intel

Voice-Controlled Stock Report

While the price plots and candlestick charts allow us to see recent price movements, they don't give us information on how a stock has performed relative to the general market. Many times, investors are interested in how well a stock has performed in comparison to a benchmark index. They're also interested in the risk of a stock, measured in how volatile a stock's price has been relative to the market as a whole.

To that end, we'll progress to a more detailed analysis of a stock's price. You'll obtain recent daily stock price information and perform regression analyses to figure out the recent performance and market risk of the stock. You'll calculate the stock's abnormal return (*alpha*, which is the relative performance of the stock compared to the market as a whole) and the market risk (*beta*, which measures how volatile the stock's return has been compared to the market as a whole) by running a regression of the stock's return on the market return.

NOTE *For detailed explanations of alpha and beta of stock, see, for example, the relevant articles on Wikipedia:* https://en.wikipedia.org/wiki/Alpha_(finance) *and* https://en.wikipedia.org/wiki/Beta_(finance).

Analyze Recent Stock Performance and Risk

You'll use the same methods we've used so far to extract recent daily stock price information from Yahoo! Finance using the *pandas_datareader* module. You'll then use a new module *statsmodels* to perform statistical analyses.

First, we'll install the third-party module and extract data. Go to your Anaconda prompt (in Windows) or a terminal (in Mac or Linux) and activate the virtual *chatting* environment. Then run the following command:

```
conda install statsmodels
```

Enter Listing 14-10 in your Spyder editor and save the script as *alpha _beta.py* in your chapter folder.

```
from datetime import date, timedelta

import statsmodels.api as sm
from pandas_datareader import data as pdr

# Set the start and end dates
end_date = date.today().strftime("%Y-%m-%d")
start_date = (date.today() - timedelta(days=180)).strftime("%Y-%m-%d")
market = "^GSPC"
ticker = "MSFT"
# Retrieve prices
sp = pdr.get_data_yahoo(market, start=start_date, end=end_date)
stock = pdr.get_data_yahoo(ticker, start=start_date, end=end_date)
# Calculate returns for sp500 and the stock
sp['ret_sp'] = (sp['Adj Close']/sp['Adj Close'].shift(1))-1
stock['ret_stock'] = (stock['Adj Close']/stock['Adj Close'].shift(1))-1
# Merge the two datasets, keep only returns
df = sp[['ret_sp']].merge(stock[['ret_stock']],\
        left_index=True, right_index=True)

# Add risk-free rate (assume constant for simplicity)
❶ df['rf'] = 0.00001
# We need a constant to run regressions
df['const'] = 1
df['exret_stock'] = df.ret_stock - df.rf
df['exret_sp'] = df.ret_sp - df.rf
# Remove missing values
df.dropna(inplace=True)
# Calculate the stock's alpha and beta
❷ reg = sm.OLS(endog=df['exret_stock'],\
            exog=df[['const', 'exret_sp']], missing='drop')
results = reg.fit()
print(results.summary())
❸ alpha = round(results.params['const']*100,3)
beta = round(results.params['exret_sp'],2)
# Print the values of alpha and beta
print(f'The alpha of the stock of {ticker} is {alpha} percent.')
print(f'The beta of the stock of {ticker} is {beta}.')
```

Listing 14-10: The script to calculate stock alpha and beta

We import the modules and then specify the start and end dates of the data you want to extract. We again use the most recent six-month period. We also provide the ticker symbols of the market index, which is an index that represents the market as a whole. The S&P 500 Index is often used, and that is what we will use. The company we'll analyze is Microsoft Corporation. We use the get_data_yahoo() method in the *pandas_datareader* module to extract daily stock price information for the market index and Microsoft, and we save the data as two *pandas* DataFrames named sp and stock, respectively.

We then calculate the daily stock returns for both the S&P 500 and Microsoft. The shift() method in *pandas* allows us to shift the index by a desired number of periods. We use shift(1) to obtain the price information of the previous trading day. This allows us to see how today compared to yesterday. Comparing the two days enables us to calculate returns. The *gross return* is the current value divided by the value at the close of the previous trading day, and the *net return* is the gross return minus one.

To calculate alpha and beta, we first merge the two datasets into one. For simplicity, we use a small constant value for the risk-free rate ❶. We then use the OLS() method in the *statsmodels* module to run a regression ❷ and print out the regression results. The alpha and beta we want are the regression coefficients on the constant and the excess return on the market, respectively ❸.

Figure 14-7 shows the regression results.

```
                         OLS Regression Results
==============================================================================
Dep. Variable:            exret_stock   R-squared:                       0.856
Model:                            OLS   Adj. R-squared:                  0.855
Method:                 Least Squares   F-statistic:                     722.1
Date:                Tue, 09 Jun 2020   Prob (F-statistic):           7.66e-53
Time:                        04:04:05   Log-Likelihood:                 362.37
No. Observations:                 123   AIC:                            -720.7
Df Residuals:                     121   BIC:                            -715.1
Df Model:                           1
Covariance Type:            nonrobust
==============================================================================
                 coef    std err          t      P>|t|      [0.025      0.975]
------------------------------------------------------------------------------
const          0.0020      0.001      1.751      0.082      -0.000       0.004
exret_sp       1.1013      0.041     26.873      0.000       1.020       1.182
==============================================================================
Omnibus:                        0.497   Durbin-Watson:                   1.890
Prob(Omnibus):                  0.780   Jarque-Bera (JB):                0.190
Skew:                           0.054   Prob(JB):                        0.909
Kurtosis:                       3.159   Cond. No.                         35.5
==============================================================================

Warnings:
[1] Standard Errors assume that the covariance matrix of the errors is correctly
specified.
```

Figure 14-7: Regression analysis results for Microsoft

Finally, we print out the values of the firm's alpha and beta as follows:

```
The alpha of the stock MSFT is 0.202 percent.
The beta of the stock MSFT is 1.1.
```

The analysis shows that the alpha and beta are 0.202 percent and 1.1, respectively. This means Microsoft has outperformed similar stocks on the market by 0.202 percent per day, and the company has a market risk slightly greater than an average firm (which has a beta of 1), which means the stock's return has been slightly more volatile than the market as a whole.

Add Voice Control

Let's add the voice control! You'll ask about a company, and the script will search for the ticker symbol, retrieve daily stock information, and calculate the alpha and beta. Then the script will let you know that information by voice. The phrase "stock report for" will trigger the stock report functionality.

Enter Listing 14-11 in your Spyder editor and save the script as *alpha_beta_hs.py* in your chapter folder.

```
from datetime import date, timedelta
import statsmodels.api as sm
from pandas_datareader import data as pdr
import requests

from mptpkg import voice_to_text, print_say

❶ def alpha_beta(firm):
    try:
        # Extract the source code from the website
      ❷ url = 'https://query1.finance.yahoo.com/v1/finance/search?q='+firm
        response = requests.get(url)
        # Read the JSON data
        response_json = response.json()
        # Obtain the value corresponding to "quotes"
        quotes = response_json['quotes']
        # Get the ticker symbol
        ticker = quotes[0]['symbol']
--snip--
        # Speak the values of alpha and beta
      ❸ print_say(f'The alpha of the stock of {firm} is {alpha} percent.')
        print_say(f'The beta of the stock of {firm} is {beta}.')

    # Start an infinite loop
❹ while True:
    # Obtain voice input from you
    print_say("How may I help you?")
    inp = voice_to_text()
    print_say(f"You said {inp}.")
    # If you want to stop, say "stop listening"
    if inp == "stop listening":
        print_say("Nice talking to you; goodbye!")
        break
    # If keywords in command, go to the stock report functionality
    elif "stock report for" in inp:
        # Locate the company name
        pos = inp.find('stock report for ')
      ❺ firm = inp[pos+len('stock report for '):]
        alpha_beta(firm)
        continue
    # Otherwise, go to the next iteration
    else:
        continue
```

Listing 14-11: Voice-control the calculation of stock alpha and beta

We import the modules, including the *requests* module and the print_say() and voice_to_text() functions.

At ❶, we start the definition of alpha_beta(), using the firm name as its argument. As before, we use the plus sign to join words together to use as search terms for the ticker symbol on Yahoo! Finance ❷. We use try and except to prevent crashes and let the user know if the entry is invalid. The script then calculates the firm's alpha and beta, as it does in *alpha_beta.py*, and both prints and speaks the alpha and beta ❸.

At ❹, we start an infinite loop that asks for your voice input. To exit the script, say, "Stop listening." Otherwise, you say, "Stock report for" followed by the company name to activate the stock report functionality. The script extracts the company name from your voice command and prepares the report for you ❺.

Here's my sample interaction:

```
How may I help you?
You said stock report for alibaba.
The alpha of the stock alibaba is 0.059 percent.
The beta of the stock alibaba is 0.61.

How may I help you?
You said stop listening.
Nice talking to you; goodbye!
```

I asked for the "stock report for Alibaba," and the script obtained the report for me and replied, "The alpha of Alibaba is 0.059 percent; the beta of the stock Alibaba is 0.61."

TRY IT OUT

Use *alpha_beta_hs.py* to obtain a stock report for British Petroleum.

Summary

In this chapter, you applied the speech recognition and text-to-speech techniques to the financial market. These skills—scraping information, forming search terms that can be used in URLs, and retrieving real-time as well as recent daily stock price information—can be applied to a huge variety of web applications. You also learned a few data analysis and visualization skills, which are also handy for many applications.

In the next chapter, you'll create talking graphical market watches for financial markets such as the US stock market or the foreign exchange market.

End-of-Chapter Exercises

1. Modify *price_plot.py* so that the start and end dates are March 1, 2021 and June 1, 2021, respectively, and the plot color is red.

2. Modify *candle_stick.py* so that the dates on the x-axis are in the format of 01-01-2021 (instead of 01/01/2021 or January 1, 2021) and rotated 15 degrees.

15

STOCK MARKET WATCH

In this chapter, you'll create a graphical, speaking app that monitors the US stock market in real time. When you run the script during trading hours, you'll see a graphical display of the major stock indexes and a couple of stocks you select. The app also lets you know the values of the indexes and the stock prices in a human voice.

To build up the necessary skills, you'll first create a graphical Bitcoin watch to display live price information, using the Python *tkinter* package. You can generalize these techniques to other financial markets such as the world stock market or the US Treasury bond market.

As always, all scripts are available through the book's resources page at *https://www.nostarch.com/make-python-talk/*, and you should make the folder */mpt/ch15/* for this chapter.

NEW SKILLS

- Retrieving live Bitcoin prices
- Using and manipulating JSON data
- Making widgets and animations using the *tkinter* package
- Generalizing these techniques to other financial markets

Bitcoin Watch

We'll start with Bitcoin because the Bitcoin price is updated 24/7, unlike the stock market, which gives live price updates only when it's open. In the process of creating a Bitcoin watch, you'll learn the necessary skills to build a market watch for other financial markets. The script tells you whenever the Bitcoin price changes or if the price moves outside preset upper or lower bounds.

You'll first learn how to read JSON data and some basics of the *tkinter* package.

How to Read JSON Data

Bitcoin prices are available online for free and are updated every minute or so day and night. We'll access Bitcoin prices through Python by using the API *https://api.coindesk.com/v1/bpi/currentprice.json*. Open the URL with a web browser, and you should see price information similar to Figure 15-1.

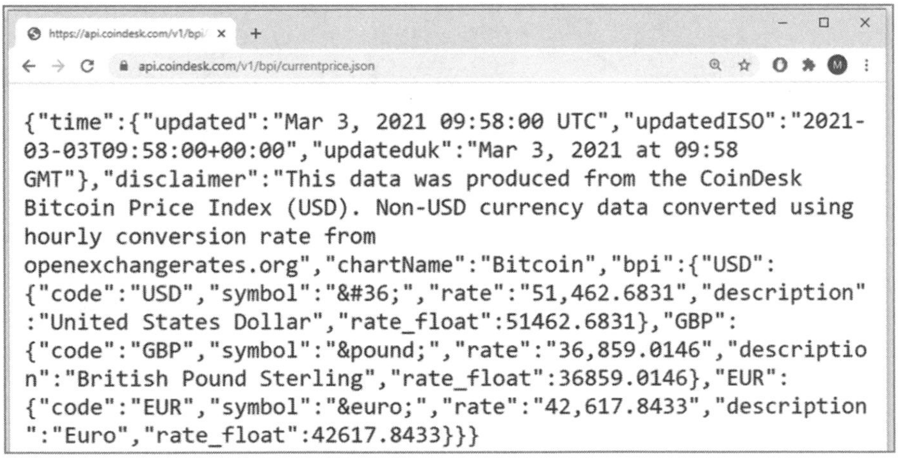

Figure 15-1: Live online information about Bitcoin price

This data is formatted in JSON and hard to read. There are so many nested dictionaries, it's hard to tell where one dictionary starts and ends. We discussed in Chapter 14 how to make the data easier to understand by using an online JSON data formatter.

Similar to what you did in that chapter, go to the online JSON data formatter website, *https://jsonformatter.curiousconcept.com/*, paste the data from Figure 15-1 into the designated space, and then click **Process**. The formatter will convert the data into a much more readable format, shown in Listing 15-1.

```
{
  ❶ "time":{
      "updated":"Mar 3, 2021 09:58:00 UTC",
      "updatedISO":"2021-03-03T09:58:00+00:00",
      "updateduk":"Mar 3, 2021 at 09:58 GMT"
  },
  ❷ "disclaimer":"This data was produced from the CoinDesk
    Bitcoin Price Index (USD). Non-USD currency data converted
    using hourly conversion rate from openexchangerates.org",
  ❸ "chartName":"Bitcoin",
  ❹ "bpi":{
      "USD":{
        "code":"USD",
        "symbol":"&#36;",
        "rate":"51,462.6831",
        "description":"United States Dollar",
        "rate_float":51462.6831
      },
      "GBP":{
        "code":"GBP",
        "symbol":"&pound;",
        "rate":"36,859.0146",
        "description":"British Pound Sterling",
        "rate_float":36859.0146
      },
      "EUR":{
        "code":"EUR",
        "symbol":"&euro;",
        "rate":"42,617.8433",
        "description":"Euro",
        "rate_float":42617.8433
      }
  }
}
```

Listing 15-1: The formatted JSON data about the Bitcoin price

The dataset is a large dictionary of four elements with keys named time ❶, disclaimer ❷, chartName ❸, and bpi ❹. The value for the bpi key is, in turn, another dictionary with three keys: USD, GBP, and EUR. These represent the Bitcoin price in US dollars, British pounds, and Euros, respectively.

We want the Bitcoin price in US dollars. The script *bitcoin_price.py*, shown in Listing 15-2, retrieves the Bitcoin price and prints it out.

```
import requests

# Specify the url to find the bitcoin price
url = 'https://api.coindesk.com/v1/bpi/currentprice.json'
# Retrieve the live information from bitcoin url
response = requests.get(url)
# Read the JSON data
response_json = response.json()
# Obtain the USD dictionary
usd = response_json['bpi']['USD']
# Get the price
price = usd['rate_float']
print(f"The Bitcoin price is {price} dollars.")
```

Listing 15-2: The script to retrieve the Bitcoin price

We import the *requests* module and specify the URL for the live Bitcoin price. We then use the get() method from the *requests* module to pull the data from the API. The json() method in the *requests* module reads the information into JSON format. We then extract the USD dictionary that contains all the Bitcoin price information in US dollars. The value we need from the dictionary is the price, and we use the rate_float key to retrieve it.

Finally, we print out the Bitcoin price. The output should be something like this:

```
The Bitcoin price is 51462.6831 dollars.
```

TRY IT OUT

Run *bitcoin_price.py* and compare the result to a Google search for the current Bitcoin price.

A Quick Introduction to the tkinter Package

Python's default standard package for building a GUI is *tkinter*, short for *Tk interface*. The *tkinter* package has a variety of *widgets*, which are various tools like buttons, labels, entries, and message boxes. Widgets appear as different types of small windows inside the top-level root window, but they can also be stand-alone entities. We'll focus on labels since we'll use them in the market watch projects.

NOTE   *For more information about Tk and* tkinter, *visit* https://docs.python.org/3/library/tkinter.html.

The *tkinter* package is in the Python standard library and needs no installation. If you are using Linux and encounter the `ModuleNotFoundError` when importing *tkinter*, execute this line of command in a terminal to install it:

```
sudo apt-get install python3-tk
```

I'll introduce you to the basics of *tkinter*, including how to set up a screen and create a label widget. The script *tk_label.py*, shown in Listing 15-3, sets up a screen and adds a label to it.

```
import tkinter as tk

# Create the root window
root = tk.Tk()
# Specify the title and size of the root window
root.title("A Label Inside a Root Window")
root.geometry("800x200")
# Create a label inside the root window
label = tk.Label(text="this is a label", fg="Red", font=("Helvetica", 80))
label.pack()
# Run the game loop
root.mainloop()
```

Listing 15-3: Create a label in the tkinter *package*

We import the *tkinter* package. We set up a root window, which is used to hold all the widgets we'll add to the script. We use the command `Tk()` and name the root window root.

Labels are a simple form of widget used to display messages or images for informational purposes. We give the root window a title, `A Label Inside a Root Window`, which will appear in the title bar. We call the `geometry()` method to specify the width and height of the root window as 800 by 200 pixels.

We initiate a label by using `Label()`, which takes the text (or image) you want to display. You can optionally specify the color and font too. We use red and set the font to `("Helvetica", 80)`.

With the `pack()` method, we specify where we want to put the label. The default is to line up widgets starting from the top center of the root window. Finally, `mainloop()` starts the game loop so that the window shows up and stays on your computer screen.

Run the script and you should see Figure 15-2.

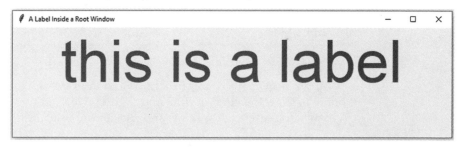

Figure 15-2: A label inside the root window in tkinter

A Graphical Bitcoin Watch

Now we'll create a graphical Bitcoin watch by using the *tkinter* package. Open your Spyder editor and save the code in Listing 15-4 as *bitcoin_tk.py* in your chapter folder.

```
import tkinter as tk
import requests

❶ import arrow

  # Specify the url to find the Bitcoin price
  url = 'https://api.coindesk.com/v1/bpi/currentprice.json'
  # Create a root window to hold all widgets
❷ root = tk.Tk()
  # Specify the title and size of the root window
  root.title("Bitcoin Watch")
  root.geometry("1000x400")
  # Create a first label using the Label() function
❸ label = tk.Label(text="", fg="Blue", font=("Helvetica", 80))
  label.pack()
  # Create a second label
  label2 = tk.Label(text="", fg="Red", font=("Helvetica", 60))
  label2.pack()

  # Define the bitcoin_watch() function
❹ def bitcoin_watch():
      # Get the live information from Bitcoin url
      response = requests.get(url)
      response_json = response.json()
      price = response_json['bpi']['USD']['rate_float']
      # Obtain current date and time information
      tdate = arrow.now().format('MMMM DD, YYYY')
      tm = arrow.now().format('hh:mm:ss A')
      # Put the date and time information in the first label
    ❺ label.configure(text=tdate + "\n" + tm)
      # Put price info in the second label
      label2.configure(text=f'Bitcoin: {price}', justify=tk.LEFT)
      # Call the bitcoin_watch() function after 1000 milliseconds
    ❻ root.after(1000, bitcoin_watch)

  # Call the bitcoin_watch() function
  bitcoin_watch()

  # Run the game loop
  root.mainloop()
```

Listing 15-4: Create a graphical Bitcoin price watch

We import the necessary functions and modules, including the *arrow* module to show the current time and date ❶. We then use the Tk() method to create a top-level root window and specify the title and the size ❷.

We create two labels using Label() ❸. We first leave the messages in both labels as empty strings because this information will fill in from the Bitcoin watch. At ❹, we define bitcoin_watch(). The function first uses the *requests* module to obtain the Bitcoin price information from the URL we provide. We also obtain the current date and time and save them in the variables tdate and tm, respectively.

At ❺, we put the current date and time information in the first label, using the escape character \n to separate the lines. We put the live Bitcoin price in the second label.

Next we set animation effects ❻. We use after() to call another function after a specified amount of time. The command after(1000, bitcoin_watch) calls the function bitcoin_watch() after 1,000 milliseconds. Calling the command within the bitcoin_watch() function itself creates an infinite loop in which all the command lines inside bitcoin_watch() will be executed every 1,000 milliseconds. The result is that the time is constantly updated, and you can see the time value changes every second. If you keep the screen live long enough, you will also see the Bitcoin price change every minute or so.

When run, the script should look similar to Figure 15-3.

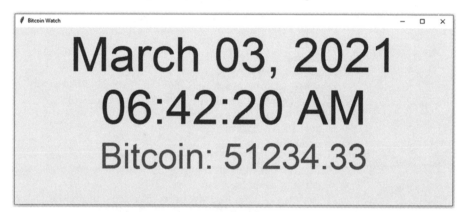

Figure 15-3: Using the after() function to create an animated Bitcoin watch

---

TRY IT OUT

Run *bitcoin_tk.py* and watch it for about three minutes to see how often the price updates.

A Talking Bitcoin Watch

Next we'll add the speech functionality. Whenever the price updates, the script will let you know in a human voice. We'll also add an alert system: when the Bitcoin price moves outside the preset upper and lower bounds, the script will alert you out loud.

Open *bitcoin_watch.py* from your chapter folder. Its differences from *bitcoin_tk.py* are highlighted in Listing 15-5.

```
--snip--
from mptpkg import print_say

# Specify the url to find the Bitcoin price
url = 'https://api.coindesk.com/v1/bpi/currentprice.json'
--snip--
# Create a second label
label2 = tk.Label(text="", fg="Red", font=("Helvetica", 60))
label2.pack()
# Set up the price bounds
response = requests.get(url)
response_json = response.json()
❶ oldprice = response_json['bpi']['USD']['rate_float']
maxprice = oldprice * 1.05
minprice = oldprice * 0.95
❷ print_say(f'The Bitcoin price is now {oldprice}!')


# Define the bitcoin_watch() function
def bitcoin_watch():
❸  global oldprice
    # Get the live information from Bitcoin url
    response = requests.get(url)
    response_json = response.json()
    price = response_json['bpi']['USD']['rate_float']
    # If there is update in price, announce it
❹  if price != oldprice:
        oldprice = price
        print_say(f'The Bitcoin price is now {oldprice}!')
    # If price goes out of bounds, announce it
❺  if price > maxprice:
        print_say('The Bitcoin price has gone above the upper bound!')
    if price < price:
        print_say('The Bitcoin price has gone below the lower bound!')
        # Obtain current date and time information
    tdate = arrow.now().format('MMMM DD, YYYY')
    tm = arrow.now().format('hh:mm:ss A')
--snip--
```

Listing 15-5: Script to create a talking graphical Bitcoin price watch

We import the modules, including the print_say() function from the local *mptpkg* package.

We retrieve a Bitcoin price to use as the starting price and save it as oldprice ❶. We set the upper and lower bounds as values 5 percent above and below the value stored in oldprice and save them as maxprice and minprice, respectively. The script announces in a human voice the price of Bitcoin at that moment ❷.

We declare oldprice a global variable so that it can be recognized both inside and outside the function bitcoin_watch() ❸. Every time bitcoin_watch()

is called, it obtains the latest Bitcoin price and compares it to the value stored in oldprice. If the values are different, the value of oldprice is updated to the new price, and the script announces the updated price ❹.

At ❺, the script checks whether the price has gone above the upper bound; if yes, it makes the announcement. Similarly, the script checks whether the price is below the lower bound and makes the announcement if it is.

This output is from running the script for a few minutes:

```
The Bitcoin price is now 51418.8064!
The Bitcoin price is now 51377.4967!
The Bitcoin price is now 51419.3027!
```

A Talking Stock Market Watch

Now we'll use these skills to build the talking, graphical, live US stock market watch. We'll make several significant changes to the Bitcoin version.

First, instead of showing just one asset, we'll cover three major players in the market: Apple, Amazon, and Tesla. We'll also show, as the main indexes we are interested in, the Dow Jones Industrial Average and the S&P 500.

Second, instead of updating every thousand milliseconds, we'll ask the script to update every two minutes. The script needs to retrieve five pieces of information instead of just one, and updating too frequently will cause information overload that could lead to the script freezing. More important, the values for the market indexes and prices for the preceding three stocks update every few seconds during the trading hours. Updating too often would make the announcements come nonstop and be distracting. You can choose to adjust the frequency that the script updates to your own liking.

Save the script in Listing 15-6 as *stock_watch.py* in your chapter folder or download it from the book's resources page.

```
import tkinter as tk

import arrow
from yahoo_fin import stock_info as si

from mptpkg import print_say

# Create a root window hold all widgets
❶ root = tk.Tk()
# Specify the title and size of the root window
root.title("U.S. Stock Market Watch")
root.geometry("1100x750")
# Create a first label using the Label() function
label = tk.Label(text="", fg="Blue", font=("Helvetica", 80))
label.pack()
# Create a second label
label2 = tk.Label(text="", fg="Red", font=("Helvetica", 60))
label2.pack()
# Set up tickers and names
tickers = ['^DJI', '^GSPC', 'AAPL', 'AMZN', 'TSLA']
```

```
     names = ['DOW JONES', 'S&P500', 'Apple', 'Amazon', 'Tesla']
     # Set up the oldprice values and price bounds
❷ oldprice = []
  maxprice = []
  minprice = []
  for i in range(5):
      p = round(float(si.get_live_price(tickers[i])), 2)
      oldprice.append(p)
      maxprice.append(p * 1.05)
      minprice.append(p * 0.95)
      if i <= 1:
          print_say(f'The latest value for {names[i]} is {p}!')
      else:
          print_say(f'The latest stock price for {names[i]} is {p} dollars!')


  # Define the stock_watch() function
❸ def stock_watch():
      # Declare global variables
      global oldprice, maxprice, minprice
      # Obtain live information about the DOW JONES index from Yahoo
  ❹ p1 = round(float(si.get_live_price("^DJI")), 2)
      m1 = f'DOW JONES: {p1}'
      # Obtain live information about the SP500 index from Yahoo
      p2 = round(float(si.get_live_price("^GSPC")), 2)
      m2 = f'S&P500: {p2}'
      # Obtain live price information for Apple stock from Yahoo
      p3 = round(float(si.get_live_price("AAPL")), 2)
      m3 = f'Apple: {p3}'
      # Obtain live price information for Amazon stock from Yahoo
      p4 = round(float(si.get_live_price("AMZN")), 2)
      m4 = f'Amazon: {p4}'
      # Obtain live price information for Tesla stock from Yahoo
      p5 = round(float(si.get_live_price("TSLA")), 2)
      m5 = f'Tesla: {p5}'
      # Put the five prices in a list p
  ❺ p = [p1, p2, p3, p4, p5]
      # Obtain current date and time information
      tdate = arrow.now().format('MMMM DD, YYYY')
      tm = arrow.now().format('hh:mm:ss A')
      # Put the date and time information in the first label
      label.configure(text=tdate + "\n" + tm)
      # Put all the five messages on the stock market in the second label
      label2.configure(text=m1 +\
          "\n" + m2 + "\n" + m3 + "\n" + m4 + "\n" + m5, justify=tk.LEFT)
      # If there is update in the market, announce it
  ❻ for i in range(5):
          if p[i] != oldprice[i]:
              oldprice[i] = p[i]
              if i <= 1:
                  print_say(f'The latest value for {names[i]} is {p[i]}!')
              else:
                  print_say\
                  (f'The latest stock price for {names[i]} is {p[i]} dollars!')
      # If price goes out of bounds, announce it
```

```
❼ for i in range(5):
        if p[i] > maxprice[i]:
            print_say(f'{names[i]} has moved above the upper bound!')
        if p[i] < minprice[i]:
            print_say(f'{names[i]} has moved below the lower bound!')
    # Call the stock_watch() function
❽ root.after(120000, stock_watch)


# Call the stock_watch() function
stock_watch()
# Run the game loop
root.mainloop()
```

Listing 15-6: Script to create a talking, graphical live US stock market watch

We import the modules, including *arrow* to show the time and date and *yahoo_fin* to obtain stock price information. We also import print_say() from the local *mptpkg* package to make announcements.

Starting at ❶, we create the *tkinter* root window and place two labels in it, as we did in *bitcoin_watch.py*. We then create three lists: oldprice, maxprice, and minprice ❷. We use oldprice to keep track of the values of the two indexes and the prices of the three stocks when we start running the script. The list maxprice holds the five upper bounds, 5 percent above the corresponding values in oldprice. Similarly, we define the five lower bounds in minprice.

The script then announces the values of the two indexes and the prices of the three stocks. Note that we put dollars after the three stock prices, but not after the two index values because index values are not measured in dollars.

We define stock_watch() at ❸, which declares oldprice a global variable. Every time the function is called, it retrieves the values we're interested in ❹. We keep two digits after the decimal for all values and save them in a list p ❺.

We obtain the time and date and put them in the first label. We put the values of the two indexes and three stocks in the second label. At ❻, we check each of the five values for updates, and we print and announce any updates. We also update the value stored in oldprice accordingly.

Starting at ❼, we check whether any of the five values has gone out of bounds. If yes, the script makes an announcement. Finally, we use after() to create the animation effect ❽. The stock_watch() function calls itself every 120,000 milliseconds, updating the screen every two minutes.

Here's the output from one interaction with the script:

```
The latest value for DOW JONES is 31477.02!
The latest value for S&P500 is 3861.02!
The latest stock price for Apple is 124.65 dollars!
The latest stock price for Amazon is 3062.5 dollars!
The latest stock price for Tesla is 692.41 dollars!
The latest value for DOW JONES is 31460.43!
The latest value for S&P500 is 3859.14!
The latest stock price for Apple is. 124.49 dollars!
```

```
The latest stock price for Amazon is 3062.32 dollars!
The latest stock price for Tesla is 690.8 dollars!
The latest value for DOW JONES is 31434.83!
The latest value for S&P500 is 3853.88!
The latest stock price for Apple is 124.26 dollars!
The latest stock price for Amazon is 3052.31 dollars!
The latest stock price for Tesla is 687.56 dollars!
```

In just a few minutes, the script has updated all five values three times. Figure 15-4 shows the final screen.

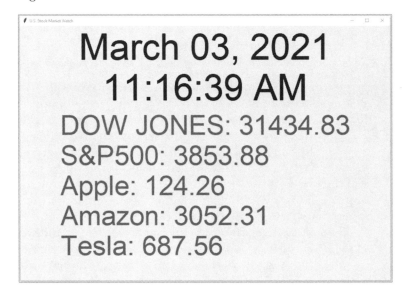

Figure 15-4: A graphical live US stock market watch

TRY IT OUT

Change the three stocks to Microsoft (ticker symbol MSFT), Goldman Sachs (ticker symbol GS), and Delta Airlines (ticker symbol DAL). Run the script after the change.

Apply the Method to Other Financial Markets

We can apply these methods to other financial markets. If the price information is available from Yahoo! Finance, the modification is minimal: we just change the ticker symbols in the scripts.

If the price information is not available from Yahoo! Finance, search online for a website that provides JSON data for the market and then use the same method we used to retrieve the Bitcoin price.

TRY IT OUT

Modify *stock_watch.py* to create a graphical watch for the Treasury bond rates. The graph should display the following four rates: 13-Week Treasury Bill rate (ticker symbol ^IRX), Five-Year Treasury Bond rate (ticker symbol ^FVX), Ten-Year Treasury Bond rate (ticker symbol ^TNX), and 30-Year Treasury Bond rate (ticker symbol ^TYX).

Summary

In this chapter, you first learned how to retrieve information from JSON data and use it to create a graphical Bitcoin watch using the *tkinter* package. You obtained the live Bitcoin price online and created widgets with animations in *tkinter*.

With these skills, you made a graphical live market watch for the US stock market with spoken alerts. The script generates a graphical display of two major US stock indexes and three stocks that you're interested in. When the prices change, the script lets you know in a human voice. The script also alerts you if an index value or a stock price goes outside the preset bounds.

You also learned how to apply this process to create a talking graphical market watch for other financial markets.

End-of-Chapter Exercises

1. Modify *bitcoin_price.py* to retrieve the price in British pounds instead of US dollars and as a string variable instead of a floating-point number.

2. Modify *tk_label.py* so that the size of the root window is 850 by 160 pixels and the message in the label displays here is your label.

3. Modify *bitcoin_tk.py* so that the screen refreshes every 0.8 seconds.

4. Modify *bitcoin_watch.py* so that the upper and lower bounds are set to 3 percent above and below the price when you start running the script.

16

USE WORLD LANGUAGES

So far, we've taught Python how to speak and listen in English. But Python can understand many other world languages. In this chapter, you'll first teach Python to talk in several other languages with the modules we've been using. I'll then introduce a useful module called *translate*, which can translate one language to another, and you'll use this to silently translate languages. Then we'll add the speech recognition and text-to-speech features so you can speak one language to the Python script and the script will say the translation in another language of your choice.

As usual, all scripts in this chapter are available at the book's resources page at *https://www.nostarch.com/make-python-talk/*. Start by creating the folder */mpt/ch16/* for this chapter.

NEW SKILLS

- Converting text to speech in major world languages
- Recognizing speech in major world languages
- Querying Wikipedia in major world languages
- Translating in text and with voice

Text to Speech in Other Languages

To work with non-English languages, we'll use *gTTS* because it supports most major world languages. The downside to using *gTTS* is that it needs a separate module to play the audio file, but the alternative (*pyttsx3*) doesn't support a wide range of non-English languages. Here we'll try out the *gTTS* module with a few examples.

Install Modules

To install the *gTTS* module in Windows, activate the virtual environment *chatting* and then execute the following command in the Anaconda prompt and follow the onscreen instructions:

```
pip install gTTS
```

If you're using Mac or Linux, you should already have installed the *gTTS* module in Chapter 4. However, Google Translate has been known to make significant changes to the module, so you should upgrade to the latest version by running the following command in a terminal with the virtual environment *chatting* activated:

```
pip install --upgrade gTTS
```

You also need to install the *pydub* module to play audio files. You need to do this step no matter whether you're using Windows, Mac, or Linux. Execute the following two lines of code in the Anaconda prompt (Windows) or a terminal (Mac or Linux), with the *chatting* virtual environment activated:

```
conda install -c conda-forge pydub
conda install -c conda-forge ffmpeg
```

Follow the instructions all the way through.

Convert Text to Speech in Spanish

The script *speak_spanish.py* in Listing 16-1 shows how the *gTTS* module converts written Spanish into spoken Spanish. Enter these lines of code in your Spyder editor and save the script as *speak_spanish.py* in your chapter folder.

```
from io import BytesIO

from gtts import gTTS
from pydub import AudioSegment
from pydub.playback import play

# Convert text to speech in Spanish
tts = gTTS(text='Buenos días',lang='es')
# Create a temporary file
voice = BytesIO()
# Save the voice output as an audio file
tts.write_to_fp(voice)
# Play the audio file
voice.seek(0)
play(AudioSegment.from_mp3(voice))
```

Listing 16-1: Script to convert written Spanish to spoken Spanish

We first import the modules, including *gTTS* and *pydub*, that will play the audio file.

Next, we use the gTTS() function to convert the Spanish phrase Buenos días to spoken Spanish. The phrase can be literally translated to *Good day*. The first argument to gTTS() specifies which phrase to convert, and the second specifies what language to use. In this case, we use es, which stands for *Español*, or *Spanish* (see Table 16-1 for a list of language codes).

The script generates a temporary file *voice* by using the BytesIO() function in the *io* module. If you instead used a fixed filename (such as *myfile.mp3*), the script may prevent you from overwriting the file when you rerun it and can crash. By using a temporary file each time you run the script, you avoid a crash.

Finally, we save the voice output as an audio file in the temporary file *voice* we just created. Then we play the audio file by using the *pydub* module. Run the script to hear Python say "Buenos días" in Spanish.

Support Text to Speech in Other Languages

The *gTTS* module can convert text to speech in most major languages. Table 16-1 provides an incomplete list of the languages that the module supports, followed by the code used in the gTTS() function.

Table 16-1: Major World Languages and the
Corresponding Code in the *gTTS* Module

Language name	Language code
Arabic	ar
Chinese	zh
Dutch	nl
English	en
French	fr
German	de
Italian	it
Japanese	ja
Korean	ko
Portuguese	pt
Russian	ru
Spanish	es

You can find a more comprehensive list at *https://cloud.google.com/ speech-to-text/docs/languages/*.

NOTE *Earlier versions of the* gTTS *module provided different accents or dialects within a language. For example, while the code* es *means Spanish,* es-es *means Spanish from Spain and* es-mx *means Spanish from Mexico. Google Translate has since deprecated this feature. If you get an error message by using accents or dialects within a language, be sure to use only the two-letter language code.*

Next, you'll create a script to choose the language you want. After that, you'll ask the script to translate a phrase from text to spoken language.

Convert Text to Speech in World Languages

The script *speak_world_languages.py* in Listing 16-2 shows you how to convert text to speech in several major world languages.

```
from io import BytesIO

from gtts import gTTS
from pydub import AudioSegment
from pydub.playback import play

# Create a dictionary of languages and the corresponding codes
❶ lang_abbre = {"english":"en",
               "chinese":"zh",
```

```
                  "spanish":"es",
                  "french":"fr",
                  "japanese":"ja",
                  "portuguese":"pt",
                  "russian":"ru",
                  "korean":"ko",
                  "german":"de",
                  "italian":"it"}
❷ lang = input("What language do you want to use?\n")
  phrase = input("What phrase do you want to convert to voice?\n")
  # Convert text to speech
  tts = gTTS(text=phrase,lang=lang_abbre[lang])
  # Create a temporary file
  voice = BytesIO()
  # Save the voice output as an audio file
  tts.write_to_fp(voice)
  # Play the audio file
  voice.seek(0)
  play(AudioSegment.from_mp3(voice))
```

Listing 16-2: Script to convert written language to spoken language

We create a dictionary *lang_abbre*, which maps different foreign languages to the corresponding codes in the *gTTS* module ❶. The script then asks what language you want to use. You can type in your choice in the IPython console ❷. Then type in the phrase you want to convert to voice at the prompt.

The script converts your phrase into an audio file and saves it in the temporary file *voice*. Then it plays the audio file by using the *pydub* module.

The following is an interaction with the script, with my text input in bold:

```
What language do you want to use?
chinese

What phrase do you want to convert to voice?
嗨,你好吗?
```

I first chose the language Chinese and then typed in the text 嗨,你好吗?, which is the Chinese phrase for *Hi, how are you?* After running the script, I heard Python speaking Chinese.

TRY IT OUT

Run *speak_world_languages.py* to speak and understand a language of your choice. Convert a phrase from text to speech. If the language of your choice is not in the dictionary *lang_abbre*, add it to the script (consult Table 16-1 for the language code).

Speech Recognition in Major World Languages

The speech recognition module we've used throughout this book is able to recognize other major world languages as well. We just need to let the script know which language we want to use.

We'll use Japanese as an example to illustrate how it works. The script *sr_japanese.py* in Listing 16-3 recognizes spoken Japanese and converts your voice into written text.

```python
import speech_recognition as sr

# Initiate speech recognition
speech = sr.Recognizer()
# Use it to capture spoken Japanese
print('Python is listening in Japanese...')
with sr.Microphone() as source:
    speech.adjust_for_ambient_noise(source)
    try:
        audio = speech.listen(source)
❶       my_input = speech.recognize_google(audio, language="ja")
        print(f"you said: {my_input}")
    except sr.UnknownValueError:
        pass
```

Listing 16-3: Speech recognition in Japanese

We first import the speech recognition module. Then we initiate speech recognition by using the `Recognizer()` function. The script prints out the message `Python is listening in Japanese` to prompt you to speak Japanese into the microphone. We use the `adjust_for_ambient_noise()` function to reduce the influence of any ambient noise on your voice input.

At ❶, we specify Japanese by passing `language="ja"` in the `recognize_google()` function. Recall from Chapter 3 that `recognize_google()` uses the Google Web Speech API; this is in contrast to other methods such as `recognize_bing()`, which uses the services of Microsoft Bing Speech, or `recognize_ibm()`, which uses the services of IBM Speech to Text. The script then prints out your voice input in Japanese.

Here's my output from interacting with the computer:

```
Python is listening in Japanese...
you said: ありがとうございます
```

I said into the microphone "Thank you" in Japanese. The script correctly captures the phrase and prints it out.

You can easily modify *sr_japanese.py* by replacing `language="ja"` (and the appropriate language titles in the prompts) with the language of your choice so that you can interact with the computer in another language. The list of world languages and their corresponding codes can be found at *https://www.science.co.il/language/Locale-codes.php*.

A Talking Wikipedia

Wikipedia supports most major world languages, detailed at *https://en.wikipedia.org/wiki/List_of_Wikipedias*. In Chapter 5, we created a talking Wikipedia in English. We'll build a version you can adapt to work with any major language. Listing 16-4 uses Chinese. Enter the following code into your Spyder editor and save it as *wiki_world_languages.py*.

```python
from io import BytesIO

import speech_recognition as sr
from gtts import gTTS
from pydub import AudioSegment
from pydub.playback import play
import Wikipedia

from mptpkg import print_say

# Create a dictionary of languages and the corresponding codes
lang_abbre = {"english":"en",
              "chinese":"zh",
              "spanish":"es",
              "french":"fr",
              "japanese":"ja",
              "portuguese":"pt",
              "russian":"ru",
              "korean":"ko",
              "german":"de",
              "italian":"it"}
Lang = input("What language do you want to use?\n")

# Initiate speech recognition
speech = sr.Recognizer()
# Request a query in a specified language
❶ print_say(f"Say what you want to know in {lang}...")
# Capture your voice query in the language of your choice
❷ with sr.Microphone() as source:
    speech.adjust_for_ambient_noise(source)
    while True:
        try:
            audio = speech.listen(source)
            my_input = speech.recognize_google(audio, language=lang_abbre[lang])
```

```
            break
        except sr.UnknownValueError:
            print_say("Sorry, I cannot understand what you said!")
# Print out what you said
❸ print(f"you said: {my_input}")
# Obtain answer from Wikipedia and print out
wikipedia.set_lang(lang_abbre[lang])
Ans = wikipedia.summary(my_input)[0:200]
print(ans)
# Convert text to speech in the language of your choice
❹ tts = gTTS(text=ans,lang=lang_abbre[lang])
# Create a temporary file
Voice = BytesIO()
# Save the voice output as an audio file
tts.write_to_fp(voice)
# Play the audio file
voice.seek(0)
play(AudioSegment.from_mp3(voice))
```

Listing 16-4: A talking Wikipedia in major world languages

We import the modules, including the *wikipedia* module we used in Chapter 5. The dictionary *lang_abbre* maps different foreign languages to the corresponding codes in the *gTTS* module. We'll also use the language codes in the *speech_recognition* module and the *wikipedia* module.

The script then asks what language you want to use ❶. You can type in your choice in the IPython console. Then speak your query into the microphone in the language you chose ❷. The script captures the voice input, converts it to written text, and stores it in my_input.

NOTE *While the three modules—gTTS, speech_recognition, and wikipedia—share the same digit language code for most languages, there could be exceptions. Double-check that the language of your choice has correct codes in all three modules.*

The script then prints your query ❸. After it does so, we set the language of Wikipedia to the language of your choice. We then send the query to Wikipedia and print the result. Finally, we convert the answer to speech and let the script say it in a human voice ❹.

Here is the output from an interaction with the script, with my written and voice inputs in bold:

```
What language do you want to use?
chinese
Say what you want to know in chinese...
美利堅合眾國（英語：United States of America，縮寫為USA，一般稱為United
States(U.S.或US),或America),中文通稱「美國」,是由其下轄50个州、華盛頓哥倫比亞
特區、五个自治領土及外島共同組成的聯邦共和国。美國本土48州和聯邦特区位於北美洲
中部，東臨大西洋，北面是加拿大，南部和墨西哥及墨西哥灣接壤，本土位於溫帶、副熱
帶地區。阿拉斯加州位於北美大陸西
```

I first typed in chinese as my choice of language. Then I said "United States of America" in Chinese into the microphone, and the script stored a short description of the United States in Chinese and both printed and spoke it.

TRY IT OUT

Run *wiki_world_languages.py* to use your chosen language and try it out. If your language is not in the dictionary *lang_abbre*, modify the script to add it.

Create Your Own Voice Translator

Now you'll create your own voice translator. When you speak to the script in any major language, the script will translate it to another language of your choice and speak it out.

We'll first make a text version with the *translate* module, then add speech recognition and text-to-speech features.

A Text-Based Translator

We first need to install the *translate* module, powered by Google Translate. The module is not in the Python Standard Library, and we need to pip install it. Open the Anaconda prompt (in Windows) or a terminal (in Mac or Linux). With the virtual environment *chatting* activated, run the following command:

```
pip install translate
```

Follow the instructions to finish the installation.

The script in Listing 16-5 translates English to Chinese, and translates Chinese to English, by using text input. Open your Spyder editor and copy the following code; then save it as *english_chinese.py* in your chapter folder.

```
# Import the Translator function from the translate module
from translate import Translator

# Specify the input and output languages
translator = Translator(from_lang="en",to_lang="zh")
# Do the actual translation
translation = translator.translate("hello all")
print(translation)
# Specify the input and output languages
translator = Translator(from_lang="zh",to_lang="en")
# Do the actual translation
translation = translator.translate("请再说一遍")
print(translation)
```

Listing 16-5: Translation between English and Chinese

We first import the `Translator()` function from the *translate* module. We need to specify the input language (here, English `from_lang="en"`) and the output language (here, Chinese with `to_lang="zh"`). We translate the phrase `hello all` from English to Chinese and print it.

Then we reverse the input and output languages to translate the phrase 请再说一遍 from Chinese to English and print it. The output is as follows:

```
大家好！
please say it again
```

We can modify the input and output languages in *english_chinese.py* to use any two major world languages. To see the languages supported by the *translate* module and their corresponding codes, check *https://www.labnol.org/code/19899-google-translate-languages/*.

A Voice-Based Translator

Next, we'll add speech recognition and text-to-speech functionality. Again, we'll hardcode the language to translate to and from, but you can easily adapt this script to any supported language.

NOTE *In Chapter 17, we'll add a voice translator functionality to our ultimate VPA, in which the script extracts the language you want to use. There we'll make the language choice dynamic.*

This version translates English to Spanish and Spanish to English. Open your Spyder editor and copy Listing 16-6. Save the script as *voice_translator.py* in your chapter folder.

```python
from io import BytesIO

from translate import Translator
import speech_recognition as sr
from gtts import gTTS
from pydub import AudioSegment
from pydub.playback import play

# Initiate speech recognition
speech = sr.Recognizer()
# Prompt you to say something in English
print('say something in English')
# Capture spoken English
with sr.Microphone() as source:
    speech.adjust_for_ambient_noise(source)
    try:
        audio = speech.listen(source)
        my_input = speech.recognize_google(audio, language="en")
        print(f"you said: {my_input}")
    except sr.UnknownValueError:
        pass
```

```
    # Specify the input and output languages
❶ translator = Translator(from_lang="en",to_lang="es")
    # Do the actual translation
    translation = translator.translate(my_input)
❷ print(translation)
    # Convert text to speech in Spanish
    tts = gTTS(text=translation,lang='es')
    # Create a temporary file
    voice = BytesIO()
    # Save the voice output as an audio file
❸ tts.write_to_fp(voice)
    # Play the audio file
    voice.seek(0)
    play(AudioSegment.from_mp3(voice))
    # Prompt you to say something in Spanish
❹ print('say something in Spanish')
    # Capture spoken Spanish
    with sr.Microphone() as source:
        speech.adjust_for_ambient_noise(source)
        try:
            audio = speech.listen(source)
            my_input = speech.recognize_google(audio, language="es")
            print(f"you said: {my_input}")
        except sr.UnknownValueError:
            pass
    # Specify the input and output languages
    Translator = Translator(from_lang="es",to_lang="en")
    # Do the actual translation
    translation = translator.translate(my_input)
    print(translation)
    # Convert text to speech in Spanish
    tts = gTTS(text=translation,lang='en')
    # Create a temporary file
    voice = BytesIO()
    # Save the voice output as an audio file
    tts.write_to_fp(voice)
    # Play the audio file
    voice.seek(0)
    play(AudioSegment.from_mp3(voice))
```

Listing 16-6: A voice translator between English and Spanish

We first import all modules. Then we initiate speech recognition by using the Recognizer() function. Next, the script prints say something in English to prompt you to speak the English phrase you want to translate.

The script captures your voice input, saves it in the variable my_input, and prints it. At ❶, we specify the input language as English and the output language as Spanish. We then translate the text stored in my_input to Spanish and print it ❷. After printing the translation, we convert the Spanish text to voice. Finally, we save the translation to an audio file and play it ❸.

Starting at ❹, we reverse the input and output languages. You can then speak a Spanish phrase to translate, and the computer will give the English translation.

Here is the output from an interaction with the script, with my voice input in bold:

```
say something in English
you said: today is a great day
Hoy es un gran día.

say something in Spanish
you said: uno dos tres
1 2 3
```

I spoke the phrase "Today is a great day" in English. The script printed and spoke the Spanish translation Hoy es un gran día. I then said in Spanish, "uno, dos, tres." The script correctly printed and spoke the English translation 1 2 3.

NOTE   *While most translations from the* translate *module are relatively accurate, it's best to avoid phrases with multiple meanings that may lead to inaccurate translations.*

TRY IT OUT

Modify *voice_translator.py* to change the language to another language of your choice. Use it to translate a phrase to English and translate a phrase from English to that language.

Summary

In this chapter, you adapted your speaking scripts to use any major world language. Along the way, you learned to convert text to speech in major world languages such as Spanish, Chinese, Japanese, French, and so on. You also learned how to perform speech recognition in major world languages. With these skills, you are able to interact with your computer in non-English languages.

You then learned how to install the *translate* module, which can translate text from one language to another. We combined the module with the speech recognition and text-to-speech features to create a voice translator. This is incredibly useful real-world functionality that can help make your deployed applications globally adaptable.

17

ULTIMATE VIRTUAL
PERSONAL ASSISTANT

In this chapter, you'll load up a virtual personal assistant (VPA) with the interesting projects in this book, like voice-controlled games, voice translators, voice music activations, and so on. You'll first add a chatting functionality to the script so you can carry out a daily conversation with the VPA. You'll create a dictionary of questions and answers. Whenever your voice command matches one of the questions in the dictionary, the VPA speaks the answer from the dictionary. This enables the VPA to answer certain questions in a very particular way, instead of obtaining an answer from Wikipedia or WolframAlpha.

After that, you'll add the following functionalities:

- The voice-activated music player from Chapter 5
- The voice-activated NPR News Now from Chapter 6
- The voice-activated radio functionality from Chapter 6
- The voice-activated Connect Four game from Chapter 13 (and the tic-tac-toe game from the exercises)
- Stock price functionality that lets you find out the latest price of US stocks and their index values from Chapter 15
- Translator functionality that renders English phrases in any major world language in Chapter 16

The whole idea of a VPA is its convenience, so we'll make adjustments in these projects so that all added functionalities are 100 percent hands-free. After a functionality is finished, the VPA will go back to the main menu and wait for your voice command.

As usual, all scripts in this chapter are available at the book's resources page, *https://www.nostarch.com/make-python-talk/*. Start by creating the folder */mpt/ch17/* for this chapter.

NEW SKILLS

- Creating a chatting functionality
- Reading JSON data saved in a JSON file
- Modularizing six versions of tic-tac-toe or Connect Four
- Understanding the difference between naming and calling a function
- Adapting the functionality of existing projects so your VPA is 100 percent hands-free

---

An Overview of the Final VPA

Let's have a look at the complete script of our final VPA. I'll then explain its individual functionalities one by one.

First you need to download several local module files. From the book's resources page (*https://www.nostarch.com/make-python-talk/*), find the following files from the */mpt/mptpkg/* directory: *mymusic.py*, *mynews.py*, *myradio.py*, *myttt.py*, *myconn.py*, *mystock.py*, and *mytranslate.py*. Put them in the same directory as your self-made local package files (refer to Chapter 5 for instructions). Make sure to place them in the package folder */mpt/mptpkg/* instead of the chapter folder */mpt/ch17/*. Later in this chapter, I'll explain the purpose of these files.

Next, open __*init__.py* from */mpt/mptpkg/*. You began this file in Chapter 5 and modified it in Chapters 7 and 8, so it should currently look something like this:

```
from .mysr import voice_to_text
from .mysay import print_say
--snip--
from .myknowall import know_all
```

Add the seven lines of code in Listing 17-1 to the end of __*init__.py*.

```
from .mymusic import music_play, music_stop
from .mynews import news_brief, news_stop
from .myradio import live_radio, radio_stop
from .myttt import ttt
from .myconn import conn
from .mystock import stock_market, stock_price
from .mytranslate import voice_translate
```

Listing 17-1: Importing functions from local modules to the local package

This code imports the 11 functions (music_play(), music_stop(), and so on) from the seven modules to the local package so you can later import them at the package level.

Open the script *vpa.py* from Chapter 8 and add the highlighted parts in Listing 17-2. Save the new script as *vpa_final.py*. You can also download the script from the book's resources.

```
import random
import json

# Ensure the following functions are imported in /mpt/mptpkg/__init__.py
from mptpkg import voice_to_text, print_say, wakeup, timer,\
alarm, joke, email, know_all, music_play, music_stop,\
news_brief, news_stop, live_radio, radio_stop, ttt,\
conn, stock_price, stock_market, voice_translate

# Open chats.json and put it in a dictionary
with open('chats.json','r') as content:
    chats = json.load(content)
# Put the script in standby
while True:
--snip--
        # The script goes back to standby if you choose
        if "back" in inp and "stand" in inp:
            print_say('OK, back to standby, let me know if you need help!')
            break
        # Activate chatting
        elif inp in list(chats.keys()):
            print_say(random.choice(chats[inp]))
            continue
        # Activate music
```

```python
    elif "music by" in inp:
        music_play(inp)
        # Say stop to stop the music anytime
        while True:
            background = voice_to_text().lower()
            if "stop" in background:
                music_stop()
                break
            else:
                continue
# Activate news
elif "npr news" in inp:
    news_brief()
    # Say stop to stop the news anytime
    while True:
        background = voice_to_text().lower()
        if "stop" in background:
            news_stop()
            break
        else:
            continue
# Activate the radio
# Put chromedriver.exe in the same folder as this script
elif "live radio" in inp:
    live_radio()
    # Say stop to stop the radio anytime
    while True:
        background = voice_to_text().lower()
        if "stop" in background:
            radio_stop()
            break
        else:
            continue
# Activate the tic-tac-toe game
elif "tic" in inp and "tac" in inp and "toe" in inp:
    ttt()
    continue
# Activate the Connect Four game
elif "connect" in inp and ('4' in inp or 'four' in inp):
    conn()
    continue
# Activate the stock price functionality
elif "stock price of" in inp:
    stock_price(inp)
    continue
# Get market indexes
elif "stock market" in inp:
    stock_market()
    continue
# Activate the voice translator
  elif "how to say" in inp and " in " in inp:
    voice_translate(inp)
    continue
```

```
# Activate the timer
elif "timer for" in inp and ("hour" in inp or "minute" in inp):
    timer(inp)
    continue
```
--snip--

Listing 17-2: Your final VPA

We first import the functions voice_to_text(), print_say(), wakeup(), and so on from the local package *mptpkg*. We already imported these functions in __*init*__*.py* from the local modules to the local package *mptpkg*, so here we import the functions at the package level directly. Further, since the custom package *mptpkg* is installed on your computer (in editable mode), the system knows where to find the files, and there is no need to tell the script where to look.

We then add the functionalities to the script using a series of elif statements. We start with the chatting functionality. We've prepared eight pairs of questions and answers and put them in the dictionary chats. If your voice input matches one of the eight questions, the chatting functionality is activated, and your VPA will speak the corresponding answer from chats.

The music functionality is activated by the phrase *music by*. The script will retrieve the artist's name you speak after saying "Music by . . ." and will play a random song by that artist.

The news functionality is activated by the phrase *NPR news*. The script will extract and play the audio file of the latest news brief from *NPR News Now*. You can say "Stop" to stop the news, and the script will go back to the main menu and ask, "How may I help you?"

The radio functionality is activated by the phrase *live radio*. The script will play streaming audio from an online radio station. You can say "Stop" anytime to return to the main menu.

The tic-tac-toe functionality is activated by the words *tic*, *tac*, and *toe* together. A game board will appear on the screen, and before the game starts, you can choose to play first or second as well as against a person, a simple computer, or a smart computer.

The Connect Four functionality is activated by the words *connect* and *four* together (or 4 in text). A game board will appear on the screen, and you can choose to play first or second as well as against a person, a simple computer, or a smart computer.

The stock price functionality is activated by the phrase *stock price of*. The script will extract the company name you speak after "Stock price of . . ." and tell you the latest price.

The stock market functionality is activated by the phrase *stock market*. The script will tell you the values of the major indexes of the US stock market.

The voice translator functionality is activated by the phrase *how to say* together with the word *in*. The script will extract the English phrase you want to translate and the foreign language into which to translate it, then give you the translation aloud.

Let's look at the individual functionalities one by one in detail.

The Chatting Functionality

This chatting functionality is new. It will allow the VPA to provide a pre-defined answer that you specify in the code, instead of an answer from Wikipedia or WolframAlpha. We're building a simple chat bot with only eight questions, but interested readers can use the principles here to create a more sophisticated chatting functionality with more questions and answers. It might also be interesting to extend this functionality with artificial intelligence.

We'll create a dictionary of questions and answers. Enter the text in Listing 17-3 and save it as the file *chats.json* in */mpt/ch17/*. These are our question-response pairs.

```
{
"how are you":["i am good","i am fine"],
"who are you":["i am a Python script","i am a computer script"],
"what are your hobbies":["a script doesn't have hobbies"],
"what's your favorite color":["blue","white"],
"hi":["hi","hello"],
"hello":["hello","hi"],
"what can you do":["lots of things, try me"],
"how old are you":["a script doesn't have age",
"good question, I don't really know the answer to that"]}
```

Listing 17-3: The eight pairs of questions and answers in the chatting functionality

The file is in JSON format, meaning it can be shared among different script languages.

To make the chatting functionality more interesting, we've prepared multiple answers to some questions. Python will read the JSON file and load the data into a dictionary object. The values are all Python lists, and the script will randomly select an answer from the list. For example, if the question is who are you, the answer will be either i am a Python script or i am a computer script.

Let's zoom in on the parts in *vpa_final.py* relevant to the chatting functionality:

```
import import random
import json
--snip--
with open('chats.json', 'r') as content:
    chats = json.load(content)
--snip--
        # Activate chatting
    ❶ elif inp in list(chats.keys()):
            print_say(random.choice(chats[inp]))
            continue
--snip--
```

We import two modules. The *random* module is used to randomly select an answer. The *json* module reads the JSON data. Both modules are in the Python Standard Library, so installation is not needed.

Then we open *chats.json* and read the content as a large string variable. We use the load() function in the *json* module to load it into the dictionary chats. When you run the VPA script, your voice is captured and converted to text and stored in the string variable inp. If your question matches one of the eight questions in chats, the chatting functionality is activated ❶. Note that list(chats.keys()) produces the list of the eight keys in chats, and if you print the list, it looks like this:

```
["how are you", "who are you", "what are your hobbies", "what's your favorite
color", "hi", "hello", "what can you do", "how old are you"]
```

The script uses inp as the key to locate the corresponding value, which is a list with one or two answers in it. The script randomly selects an answer from the list and speaks it out.

Here's one example interaction, with my voice input in bold:

```
--snip--
how may I help you?
you just said hello
hello

how may I help you?
you just said who are you
i am a computer script

how may I help you?
you just said what can you do
lots of things, try me

how may I help you?
you just said how old are you
a script doesn't have age
--snip--
```

After the computer asked, "How may I help you?" I said, "Hello" to the microphone. Since hello is one of the eight questions, the chatting functionality was activated, and the computer selected one of the two answers (in this case, hello).

I then asked three more questions: Who are you? What can you do? How old are you? They all activated the chatting functionality.

TRY IT OUT

Run *vpa_final.py* and ask a question to activate the chatting functionality. Then add two of your own question-and-answer pairs to *chats.json*. Run *vpa_final.py* again and activate the chatting functionality twice by asking the two questions.

The Music Functionality

We'll modify the script *play_selena_gomez.py* from Chapter 5 and add music functionality to our final VPA. You'll create a music module and import it to the main script.

Create a Music Module

Open the file *mymusic.py* you just downloaded from the book's resources and saved in your local package folder */mpt/mptpkg*. The code is shown in Listing 17-4.

```
import os
import random
❶ from pygame import mixer

from mptpkg import print_say

# Define a function to play music
❷ def music_play(v_inp):
    # Extract artist name
    pos = v_inp.find("music by ")
    v_inp = v_inp[pos+len('music by '):]
    # Separate first and last names
    names = v_inp.split()
    # Extract the first name
    firstname = names[0]
    # Extract the last name
    if len(names)>1:
        Lastname = names[1]
    # If no last name, use first name as placeholder
    else:
        lastname = firstname
    # Create a list to contain songs
    mysongs = []
    # If either first name or last name in the filename, put in list
    with os.scandir("../ch05/chat") as files:
        for file in files:
            if (firstname in file.name.lower() or lastname\
                in file.name.lower()) and "mp3" in file.name:
                mysongs.append(file.name)
    # Let you know if no song by the artist
    if len(mysongs) == 0:
        print_say(f"I cannot find any song by {names}.")
    else:
        # Randomly select one from the list and play
        mysong = random.choice(mysongs)
        print_say(f"play the song {mysong} for you.")
        mixer.init()
        mixer.music.load(f'../ch05/chat/{mysong}')
        mixer.music.play()

    # Define a function to stop music
❸ def music_stop():
```

```
try:
    mixer.music.stop()
except:
    print('no music to stop')
```

Listing 17-4: The script to add music functionality

In Chapter 5, you created the subfolder */chat/* in your chapter folder */mpt/ch05/* and saved some MP3 files in it. Each filename should contain the artist's name—for example, *SelenaGomezWolves.mp3* or *katy_perry_roar.mp3*—so that the Python script can locate it. A typical song is about four minutes long, which is a long time if you're given a song that you don't like, so you also learned how to stop the song while it's playing. The *playsound* and *pydub* modules don't allow the script to execute the next line of code while the song is playing, but with *pygame*, the script does move to the next line of code while the song is playing, allowing you to stop a song.

NOTE   *If you cannot install* pygame *on your computer, you can use the* vlc *module, which also allows you to stop the song while it is playing. See Appendix A for instructions on how to install the four modules that play audio files:* pygame, vlc, playsound, *and* pydub.

At ❶, we import the mixer module from *pygame*, which can play audio files. At ❷, we start defining the music_play() function, which takes a voice command v_inp as its argument. We locate the phrase *music by* in the voice command and use that to extract the artist name.

We use the split() function to separate the first name and last name and associate them with the variables firstname and lastname. The script then goes into the appropriate folder and selects a song with the artist's first name or last name to play. Note here that we use ../ch05/chat to access the subfolder */chat* in the parallel folder */mpt/ch05*.

We also define a music_stop() function, which will stop the music playing ❸. We use try and except here in case the script misunderstands your voice input and tells you that no song by the artist can be found. If that happens, you can still say "Stop" to go back to the main menu without crashing the script.

Activate the Music Functionality

Next, you'll add the music module to the final VPA. Here's the part of *vpa_final.py* that's relevant for the music functionality:

```
--snip--
from mptpkg import music_play, music_stop
--snip--
        # Activate music
    ❶ elif "music by" in inp:
            music_play(inp)
            # Say stop to stop the music any time
```

```
❷ while True:
      background = voice_to_text().lower()
      if "stop" in background:
          music_stop()
          break
      else:
          continue
--snip--
```

We import music_play() and music_stop(), which you just created, and then check for the activation phrase *music by* ❶. Once activated, the music_play() function is called, with your voice input taken as the argument.

While the music is playing, the script continues to execute the next line of code, which starts an infinite loop listening for your voice input in the background ❷. Any detected voice input is converted to the variable background. If the word *stop* is detected, the music_stop() function is called. If the word *stop* isn't detected, the script goes to the next iteration and continues listening for background voice input.

WARNING *Make sure to keep your speaker volume relatively low. If it's too high, the music will drown out your voice input, and it will be hard for the script to pick up your command and stop the music.*

Here's an example interaction with the music functionality, with my voice input in bold:

```
--snip--
how may I help you?
you just said play music by katy perry
play the song KatyPerry- Hey Hey Hey.mp3 for you
```

After about one minute of that tune, I said, "Stop playing." The music stopped playing, and the script went back to the main menu and asked, "How may I help you?"

NOTE *Even after the song finishes playing, you need to say "Stop" to go back to the main menu. If the script misunderstands your voice input and tells you that no song by the artist can be found, you also need to say "Stop" to go back to the main menu.*

TRY IT OUT

Save several songs by your favorite artist in the subfolder */mpt/ch05/chat*. Run *vpa_final.py* and activate the music functionality. Stop the song after a minute or so.

The News Brief Module

We'll modify the script *npr_news.py* from Chapter 6 and add a news functionality to our final VPA. You'll create a news module and import it to the main script.

Create a News Module

The script *mynews.py* in Listing 17-5 creates the news module. This file is available from the book's resources and needs to be saved in the local package directory.

```
from random import choice

import requests
import bs4
❶ from pygame import mixer

  # Define news_brief() function
❷ def news_brief():
      # Locate the website for the NPR news brief
      url = 'https://www.npr.org/podcasts/500005/npr-news-now'
      # Convert the source code to a soup string
      response = requests.get(url)
      response.raise_for_status()
      soup = bs4.BeautifulSoup(response.text, 'html.parser')
      # Locate the tag that contains the mp3 files
      casts = soup.findAll('a', {'class': 'audio-module-listen'})
      # Obtain the weblink for the mp3 file related to the latest news brief
      cast = casts[0]['href']
      pos = cast.find("?")
      # Download the mp3 file
    ❸ mymp3 = cast[0:pos]
      x = choice(range(1000000))
      mymp3_file = requests.get(mymp3)
      with open(f'f{x}.mp3','wb') as f:
          f.write(mymp3_file.content)
      # Play the mp3 file
      mixer.init()
      mixer.music.load(f'f{x}.mp3')
    ❹ mixer.music.play()

  # Define the news_stop() function
❺ def news_stop():
      try:
          mixer.music.stop()
      except:
          print('no news to stop')
```

Listing 17-5: The script to create a news functionality

At ❶, we import mixer from *pygame*. We'll use the *pygame* module so that we can stop the news brief anytime. At ❷, we define news_brief(). When this function is called, the script goes to the NPR news website, extracts the MP3 file associated with the latest news brief, and saves it on your computer ❸. The script uses music.play() to play the audio file ❹.

We also define a news_stop() function that will stop playing the news file ❺.

Activate the News Functionality

Let's add the functionality you just created to the final VPA. Here are the parts of *vpa_final.py* relevant to the news functionality:

```
--snip--
from mptpkg import news_brief, news_stop
--snip--
        # Activate news
        elif "npr news" in inp:
            news_brief()
            # Say stop to stop the news any time
            while True:
                background = voice_to_text().lower()
                if "stop" in background:
                    news_stop()
                    break
                else:
                    continue
--snip--
```

We import news_brief() and news_stop() from *mynews*. We check for the activation phrase *NPR News* in your voice command. It's a good idea to say "Play NPR News" or "Tell me the latest NPR news" instead of just "NPR news," because the first word or two may be cut off due to timing. Putting something in front of "NPR News" provides a buffer.

Once activated, the news_brief() function is called, which extracts the news brief audio file from the *NRR News Now* website and plays it using *pygame*.

While the news is broadcasting, the script starts an infinite loop to listen for your voice input in the background, listening for the word *stop*. If the word is detected, the news_stop() function is called. Otherwise, the script goes to the next iteration and continues listening for background commands.

As with to the music-playing functionality, you need to keep your speaker volume low so you can stop the audio by using voice input. After the news brief is finished, you need to say "Stop" to go back to the main menu.

TRY IT OUT

Run *vpa_final.py* and activate the news functionality. Say "Stop" when the news is finished to go back to the main menu.

The Live Radio Module

We'll modify *play_live_radio.py* from Chapter 6 and add a radio module to our final VPA. As usual, you'll create the radio module and import it to the main script.

Create a Radio Module

Frist we'll create a radio module. The script *myradio.py* is shown in Listing 17-6.

```
# Put chromedriver.exe in the same folder as vpa_final.py
from selenium import webdriver
from selenium.webdriver.chrome.options import Options

❶ def live_radio():
    global button
    chrome_options = Options()
    chrome_options.add_argument("--headless")
    browser = webdriver.Chrome(executable_path='./chromedriver',\
                               chrome_options=chrome_options)
    browser.get("https://onlineradiobox.com/us/")
    button = browser.find_element_by_xpath('//*[@id="b_top_play"]')
    button.click()

❷ def radio_stop():
    global button
    try:
        button.click()
    except:
        print('no radio to stop')
```

Listing 17-6: The script to create livestreaming radio functionality

First, you need to put the file *chromedrive.exe in* the same folder as the VPA script (that is, in */mpt/ch17*). At ❶, we define the live_radio() function. We make button a global variable so we can use it again later in another function. We use the headless option, which provides the same functionalities as the regular Chrome browser but does not display the browser window on the desktop. Then we define button as the play button on the online radio station Online Radio Box. The button is clicked via voice control so that the radio starts streaming when live_radio() is called.

At ❷, we define a radio_stop() function that stops the radio playing. Note here that we need to make button a global variable as well so that it can be modified in radio_stop().

Activate the Radio Functionality

Next, add the radio functionality you just created to the final VPA. Here are the relevant parts of *vpa_final.py*:

```
--snip--
from mptpkg import live_radio, radio_stop
```

```
--snip--
        # Activate the radio
        # Put chromedriver.exe in the same folder as this script
        elif "live radio" in inp:
            live_radio()
            # Say stop to stop the radio anytime
            while True:
                background = voice_to_text().lower()
                if "stop" in background:
                    radio_stop()
                    break
                else:
                    continue
--snip--
```

We first import the live_radio() and radio_stop() functions you just created from the local *mptpkg* package. We listen for the activation phrase *live
radio*. Again, it's a good idea to include a word or two in front of "live radio"
to provide a buffer.

Once activated, live_radio() is called, which goes to Online Radio Box
and clicks the play button to stream the audio.

While the radio is playing, the script starts an infinite loop to listen
for background voice input, which if detected is stored in background. If the
word *stop* is detected, radio_stop() is called to press the play button again so
that the audio stops streaming. Otherwise, the script goes to the next iteration and listens for background voice commands.

TRY IT OUT

Run *vpa_final.py* and activate the radio functionality. Stop the radio after a
minute or so.

The Tic-Tac-Toe Module

We'll add a tic-tac-toe module so you can voice-activate the game and play
with the computer 100 percent hands-free. Here, we use one script to offer
six versions of the tic-tac-toe game: you can choose to play against another
person, a simple computer that makes random moves, or a smart computer
that thinks three steps ahead (recall Chapter 13). You can also choose to go
either first or second.

You'll create a tic-tac-toe module and import it to the main script.

Create a Tic-Tac-Toe Module

First we'll create a local tic-tac-toe module. The script *myttt.py* is based on the
scripts *ttt_hs.py* in Chapter 10 and *ttt_think.py*, which is the answer to question
#5 in the end-of-chapter exercises in Chapter 13 and is available at the book's
resources website. I highlight the key parts of *myttt.py* in Listing 17-7.

```
--snip--
def ttt():
    t.setup(600,600,100,200)
--snip--
    # Define the smart_computer() function
  ❶ def smart_computer():
        if turn == "blue":
            nonturn = "white"
        else:
            nonturn = "blue"
        # Choose center at the first move
        if "5" in validinputs:
            return "5"
--snip--
        for move in valids:
            tooccupy = deepcopy(occupied)
            tooccupy[turn].append(move)
            if win_game(tooccupy,turn) == True:
                winner.append(move)
--snip--
    # Obtain move from a human player
  ❷ def person():
        print_say(f"Player {turn}, what's your move?")
        return voice_to_text().lower()
    # Obtain a move from a simple computer
  ❸ def simple_computer():
        return choice(validinputs)
    # Ask you for your choice of opponent
  ❹ while True:
        print_say('''Do you want your opponent to be a person,
        a simple computer, or a smart computer?''')
        which_player = voice_to_text().lower()
        print_say(f"You said {which_player}.")
        if 'person' in which_player:
            player = person
            break
        elif 'simple' in which_player:
            player = simple_computer
            break
        elif 'smart' in which_player:
            player = smart_computer
            break
    # Ask if you want to play first or second
  ❺ while True:
        print_say("Do you want to play first or second?")
        preference = voice_to_text().lower()
        print_say(f"You said {preference}.")
        if 'first' in preference:
            preference = 1
            break
        elif 'second' in preference:
            preference = 2
            break
```

```
        # Add a dictionary of words to replace
        to_replace = {'number ':'', 'cell ':'', 'column ':'',
                      'one':'1', 'two':'2', 'three':'3',
                      'four':'4', 'for':'4', 'five':'5',
                      'six':'6', 'seven':'7', 'eight':'8','nine':'9'}
    # Start game loop
    while True:
        # See whose turn to play
      ❻ if (preference+rounds)%2 == 0:
            print_say(f"Player {turn}, what's your move?")
            inp = voice_to_text().lower()
        else:
          ❼ inp = player()
            if inp == None:
                inp = choice(validinputs)
      ❽ print_say(f"Player {turn} chooses {inp}.")
--snip--
        # If the move is a not valid one, remind
      ❾ if inp not in validinputs:
            print_say("Sorry, that's an invalid move!")
        # If the move is valid, go ahead
        else:
            # Go to the cell and place a dot of the player's color
--snip--
  ❿ try:
        bye()
    except Terminator:
        print('exit turtle')
```

Listing 17-7: The script to create the tic-tac-toe functionality

Unlike in previous tic-tac-toe versions, here we don't use the *messagebox* module to remind us about wins, ties, and invalid moves because we cannot use voice commands to remove the message box from the screen. You need to physically click the box to make it disappear. Instead we'll just print and announce wins, ties, and invalid moves.

We define the ttt() function, which we'll call from the VPA script to draw the game board and ask whether you want to play against a person, a simple computer, or a smart computer. After that, the script asks whether you want to play first or second. Once the game is over, the board disappears from the screen, and the script goes back to the main menu of the VPA automatically.

In the ttt() function, we use the smart_computer() function ❶, which is based on the best_move() function in *ttt_think.py* but gives you the option to go first or second. We change blue and white to turn and nonturn, respectively, so the computer can be the white player if it plays second. We also allow the smart computer to occupy cell 5 if it's empty even if it plays second because doing so increases its chance of winning the game.

We then define the person() function ❷, which allows a human player to make a move by using voice commands. Similarly, the simple_computer() function allows the computer to make a random move ❸.

At ❹, we start an infinite loop. At each iteration, the script asks whether you want to choose a person, a simple computer, or a smart computer as your opponent. If your answer includes *person*, the variable player will be assigned a value of person. If your answer includes *simple* or *smart*, player will be assigned a value of simple_computer or smart_computer. Later, when we call the player() function, one of the three functions person(), simple_computer(), or smart_computer() will be called, depending on which function name is stored in player.

Pay attention to the difference between a function name and the calling of a function. For example, smart_computer is just a function name, while smart_computer() calls the function and executes all command lines in it. What a difference the parentheses make!

At ❺, we start an infinite loop to determine whether you want to play first or second. If your answer includes *first*, the variable preference will be assigned a value of 1. If your answer includes *second*, preference is assigned a value of 2.

We then start the game loop. At each iteration, we first determine whether you or your opponent has the turn, based on the values of preference and rounds ❻. For example, if you choose to play first, the value of preference is 1, and when the game starts, the value of rounds is 1. So the condition (preference+rounds)%2==0 is met, and you'll have the first turn at the beginning of the game.

When it's your opponent's turn ❼, the player() function is called. This means one of the three functions, person(), simple_computer(), or smart _computer(), is called, depending on the value stored in the player variable. The script announces the move ❽. If the move is not valid, the script asks you or your opponent to choose again ❾. Otherwise, a piece is placed on the game board.

Finally, when the game ends, we do not include the done() function in the script. As you may recall from the script *guess_letter.py* in Chapter 12, without done(), the script goes to the bye() function after the while loop is finished. This way, the game board will disappear from the screen ❿, and you can go back to the main menu of your VPA script.

Activate Tic-Tac-Toe

Let's now add the tic-tac-toe functionality to the final VPA. Here are the relevant parts of the script *vpa_final.py*:

```
--snip--
from mptpkg import ttt
--snip--
        # Activate the tic-tac-toe game
        elif "tic" in inp and "tac" in inp and "toe" in inp:
            ttt()
            continue
--snip--
```

We import the ttt() function you just created from the local *mptpkg* package. To activate the tic-tac-toe game, you need to include *tic*, *tac*, and *toe* in your voice command. Once the game is over, the game board disappears, and you'll go back to the main menu.

Here's an example of one interaction, with my voice input in bold:

```
--snip--
How may I help you?
You just said play tic-tac-toe.

Do you want your opponent to be a person, a simple computer, or a smart
computer?
You said simple computer.

Do you want to play first or second?
You said first.

Player blue, what's your move?
Player blue chooses 5.
Player white chooses 9.

Player blue, what's your move?
Player blue chooses number 7.
Player white chooses 6.

Player blue, what's your move?
Player blue chooses number three.
Congrats player blue, you won!

How may I help you?
--snip--
```

I activated the game by saying "Play tic-tac-toe." I then chose to play first against a simple computer as my opponent. I won the game by occupying cells 5, 7, and 3.

TRY IT OUT

Run *vpa_final.py* and activate the tic-tac-toe functionality. Play a game with the smart computer and let the computer move first.

The Connect Four Module

At this point, adding the Connect Four module should be straightforward. We can modify the tic-tac-toe module and change the game to Connect Four. Then you'll import the local module to the main script.

Create a Connect Four Module

First we'll create a Connect Four module. The script *myconn.py* is based on *conn_think_hs.py* in Chapter 13 and *myttt.py*, which you just created. Again, we won't use *messagebox* to remind us about wins, ties, and invalid moves. We'll define a conn() function so that when the function is called, the game appears onscreen and you can start playing.

As in the tic-tac-toe module, you can choose who goes first and who your opponent is. We change red and yellow to turn and nonturn, respectively, so that the computer can be the yellow player if it plays second.

To save space, I won't explain *myconn.py* in detail here, but it's available at the book's resources, in the folder */mpt/mptpkg*. Open it now and take a look; then go back to the main script for the VPA.

Activate Connect Four

Add the Connect Four module you just created to the final VPA, shown here in *vpa_final.py*:

```
--snip--
from mptpkg import conn
--snip--
        # Activate Connect Four
        elif "connect" in inp and ('4' in inp or 'four' in inp):
            conn()
            continue
--snip--
```

We import the conn() function you just created from the local *mptpkg* package. We listen for the activation phrase *Connect Four* in your voice command. Note that the script may convert your voice as either connect four or connect 4. As a result, we need to use '4' in inp or 'four' in inp to cover both cases.

Here is one sample output from a game:

```
--snip--
How may I help you?
You just said play connect four.

Do you want your opponent to be a person, a simple computer, or a smart
computer?
You said smart computer.

Do you want to play first or second?
You said second.
Player red chooses 4.

Player yellow, what's your move?
Player yellow chooses number three.
Player red chooses 1.

Player yellow, what's your move?
```

```
Player yellow chooses number three.
Player red chooses 5.

Player yellow, what's your move?
Player yellow chooses number three.
Player red chooses 3.

Player yellow, what's your move?
Player yellow chooses number two.
Player red chooses 7.

Player yellow, what's your move?
Player yellow chooses number two.
Player red chooses 6.
Congrats player red, you won!

How may I help you?
--snip--
```

I chose to play second against the smart computer. By connecting four discs horizontally in columns 4, 5, 7, and 6, the smart computer wins the game.

TRY IT OUT

Run *vpa_final.py* and activate the Connect Four functionality. Play a game with the simple computer and let the computer play second.

The Stock Price Module

Now let's add stock price functionality to our final VPA, building the module and then importing it.

Create a Stock Market–Tracking Module

First we'll create stock-monitoring functionality. The script *mystock.py* has the code shown in Listing 17-8.

```
import requests
from yahoo_fin import stock_info as si

from mptpkg import print_say

# Define stock_price() function
❶ def stock_price(v_inp):
    # Extract company name
    pos = v_inp.find("stock price of")
    myfirm = v_inp[pos+len("stock price of "):]
    # Extract the source code from the website
```

```
# Prevent crashing in case there is no result
try:
    # Extract the source code from the website
  ❷ url = 'https://query1.finance.yahoo.com/v1/finance/search?q='+myfirm
    response = requests.get(url)
    # Read the JSON data
    response_json = response.json()
    # Obtain the value corresponding to "quotes"
    quotes = response_json['quotes']
    # Get the ticker symbol
    ticker = quotes[0]['symbol']
    # Obtain real-time stock price from Yahoo
  ❸ price = round(float(si.get_live_price(ticker)),2)
    # Speak the stock price
    print_say(f"the stock price for {myfirm} is {price} dollars")
    # If price is not found, the script will tell you
except:
    print_say("sorry, I cannot find what you are looking for!")


  # Define stock_market() function
❹ def stock_market():
    # Obtain real-time index values from Yahoo
    dow = round(float(si.get_live_price('^DJI')),2)
    sp500 = round(float(si.get_live_price('^GSPC')),2)
    # Announces the index values
    print_say(f"The Dow Jones Industry Average is {dow}.")
    print_say(f"The S&P 500 is {sp500}.")
```

Listing 17-8: The script to create stock market–tracking functionality

At ❶, we define the stock_price() function, saving the voice command v_inp as the argument. We then locate the company name in your voice command and use that to extract the ticker symbol of the firm's stock ❷. The script goes to Yahoo! Finance and obtains the stock price based on the ticker symbol ❸. Finally, the script prints and announces the stock price.

We also define stock_market() ❹. When this function is called, it will retrieve the latest values of the Dow Jones Industrial Average and the S&P 500. The script then prints and announces the two values.

Activate the Stock Market–Tracking Functionalities

Now add the stock-monitoring module you just created to the final VPA. Here are the relevant parts of *vpa_final.py*:

```
--snip--
from mptpkg import stock_market, stock_price
--snip--
        # Activate the stock price functionality
        elif "stock price of" in inp:
            stock_price(inp)
            continue
        # Get market indexes
```

```
        elif "stock market" in inp:
            stock_market()
            continue
--snip--
```

We first import the stock_price() and stock_market() functions and listen for the activation phrase *stock price of* in your voice command, such as, "Tell me the stock price of General Motors." The stock_price() function uses your voice command as the argument and tells you the latest price for the company's stock.

We then listen for the activation phrase *stock market* for the stock_market() function. The script retrieves the latest values of the market indexes and announces them to you.

The following is one interaction with the stock module, with my voice input in bold:

```
--snip--
how may I help you?
you just said tell me the stock price of general motors
the stock price for general motors is 24.39 dollars

how may I help you?
you just said tell me about the stock market
the Dow Jones Industry Average is 26075.3
the S&P 500 is 3185.04

how may I help you?
--snip--
```

TRY IT OUT

Run *vpa_final.py* and find the latest stock price of Goldman Sachs. Then find the values of the Dow Jones Industrial Average and S&P 500.

The Voice Translator Module

We'll finally add the translator functionality so that your VPA can translate an English phrase into a foreign language of your choice.

Create a Translator Module

First we'll create a translator module. The script *mytranslate.py* is shown in Listing 17-9.

```
from mptpkg import import print_say

❶ lang_abbre = {"english":"en",
                "chinese":"zh",
```

```
                    "spanish":"es",
                    "french":"fr",
                    "japanese":"ja",
                    "portuguese":"pt",
                    "russian":"ru",
                    "korean":"ko",
                    "german":"de",
                    "italian":"it"}

# Import the platform module to identify your OS
import platform

# If you are using Windows, use gtts
if platform.system() == "Windows":
    import random

    from translate import Translator
    from gtts import gTTS
    from pydub import AudioSegment
    from pydub.playback import play

  ❷ def voice_translate(inp):
        # Extract the phrase and the language name
        ps1 = inp.find('how to say')
        ps2 = inp.rfind(' in ')
        try:
            eng_phrase = inp[ps1+10:ps2]
            tolang = inp[ps2+4:]
            translator = Translator(from_lang="english",to_lang=tolang)
            translation = translator.translate(eng_phrase)
            tts = gTTS(text=translation, lang=lang_abbre[tolang])
            print_say(f"The {tolang} for {eng_phrase} is")
            print(translation)
            x = random.choice(range(1000000))
            tts.save(f'file{x}.mp3')
            play(AudioSegment.from_mp3(f"file{x}.mp3"))
        except:
            print_say("Sorry, cannot find what you are looking for!")

# If you are not using Windows, use gtts-cli
if  platform.system() == "Darwin" or platform.system() == "Linux":
    import os
    from translate import Translator
    from gtts import gTTS

    def voice_translate(inp):
        # Extract the phrase and the language name
        ps1 = inp.find('how to say')
        ps2 = inp.rfind(' in ')
        try:
            eng_phrase = inp[ps1+10:ps2]
            tolang = inp[ps2+4:]
            translator = Translator(from_lang="english",to_lang=tolang)
            translation = translator.translate(eng_phrase)
            print_say(f"The {tolang} for {eng_phrase} is")
```

```
        print(translation)
        tr = translation.replace('"','')
        ab = lang_abbre[tolang]
    ❸ os.system(f'gtts-cli --nocheck "{tr}" --lang {ab} | mpg123 -q -')
    except:
        print_say("sorry, cannot find what you are looking for!")
```

Listing 17-9: The script to create a voice translator functionality

We start by importing the needed modules. In particular, we import *platform* to identify your operating system. At ❶, we create a dictionary lang_abbre, which maps several world languages to their language codes in Google Translate. Listing 17-9 includes 10 languages, and you can add more to the dictionary if you prefer.

If you're using Windows, at ❷, we start the definition of the voice _translate() function, which takes your voice command as the argument. Your voice command should contain *how to say* and *in*. For example, you can ask, "Python, how to say *thank you* in Japanese?" The script locates the positions of *how to say* and *in* in your voice. It then extracts the English phrase you want to translate and the target language and stores them in variables eng_phrase and tolang, respectively.

NOTE   *While the string method find() locates the position of the first occurrence of a substring, the rfind() method returns the position of the last occurrence. We use rfind(' in ') in this script in case you include the word in in the English phrase you want to translate, such as "How to say the cat in the hat in Spanish?"*

We then use the Translator() class from *translate* to translate the English phrase to the language you want in text. Next, the script converts the translation into voice. It saves the voice translation into an MP3 file and uses the *pydub* module to play it.

If you're using Mac or Linux, the process is similar except that you don't need to create and play the audio file. Instead, we use the command line method gtts-cli to play the audio file directly without saving and retrieving the audio file, similar to what we did in Chapter 4 ❸. Since we convert a foreign language to speech, we need to add the --lang option, followed by the abbreviation for the language.

Activate the Voice Translator

Next, you'll add the voice translator module you just created to the final VPA, shown here:

```
--snip--
from mptpkg import voice_translate
--snip--
        # Activate the voice translator
        elif "how to say" in inp and " in " in inp:
            voice_translate(inp)
            continue
--snip--
```

We import the voice_translate() function you just created and listen for the activation phrase. Once the translator functionality is activated, voice_translate() is called, using your voice input as the argument. The function tells you the translation in a human voice.

The following is one interaction with the functionality, with my voice input in bold:

```
--snip--
how may I help you?
you just said how to say good afternoon in japanese
the japanese for good afternoon is
こんにちは
--snip--
```

TRY IT OUT

Run *vpa_final.py* and ask it how to say "thank you" in a foreign language you understand; then check that the translation is correct. If the foreign language is not in the script *mytranslate.py*, add the language to it.

Summary

In this chapter, you added several projects created earlier in the book to your VPA. Along the way, you learned how to modify existing projects, modularize them, and use their functionality in your VPA. You learned how to use voice control to activate a functionality so that everything is 100 percent hands-free, and how to return to the main menu after the functionality is finished. You also efficiently included six versions of the tic-tac-toe or Connect Four game in a single module by allowing the script to ask you a couple of questions before the game starts. With these skills, you'll be able to create your own functionalities and add them to your VPA.

A

INSTALL MODULES
TO PLAY AUDIO FILES

In this appendix, I'll discuss the various modules for playing audio files in Python. While there is no feasible way to account for all the differences in hardware and operating system combinations, I have tested the instructions in this book on a variety of hardware and software platforms. In doing so, I encountered various problems, and I want to help you avoid those problems.

There are two types of modules when it comes to playing audio files. The first type (which we can call *blocking*) will take control of the script and won't let your execution move to the next line of code until the audio file is finished playing. We'll discuss two modules in this category: *playsound* and *pydub*. You need to make only one of them work for this book. The second type won't take control of the script; it simply moves on to the next line of code as soon as the audio file starts playing (we can refer to this as *non-blocking*). We'll look at two modules in this category: *vlc* and *pygame*. Similarly, you need to make only one of them work for this book.

Both module types are used in this book. The blocking type is the most common, and we use it to play most audio files in our scripts. The non-blocking type is useful when the audio file is long and you want the option of pausing or stopping while it's playing. We use this in Chapter 6 in the script *news_brief_hs.py* and in the music-playing functionality in our ultimate VPA script, *vpa_final.py*, in Chapter 17 .

Next, we'll discuss how to install these four modules in different operating systems.

Install the playsound Module

The *playsound* module is easy to use since the required lines of code are minimal. However, installing in Mac or Linux may be difficult, even though I have managed to install it in all three operating systems.

Windows

To install *playsound* in Windows, execute the following command in an Anaconda prompt with your *chatting* virtual environment activated:

```
pip install playsound
```

Follow the instructions.

Mac

To install *playsound* in Mac, execute the following two commands in a terminal with your *chatting* virtual environment activated:

```
pip install playsound
conda install -c conda-forge pygobject
```

Follow the instructions.

Linux

To install *playsound* in Linux, execute the following three commands in a terminal with your *chatting* virtual environment activated:

```
pip install playsound
conda install -c conda-forge pygobject
conda install gstreamer
```

Follow the instructions.

Install the pydub Module

The *pydub* module is easy to install in Mac or Linux. However, installing in Windows may be difficult, even though I have managed to install it in all three operating systems. To install *pydub*, execute the following commands in your Anaconda prompt (Windows) or a terminal (Mac and Linux) with your *chatting* virtual environment activated:

```
conda install -c conda-forge pydub
conda install -c conda-forge ffmpeg
```

Install the pygame Module

Since software is constantly being updated, the installation instructions are likely to change. I suggest you refer to the Pygame official website, *https://www.pygame.org/wiki/GettingStarted/*, for instructions if you get stuck.

Windows

Execute this command in your Anaconda prompt with your *chatting* virtual environment activated:

```
pip install pygame
```

Follow the instructions.

Mac

Recent versions of macOS require the installation of Pygame 2. To install, execute this command in a terminal with your *chatting* virtual environment activated:

```
pip install pygame==2.0.0
```

Then follow the instructions.

Linux

In Linux, execute the following three commands in a terminal with your *chatting* virtual environment activated:

```
sudo apt-get install python3-pip python3-dev
sudo pip3 install pygame
pip install pygame
```

Install the vlc Module

For the *vlc* module, you need to have VLC Media Player installed on your computer no matter which operating system you are using. Go to the VLC website at *https://www.videolan.org/index.html* to download the software and install it.

In Linux, you can install the app by running this command in a terminal:

```
sudo apt-get install vlc
```

With your *chatting* virtual environment activated in an Anaconda prompt (Windows) or a terminal (Mac or Linux), install the Python *vlc* module by running the following command:

```
pip install python-vlc
```

Sample Scripts to Test the Four Modules

In this section, we provide a sample script for each of the four modules to test that the modules are running successfully. Again, you need to install only one out of *playsound* and *pydub* and one out of *vlc* and *pygame* for this book.

Go to the book's resources and download the file *hello.mp3* for testing purposes. Be sure to place the file in the same folder as the testing scripts created next.

The playsound Module

Enter the following lines of code in your Spyder editor. Save the script as *test_playsound.py* and run it. Alternatively, you can download it from the book's resources.

```
from playsound import playsound
playsound("hello.mp3")
```

If successful, you should hear a human voice saying, "Hello, how are you?"

The pydub Module

Enter the following lines of code in your Spyder editor. Save the script as *test_pydub.py* and run it. Alternatively, you can download it from the book's resources.

```
from pydub import AudioSegment
from pydub.playback import play
play(AudioSegment.from_mp3("hello.mp3"))
```

If successful, you should hear a human voice saying, "Hello, how are you?"

The pygame Module

Enter the following lines of code in your Spyder editor. Save the script as *test_pygame.py* and run it. Alternatively, you can download it from the book's resources.

```
from pygame import mixer
mixer.init()
mixer.music.load("hello.mp3")
mixer.music.play()
```

If successful, you should hear a human voice saying, "Hello, how are you?"

The vlc Module

Enter the following lines of code in your Spyder editor. Save the script as *test_vlc.py* and run it. Or you can download it from the book's resources.

```
from vlc import MediaPlayer
player=MediaPlayer("hello.mp3")
player.play()
```

If successful, you should hear a human voice saying, "Hello, how are you?"

B

SUGGESTED ANSWERS TO END-OF-CHAPTER EXERCISES

This appendix provides suggested answers to all end-of-chapter exercises in this book. If you get stuck on any chapter questions, you can study the answers here and move on. While most chapters have end-of-chapter exercises, Chapters 8, 16, and 17 do not, but they do have a lot of try-it-out questions to help you practice.

Chapter 1

1. Add this line of code:

```
print("Here is a third message!")
```

2. Here are the outputs, respectively:

```
2
9
2
2.3333333333333335
1
4
20
```

3. Add this line of code:

```
print(55 * 234)
```

Chapter 2

1. Here are the outputs:

```
<class 'str'>
<class 'str'>
Kentucky Wildcats
WildcatsKentucky
Wildcats @ Kentucky
WildcatsWildcatsWildcats
```

2. The outputs are as follows:

```
<class 'float'>
<class 'float'>
3.46
-2.4
3.0
```

3. Here are the outputs:

```
<class 'int'>
57
0.0
```

4. The outputs are shown here:

```
<class 'bool'>
8<7
False
<class 'str'>
<class 'str'>
```

5. These are the outputs:

```
-23
56
-23.0
8.0
```

6. Here are the outputs:

```
1
0.0
False
```

7. The outputs are as follows:

```
False
True
True
True
```

8. Here are the answers:

global: No, because it's a Python keyword

2print: No, because you can't start a variable with a number

print2: Yes

_squ: Yes

list: No, because list() is a Python built-in function

9. Here is the output:

```
this is A1
this is A2
```

10. The output is as follows:

```
this is A1
this is A2
this is C1
this is C2
```

11. This is the output:

```
this is A1
this is A2
this is B1
this is B2
this is C1
this is C2
```

12. The answers are shown here:

a.

```
0
1
2
3
4
```

---

b.

```
10
11
12
13
14
```

---

c.

```
10
12
14
```

---

13. 270

14. See the new script *import_local_module1.py* from the book's resources.

15. The range and the average of the grades are 29 and 82.625, respectively. You can use the following lines of code to get the answers:

```
midterm = [95, 78, 77, 86, 90, 88, 81, 66]
print("the range is", max(midterm)-min(midterm))
print("the average is", sum(midterm)/len(midterm))
```

---

16. The outputs are as follows:

```
rsity
y
University
rsity of Kentucky
```

---

17. If email = John.Smith@uky.edu, then email.find("y") returns 13.

18. The answers are shown here:

```
[2, 3, 5, 9]
5
3
```

---

19. The outputs are as follows:

```
["a", "hello", 2]
[1, "a", "hello", 2, "hi"]
```

---

20. 10

21. (9,)

22. One way is to use the `enumerate()` method as follows:

```
lst = [1, "a", "hello", 2]
newdict = {}
for i, x in enumerate(lst):
    newdict[i] = x
print(newdict)
```

Another way is as follows:

```
lst = [1, "a", "hello", 2]
newdict = {i:lst[i] for i in range(len(lst))}
print(newdict)
```

Chapter 3

1. Change

```
if inp == "stop listening":
    print('Goodbye!')
```

to

```
if inp == "quit the script":
    print('Have a great day!')
```

2. Add the following to the end of the script:

```
elif "open text" in inp:
    inp = inp.replace('open text ','')
    myfile = f'{inp}.txt)'
    open_file(myfile)
    continue
```

3. Change

```
import speech_recognition as sr
speech = sr.Recognizer()
def voice_to_text():
    voice_input = ""
    with sr.Microphone() as source:
        speech.adjust_for_ambient_noise(source)
        try:
            audio = speech.listen(source)
            voice_input = speech.recognize_google(audio)
```

```
        except sr.UnknownValueError:
            pass
        except sr.RequestError:
            pass
        except sr.WaitTimeoutError:
            pass
    return voice_input
```

to

```
from mysr import voice_to_text
```

Make sure you put the script *mysr.py* in the same folder as *voice_open_file.py*.

Chapter 4

1. See *pyttsx3_adjust1.py*, shown here:

```
import pyttsx3
engine = pyttsx3.init()
voices = engine.getProperty('voices')
engine.setProperty('voice', voices[0].id)
engine.setProperty('rate', 160)
engine.setProperty('volume', 0.8)
engine.say("This is a test of my speech id, speed, and volume.")
engine.runAndWait()
```

2. See *area_hs1.py*, shown here:

```
# Put mysr.py and mysay.py in the same folder as this script
from mysr import voice_to_text
from mysay import print_say
# Ask the base length of the triangle
print_say('What is the base length of the triangle?')
# Convert the voice input to a variable inp1
inp1 = voice_to_text()
print_say(f'You just said {inp1}.')
# Ask the height of the triangle
print_say('What is the height of the triangle?')
# Save the answer as inp2
inp2 = voice_to_text()
print_say(f'You just said {inp2}.')
# Calculate the area
area = float(inp1)*float(inp2)/2
# Print and speak the result
print_say(f'The area of the triangle is {area}.')
```

Chapter 5

1. Change

```
elif re2 == "too high":
    print_say("Is it 1?")
    while True:
        re3 = voice_to_text()
        print_say(f"You said {re3}.")
        if re3 in ("too high", "that is right", "too small"):
            break
    if re3 == "too small":
        print_say("It is 2!")
        sys.exit
    elif re3 == "that is right":
        print_say("Yay, lucky me!")
        sys.exit
```

to

```
elif re2 == "too high":
    print_say("Is it 2?")
    while True:
        re3 = voice_to_text()
        print_say(f"You said {re3}.")
        if re3 in ("too high", "that is right", "too small"):
            break
    if re3 == "too high":
        print_say("It is 1!")
        sys.exit
    elif re3 == "that is right":
        print_say("Yay, lucky me!")
        sys.exit
```

2. Change

```
print(answer)
```

to

```
print(answer[0:300])
```

3. Change

```
from pygame import mixer
```

to

```
import platform
```

and change

```
mixer.init()
mixer.music.load(f"./chat/{mysong}")
mixer.music.play()
```

to

```
if platform.system() == "Windows":
    os.system(f"explorer ./chat/{mysong}")
elif platform.system() == "Darwin":
    os.system(f"open ./chat/{mysong}")
else:
    os.system(f"xdg-open ./chat/{mysong}")
```

4. Change

```
and "mp3" in file.name
```

to

```
and "wav" in file.name
```

Chapter 6

1. See *parse_local2.py*, shown here:

```
from bs4 import BeautifulSoup
textfile = open("UKYexample.html", encoding='utf8')
soup = BeautifulSoup(textfile, "html.parser")
ptags = soup.findAll("p")
atag = ptags[1].find("a")
print(atag['class'])
print(atag['href'])
```

2. See *scrape_live_web2.py*, shown here:

```
from bs4 import BeautifulSoup
import requests
url = 'http://libraries.uky.edu'
page = requests.get(url)
soup = BeautifulSoup(page.text, "html.parser")
div = soup.find('div', class_="sf-middle")
contact = div.find("div", class_="dashing-li-last")
area = contact.find('span', class_="featured_area")
print(area.text)
atag = contact.find('span', class_="featured_email")
print(atag.text)
```

3. See *voice_podcast.py*, shown here:

```python
from io import BytesIO
import requests
import bs4
from pygame import mixer
# Import functions from the local package
from mptpkg import voice_to_text, print_say
def podcast():
    # Break a long url into multiple lines
    url = ('https://goop.com/the-goop-podcast/'
        'gwyneth-x-oprah-power-perception-soul-purpose/')
    # Convert the source code to a soup string
    response=requests.get(url)
    soup = bs4.BeautifulSoup(response.text, 'lxml')
    casts = soup.findAll\
    ('audio', {'class':'podcast-episode__audio-player'})
    casts = str(casts)
    start = casts.find("https")
    end = casts.find(".mp3")
    cast= casts[start:end+4]
    # Play the mp3 using the pygame module
    mymp3 = requests.get(cast)
    voice = BytesIO()
    voice.write(mymp3.content)
    voice.seek(0)
    mixer.init()
    mixer.music.load(voice)
    mixer.music.play()
while True:
    print_say('Python is listening...')
    inp = voice_to_text().lower()
    print_say(f'you just said: {inp}')
    if inp == "stop listening":
        print_say('Goodbye!')
        break
    # If "podcast" in your voice command, play podcast
    elif "podcast" in inp:
        podcast()
        # Python listens in the background
        while True:
            background = voice_to_text().lower()
            # Stops playing if you say "stop playing"
            if "stop playing" in background:
                mixer.music.stop()
                break
```

Chapter 7

1. Here is a script:

```python
import arrow
from mptpkg import print_say
```

```
dt = arrow.now().format('MMMM D, YYYY')
tm = arrow.now().format('hh:mm:ss A')
print_say(f'today is {dt}, and the time now is {tm}.')
```

2. Change

```
elif "stop" in voice_input:
```

to

```
elif "quit the script" in voice_input:
```

Chapter 9

1. The changes are as follows:

```
import turtle as t

t.Screen()
t.setup(500,400,100,200)
t.bgcolor('blue')
t.title('Modified Screen')
t.done()
t.bye()
```

2. Change

```
t.forward(200)
t.backward(300)
```

to

```
t.backward(100)
t.forward(250):
```

3. The changes are as follows:

```
import turtle as t

t.Screen()
t.setup(600,500,100,200)
t.title('Python Turtle Graphics')
t.hideturtle()
t.up()
t.goto(100,100)
t.dot(60,'lightgreen')
t.goto(-100,-100)
t.dot(60,'lightgreen')
t.done()
```

```
try:
    t.bye()
except Terminator:
    pass
```

4. Change

```
t.pencolor('blue')
t.pensize(5)
```

to

```
t.pencolor('red')
t.pensize(3)
```

5. The code is as follows:

```
import turtle as t
t.Screen()
t.setup(600,500,100,200)
t.bgcolor('green')
t.title('Python Turtle Graphics')
t.hideturtle()
t.tracer(False)
t.pensize(6)
t.goto(200,0)
t.goto(200,100)
t.goto(0,100)
t.goto(0,0)
t.update()
t.done()
try:
    t.bye()
except Terminator:
    pass
```

Chapter 10

1. Change

```
t.goto(center)
t.write(cell,font = ('Arial',20,'normal'))
```

to

```
t.goto((center[0]-80, center[1]-80))
t.write(cell,font = ('Arial',15,'normal'))
```

2. Change

```
print(f'(x, y) is ({x}, {y})')
```

to

```
print(f'(x, y) is ({x}, {y})')
print('x+y is ', x+y)
```

3. Change

```
print('row number is ', row)
```

to

```
print(f'you clicked on the point ({x}, {y})')
print('row number is ', row)
```

4. Change

```
# The blue player moves first
turn = "blue"
```

to

```
# The white player moves first
turn = "white"
```

5. Delete the following from the script:

```
if '1' in occupied[turn] and '5' in occupied[turn] and '9' in
occupied[turn]:
    win = True
if '3' in occupied[turn] and '5' in occupied[turn] and '7' in
occupied[turn]:
    win = True
```

Chapter 11

1. Change

```
done()
```

to

```
rownum = 1
for y in range(-250, 300, 100):
```

```
        goto(325,y)
        write(rownum,font=('Arial',20,'normal'))
        rownum += 1
done()
```

2. Change

```
sleep(0.05)
```

to

```
sleep(0.025)
```

3. Delete the definition of the vertical4() function and delete the following from the script:

```
if vertical4(x, y, turn) == True:
    win = True
```

4. Add the following to the dictionary to_replace:

```
'column ':'',
```

5. See *conn_hs_2player.py* at *https://nostarch.com/make-python-talk/*.

Chapter 12

1. Change

```
coins[i].goto(-100 + 50 * i, 0)
```

to

```
coins[i].goto(-100 + 50 * i, -10)
```

2. Change

```
coins[-(i+1)].hideturtle()
```

to

```
coins[i].hideturtle()
```

3.

```
['H', 'i', ' ', 'P', 'y', 't', 'h', 'o', 'n']
```

Chapter 13

1. Change

```
# The red player moves first
turn = "red"
```

to

```
# The yellow player moves first
turn = "yellow"
```

Then, delete

```
# Computer moves first
computer_move()
```

Also, delete

```
# Take column 4 in the first move
if len(occupied[3]) == 0:
    return 4
```

The complete script is in *conn_think1_second.py* at *https://nostarch.com/make-python-talk/*.

2. See *ttt_think1.py* at the book's resources website.
3. See *ttt_think2.py* at the book's resources website.
4. The values are as follows:

```
cnt = {2:7, 1:5, 4:6}
```

Note that since both values 4 and 5 appear once, only one of them shows up in the dictionary cnt because a dictionary cannot have two elements with the same key: maxcnt = 4, and cnt[maxcnt] = 6.

5. See *ttt_think.py* at the book's resources website.
6. See *ttt_simulation.py* and *ttt_ml.py* at the book's resources website.
7. See *outcome_ttt_think.py* and *outcome_ttt_ml.py* at the book's resources website.
8. The yellow player has won the 10th game. Four discs are connected horizontally (in columns 2, 3, 4, and 5).

Chapter 14

1. Change

```
start_date = "2020-09-01"
end_date = "2021-02-28"
```

to

```
start_date = "2021-03-01"
end_date = "2021-06-01"
```

and change

```
plt.plot(stock['Date'], stock['Adj Close'], c = 'blue')
```

to

```
plt.plot(stock['Date'], stock['Adj Close'], c = 'red')
```

2. Change

```
formatter = mdates.DateFormatter('%m/%d/%Y')
```

to

```
formatter = mdates.DateFormatter('%m-%d-%Y')
```

and change

```
plt.setp(fig.get_xticklabels(), rotation = 10)
```

to

```
plt.setp(fig.get_xticklabels(), rotation = 15)
```

Chapter 15

1. Change

```
usd = response_json['bpi']['USD']
# Get the price
price = usd['rate_float']
print(f"The Bitcoin price is {price} dollars.")
```

to

```
gbp = response_json['bpi']['GBP']
# Get the price
price = gbp['rate']
print(f"The Bitcoin price is {price} pounds.")
```

2. Change

```
root.geometry("800x200")
# Create a label inside the root window
label=tk.Label(text="this is a label", fg="Red", font=("Helvetica", 80))
```

to

```
root.geometry("850x160")
# Create a label inside the root window
label=tk.Label(text="here is your label", fg="Red", font=("Helvetica",
80))
```

3. Change

```
root.after(1000, bitcoin_watch)
```

to

```
root.after(800, bitcoin_watch)
```

4. Change

```
maxprice = oldprice * 1.05
minprice = oldprice * 0.95
```

to

```
maxprice = oldprice * 1.03
minprice = oldprice * 0.97
```

INDEX

Gmail passwords, 150
Gmail SMTP, 151
Google search project, 64–65
Google Translate, 310, 312, 317–318
Google Web Speech API, 58, 97
goto() function, 175
graphics *See turtle* screens
grid_lines.py script, 181–182
gtts-cli tool, 76–77, 344
gTTs() function, 311
gTTS module
    installation, 46, 75, 310
    language codes, 312
    using, 74
gtts_slow.py script, 83
Guess the Number project, 94–98
guess-the-word project, 228–239
    game board drawing, 228–229
    guessing the letters, 231–234
    load coin pieces, 230–231
    rules description, 228
    rules implementation, 234–237
    voice-controlled version, 237–239
guess_hs.py script, 94, 95–97
guess_letter.py script, 232–233, 234
guess_word_board.py script, 228–229, 230, 232
guess_word_hs.py script, 237–238
guess_word.py script, 234–236

H

hash mark (#), 9
headless option, 128
help() command, 40, 45
hideturtle() function, 176
horizontal4() function, 216, 245
HTML (HyperText Markup Language)
    parsing, 98–101, 114–116, 121–122
    scraping live pages, 116–117
    tags, 112–113
    web page content, 113–114
HTTP (HyperText Transfer Protocol) requests, 277
HuffPost quotes list, 149
hyperlinks, 113, 114

HyperText Markup Language *See* HTML (HyperText Markup Language)
HyperText Transfer Protocol (HTTP) requests, 277

I

IBM Speech to Text, 58
if statements, 19–20
image scaling, 230–231
import statement, 43
importing modules and functions, 42–44
import_local_module.py script, 44
indentations, 9, 21–22
index() method, 31–32
IndexError errors, 216
indexes and indexing
    dictionaries, 34
    game board, 216
    shift() method, 291
    strings, 24, 25–26
    timestamps as, 281
    tuples, 37
IndexOutOfBounds errors, 216
init() function, 75
__init__.py file, 91–92, 323
input() function, 39
install command, 92
int() function, 17, 142
int type, 16
integer quotient (//) operator, 10
integers, 15–16, 18
Intelligent Connect Four project. *See also* Connect Four project, 241–267
    machine-learning design, 252–257
    testing effectiveness of, 257–263
    Think-Three-Steps-Ahead design, 242–252
    voice-controlled, 264–267
io module, 124
IPython (interactive Python) console, 7, 39
items() method, 35

Make Python Talk is set in New Baskerville, Futura, Dogma, and TheSansMono Condensed. The book was printed and bound by Sheridan Books, Inc. in Chelsea, Michigan. The paper is 60# Finch Offset, which is certified by the Forest Stewardship Council (FSC).

The book uses a layflat binding, in which the pages are bound together with a cold-set, flexible glue and the first and last pages of the resulting book block are attached to the cover. The cover is not actually glued to the book's spine, and when open, the book lies flat and the spine doesn't crack.